W9-AUJ-112

83-129
167-204

181
131-165

Religion in the National Agenda

Religion in the National Agenda

What We Mean by Religious, Spiritual, Secular

C. John Sommerville

BAYLOR UNIVERSITY PRESS

© 2009 by Baylor University Press
Waco, Texas 76798-7363

All Rights Reserved. No part of this publication may be reproduced, stored
in a retrieval system, or transmitted, in any form or by any means,
electronic, mechanical, photocopying, recording or otherwise, without
the prior permission in writing of Baylor University Press.

Cover Design by David Alcorn

Library of Congress Cataloging-in-Publication Data

Sommerville, C. John (Charles John), 1938-
  Religion in the national agenda : what we mean by religious, spiritual,
secular / C. John Sommerville.
     p. cm.
  Includes index.
  ISBN 978-1-60258-163-0 (hardback : alk. paper)
  1. Religion. 2. Spirituality. 3. Secularism. 4. Religion and science. 5.
Religion and politics. I. Title.

  BL51.S62188 2008
  200--dc22
                            2008011908

Printed in the United States of America on acid-free paper with a
minimum of 30% pcw recycled content.

FOR RICHARD AND APRIL HORNER

Contents

Preface

Many Western societies today are searching for a definition of religion that will guide them in determining legal, political, and educational issues in this day of increasing social and cultural diversity. When natural scientists and social scientists study religion, they need to be able to pin the subject down. Oddly, this is not something that religious studies can help us with. It is itself a field in search of definition, for defining religion is not an empirical matter but a question of language usage. Religion is one of those things that must be defined *before* we can identify cases.

Experts frequently declare that defining religion is impossible. Indeed it has proved impossible to reach entire agreement when trying to define the *thing*. This book will, instead, show how we define the *word*. This is the difference between real (or referential) and nominal definitions. And this will also aid in defining spiritual and secular, which are similarly controversial today. We need to recognize that these are words, whatever else they are, and find in our usage the key to defining the subject. It has been complained that this is taking the dominant modern discourse to be the nature of reality. But culture and language have their rules. Scholars might try to correct matters with definitions that reach for transcendence. But religion has proved to be a tough word, which is resisting our well meant revisions.

After showing our present usage, this book will show how nominal definitions of religion or religious do all the work that definitions need to do, in clarifying problems encountered in education, law, political philosophy and debate, cosmology, psychology, anthropology, sociology, theology, and so on.

Of course we are considering English words, which seems to open us to accusations of ethnocentrism, of projecting a Western sense of things onto the rest of the world. Actually, it is quite the contrary. By admitting that our words primarily describe Western understandings, we thereby respect the cultural diversity we talk about. None of us speaks language-in-general, so it is rather the effort to offer a culture-free and referential definition that is imperialistic.

In dealing with the applications of our usage in other fields we cannot possibly be comprehensive, but I have chosen examples that will be familiar to readers and that reveal my theme. We will not address all the subjects that scholars in those fields are concerned with, but we will try to clarify the terms they are using in their thinking and research. Thus we will show the practical value of what may at first seem an abstract definition.

Among those who have helped me with information and encouragement I would especially like to mention Diogenes Allen, Michael Armer, Roger Blashfield, Jerald Brauer, Clarke Cochran, Donald Dewsbury, Richard Fenn, Charles Glenn, Frederick Gregory, Michael Eldridge, David Hackett, Hans Hillerbrand, Peter Iver Kaufman, James Keesling, Kirk Ludwig, Ernst Mayr, D. Z. Phillips, H. Jefferson Powell, Richard L. Pratt Jr., Hilary Putnam, Lawrence Sullivan, Kenneth Wald, and Robert Wuthnow. The Earhart Foundation repeatedly gave needed financial assistance, and the Center for the Study of World Religions at Harvard offered the opportunity to be part of a community of interested scholars. Groups that welcomed presentations on the subject included the philosophy and religion departments at the University of Florida, the American Society for Church History, the Rutgers Center for Historical Analysis, and the Conference on Faith and History. I would also like to acknowledge the help that my editor, Carey Newman, has offered at every step, as well as the suggestions by anonymous readers.

Chapters 2, 4, 8, and 9 draw from articles I published as "Resurrecting Religion in a New (Hermeneutical) Dimension," *Fides et Historia* 30 (1999): 21–30, with rejoinder to critics in 31 (1999): 167–68; "Defining Religion and the Present Supreme Court," *Journal of Law and Public Policy* (Florida) 6 (1994): 167–80; "Is Religion a Language Game? A Real-World Critique of the Cultural-Linguistic Theory," *Theology Today* 51 (1995): 594–99; "Secular Society/Religious Population: Our Tacit Rules for Using the Term 'Secularization,'" *Journal for the Scientific Study of Religion* 37 (1998): 249–53. I thank all these journals for permission to include this information, as well as Oxford University Press, for arguments made in *The Decline of the Secular University* (2006).

CHAPTER ONE

Growing Confusion over Religion and Spirituality

A half century ago, it would have surprised scholars to think that religion would be an interest and a concern in the third millennium. Modernization of institutions and modernism in culture were widely thought to be sweeping it aside, to make way for a more rational and technical civilization. But religions are more in the news today than they were then, showing remarkable powers of adaptation. As a matter of increased discussion, the question of defining religion becomes a more pressing concern for legal, political, and educational institutions. At the same time, religion is becoming, for some, a more troubling reality. The popularity of "spirituality" is undoubtedly one response to religion's sometimes frightening aspects.

There is much talk these days about "spirituality" and how it differs from religion. Everyone agrees that the talk is quite vague. That is partly because the definition of religion itself is quite vague. Religious Studies scholars routinely admit that we cannot define religion, or that *they* cannot, at least. They know about too many "religions" to imagine that there are common features in them all. And if spirituality is commonly specified by contrast to religion, that seems to make any close definition of spirituality out of the question.

The public is also becoming increasingly aware of the diverse forms that religion may take. In 1965, U.S. immigration quotas against Asians were revised, and Americans became more aware of a variety of cultural traditions. At the same time, there was an upsurge of interest in Native American religions, in drug-induced mystical states, and in the designer faiths of New Age spirituality. In the light of such developments, we see that defining the subject is full of ambiguities. Many think it is impossible. If this is the case, it will make increasing trouble for judges, legislators, and educators who must make judgments in this area, as well as for scientists and scholars who want to study the subject.

Actually, it is not the case. This book will offer definitions of religious or religion (in chapter 2) which are both academically precise and consistent with common usage. First, however, we must explain how the subject became confused. Then we will indicate why we expect success in this effort where others have admitted failure. Essentially, it is because we are taking a novel approach to the problem. We are offering a nominal rather than a real definition of religion. That is, while others have tried to define the *thing*, we will define the *word*, which is all that can be done with something as elusive as religion. It was the attempt to define the *thing* that caused the trouble.

One would think that scholars in religious studies or comparative religion would be the ones to ask for guidance on this question. But the answer is not derived from a study of cases, but from a consideration of language usage. Religion is something that must be defined *before* we can identify cases. We decide whether something is actually a religion, not by studying the thing, but by consulting English usage. As we will see, scholars commonly complain that our word "religion" is a Western term that does not really fit Asian cultures. They think that our definition is ideological and that imposing it on other cultures is imperialistic. But beyond that, their reaction is puzzling. They may go on using it after that disclaimer, or redefine the term so that only scholars can use it confidently, or offer substitutes that may be equally Western.

We will be doing something different. We will be offering a nominal definition, drawn from common English usage that has remained fairly stable over a long period. At first it will seem that this definition privileges Western monotheism. Indeed it may. That is not because of personal bias but because English and other Western languages do appear to privilege that perspective. Thus, if we want to use the word without unwieldly qualifications, we must be aware of this. We can still express our respect for other cultures and their traditions, but we should do so in other ways than by creating incoherence in our own.

"Religion" is first of all a word. This book is about what our use of the word suggests about the thing as we understand it. This may seem an odd way to proceed, but religion is an odd word. It deals with the oddest of things. Everyone who has offered a definition has remarked on this, but no one yet has used all the help that our usage offers in opening our understanding. Dealing with the word will not leave us with a vacuous definition. After defining the word in chapter 2, later chapters will show how our nominal definition does all the work that a definition needs to do. For it will clarify the scholarly, scientific, theological, educational, legal, and political questions that have been left hanging in our current confusion. Any prospective science of comparative religion will still have to make other arrangements. What we nominally call "sciences" require real or referential definitions, to be sure that everyone agrees on cases.

It must be said that not everyone wants greater clarity in defining religion. Judges may feel that old laws give religion an advantage which is now obsolete. Some legal writers are encouraging them to expand the definition to include more general rights of privacy or of conscience. Scholars are often fearful that strict definitions of religion may privilege Western traditions and seem prejudicial to others. For they rightly see that nominal definitions are necessarily culture-specific, though they may forget this later. Theologians may think that more of us are religious than think we are. They are sometimes accused of extending their empire by redefinition rather than conversion. All of them may like some ambiguity in the word. But I will argue that the English-speaking public is not all that uncertain in this area.

Religion concerns us all in one way or another: some are concerned about being allowed to express their own beliefs, while some do not want to be bothered by those of others. Those of majority faiths, of minority faiths, and of no faith may all be nervous about the vitality of religions today. Fifty years ago journalists were too polite to mention religion. It would amaze them to see how our news industry has drifted toward constant coverage, both as an element in the public and the private spheres, and how religions are implicated in our culture wars, often on both sides. As we try to control our world, our laws and regulations take the form of words, so that the way we define "religion" and "religious" will be critical in coping with this troubling situation. Concentrating on words does not mean we are neglecting the real world. When political debate, law, education, science, and journalism turns on the meaning of words, we see that words impact that real world. This is because words cannot be changed unilaterally. In fact, they change very slowly.

Sophistication, cosmopolitanism, and diversity have increased our confusion. Faculty in religious studies are the first to admit the difficulties. Since they have not found features that all religions share, some have advocated eliminating the word altogether. Journalists are often unsure whether some group should be described as religious, cultic, or mentally unhinged. Artists may insist that their works are spiritual, but they would object to calling them religious. We do not know whether to say that a movie that treats religious subjects, using all of Hollywood's special-effects technology, can be truly said to be creating a religious experience. Scientists wonder whether "religion" can be reduced to some other conceptual level—perhaps psychological, neurological, or sociological (see chapters 6 and 7). Judges puzzle over whether certain claims for conscientious objector status qualify as religious, and whether prisoners' demands really qualify as religious freedoms (chapter 4). Teachers and school principals are nervous about the line between teaching religion and teaching about religion, and they may try to leave the whole subject alone (chapter 3).[1]

Even churches today need help in defining religion. In 2001, the Annual Meeting of the Unitarian Universalist Association in the

United States split when conservative members questioned whether it had ceased to be a religion. They claimed that some members showed such hesitation over the bare use of the term God, much less any worship of "the source of being," that there was doubt about whether the denomination was justified in receiving a tax exemption as a religion.[2] And we note the recent proliferation of terms in this area, which must be a significant fact about our culture. Are there, in fact, real or consistent differences between religion and spirituality, mysticism, myth, piety, worldview, ritual, magic, philosophy and the like?

What Our Use of "Spirituality" Tells Us

Here we have stumbled on an interesting fact. The growing popularity of the term "spirituality" turns out to be evidence that there is a limit to our confusion about the term religion. It indicates that we would rather employ another word than stretch an old one out of shape. Professor of Religious Studies Wade Clark Roof interviewed California baby boomers on their religious or spiritual quests, and he noted their preference for the term "spirituality." Though they were hazy on the term, he gathered that they meant a rejection, not of religion perhaps, but of organized or institutional religion, which seemed lifeless and external. Having been disappointed with churches, it excited them to think that spirituality indicated something more vital and personal. They embraced spirituality as part of their identity "against a background of fragmentation and commodification of the self in modern society."[3]

Roof noticed that those who use this language may not want it defined, since a central feature of the experience is a questing mentality: "The spiritual comprehends but cannot be contained by intellect, cognition, or institutional structure; it reaches out for unity and the ordering of experience; it abhors fixity in the interest of transformation."[4] Sociologist Robert Wuthnow found much the same in a study of a hundred artists who were identified as expressing "spiritual" interests in their work. He noted that they were drawn to the term in reaction against the technical, rational, and commercial character of modern society. But they also reported resistance to organized religion. "Spirituality" connoted something more intrinsic or personally authentic. It also helped that spirituality was not subject to the philosophical or moral criticisms directed at historical religions.[5]

Other scholars have tried to discover how the word "spirituality" is being used. One group of researchers reported their findings under the title "Religion and Spirituality: Unfuzzying the Fuzzy." The self-reports they collected most often linked spirituality to "relationship to a Higher Power of some kind," as with religion, but the subjects wanted to distance themselves from the institutional forms of religion. "Spiritual" seemed individual and more creative.[6] Another scholar tried to probe more deeply by observing that "human existence is spiritual insofar as it intentionally engages reality as a maximally inclusive whole and makes the cosmos an intentional object of thought and feeling." It makes one's life "the project of one's most vital and enduring self."[7] As the word becomes more popular, we may doubt that it always carries that whole freight. But in any event, it seems to involve wholeness and other classic mystical themes.

As we will see in chapter 2, spirituality does not entirely capture the sense of religion in English. To anticipate our definition in briefest terms, we will find that, in English, religion is our word for a certain kind of response to a certain kind of power (the power and the response both being beyond anything else in our experience). Spirituality, on the other hand, does not seem to require the same kind of ethical or existential response. For those who seem to understand the distinction intended between religion and spirituality, spirituality is more like an aesthetic category. It is an awareness or apprehension, like a feeling for beauty.

The fact that neuroscientists are eager to study spirituality is an unconscious recognition of its aesthetic and psychological character. Neuroscientists must be guided by our linguistic usage in identifying the subjects of their study. They must study the feelings that are popularly identified as spiritual. It is feelings that might register in physical measurement. So language guides their efforts to reduce the spiritual to physicalist terms.

The ethical or existential aspect of a truly *religious* response will create greater difficulties for scientific naturalism or physical measurement. Just as neuroscience will never explain itself—never explain the choices that science makes or the truths of its statements, in terms of neural impulses—it cannot promise to explain religion itself, but only its spiritual aspects. That is, religion has that area of existential response to consider, besides the awareness that might have triggered it. But we are getting ahead of our story. We will take up the issue of naturalistic explanations of religious phenomena in chapter 6.

The lack of an ethical dimension in spirituality is hinted at by one of the foremost scholars of secularization, Steve Bruce. While he has no desire to promote religion, he notes that

> the weakness of community in [the spirituality of] the New Age is not an accident but an inevitable consequence of its solipsistic basis of authority. . . . This explains why, for all the talk of counter-cultural and alternative community, New Age spirituality has not produced its alternative schools and communes. . . . Only a religion that has an authoritative reference point outside the individual is capable of providing a challenge to any status quo.[8]

We conclude that the popular use of the term "spirituality" shows that people do have a tacit definition of "religion" and that they employ a different term to register a distinction. This is evidence against the idea that words are always in flux or can mean whatever we like. Words must communicate. They are part of our social, not our individual, life. Common words like "religion" may be played with metaphorically, but their serious use will not be forgotten. They can spring back to their original shape. We hope to discern that more enduring form.

If part of the popularity of the term "spiritual" is the unpopularity of religion among certain groups, we may notice that religion has very frequently been unpopular. After all, it tends to make demands. We have often heard that religion persists because it is popular, and no doubt that is true too! In its confirming mode, religion can be a great comfort. In its judgmental mode, religion can be bitterly resisted. It might be difficult to characterize the present mood in American society in this respect. Teachers are supposed to affirm their students; politicians are supposed to flatter the voters; commercial advertising praises us as customers; few churches may have heard of fire and brimstone. But when we need to find figures to demonize, by way of registering our hostility, one of the tempting groups just might be religious figures, past and present, foreign and domestic, if one can judge by our books and movies.

Growing Suspicions of Religion

While there is more public discussion of religion in our politics and our media, it is strongly ambivalent. So tendentious definitions may prejudice things in this regard. Yale law professor Stephen L. Carter has protested the current treatment of religion in our media and public discourse: "The wrongs that religious regimes have done are not worse than the wrongs that secular regimes have done; they are, all through history, just about the same. The difference is that we expect more from the religious, or at least we should."[9] In fact, recent secular regimes have been notably more murderous than regimes in the smaller populations of the past, yet fear of religion is not at all unrealistic. The mass suicides at Jonestown and Heaven's Gate show the hold that religious beliefs can exercise. The wars and civil wars that have revived after the end of the twentieth century's ideological wars mostly involve religious identities. These may be only a justification for cynical leaders whose religion is only extrinsic, but religious beliefs and identities can indeed be the ultimate motivating forces.

It is sometimes denied that there is prejudice against religion in America, on the basis of an increased use of pious rhetoric in politics. Philosopher Richard Rorty rightly claimed that "no uncloseted atheist is likely to get elected anywhere in the country."[10] That does not mean, however, that Americans accept religion implicitly. It is one thing for politicians to ask God to bless America; it is quite another to admit seeking religious guidance. Political opponents are quick to call attention to any religious particularity of their rivals.

As a president of Emory University has remarked, "I could maybe get away with saying that Emory is a United Methodist university, but, if I said it was a Christian university, all hell would break loose."[11]

So we have reached the point where a senator warns that government programs to combat drug addiction need to be cautious in allowing religious counseling, whatever the success rate of such treatment. The media understood him to mean that a change from drugs to religion might be a change for the worse.[12] We may be horrified at China's current suppression of Falun Gong which has meant the torture and death of several hundred persons for their beliefs. But American companies doing business there do not protest when the Chinese government interrogates their own workers for this heresy.[13]

Whatever the degree of religion's current unpopularity, it is doubtless connected to the dominance of news discourse. Daily news product does not report on the world so much as on what has gone wrong with the world. Therefore one is less likely to hear of the normal business of religion in reconciliation or support than of something bizarre and disruptive, and we may mistake that for the typical picture. This can result in a generalized suspicion of religion.[14] The entertainment industry encourages a similar wariness of religion. Movies seldom treat religion as an ordinary part of life. When a character is identified as religious, that becomes the single dimension of the role whether for good or, often, for bad. Even conventional churchgoers have their suspicions of religion. They do not want to be associated with people who will risk everything for beliefs which make no sense to them. They may protest their difference, in an exercise of what sociologists call "boundary maintenance." Americans United for Separation of Church and State, representing mainline churches along with other groups, exists to file legal complaints against those churches that get too far into the political arena. Studies have shown, however, that they are thirty times more likely to complain against churches whose greater conviction marks them as unconventional.[15]

Clearly, one element in our fears is the matter of the power of religion. In the next chapter we will see that power is involved in the very definition of "religion." But it is not the human power of religion that is essential. Religion is understood as a *response* to a transcendent power, rather than as a human *exercise* of power. On the other hand, religious commitment seems to be the only force left in the world that can challenge our globalizing bureaucratic and commercial world order. With the imbalance of power in the world and the defeat of class conflicts, there is nothing besides religion that could disrupt a domineering order. Those who are comfortable with that order see religion as a threat, while those who resent what they see as imperialism may see religion as their hope.

Secular groups may use terms like "spirituality," "cult," and "fundamentalist" to disguise an opposition to religion more generally. But the fears may find raw expression, as they did, rather puzzlingly, at the impeachment trial of President Clinton.[16] Some of his supporters saw advantages in demonizing religion. At a rally at New York University, legal philosopher Ronald Dworkin warned that "there's the smell of brimstone in the air"—brimstone being something one seldom meets outside religion. Harvard's Alan Dershowitz declared that to vote against Clinton's impeachment

> is not a vote for Bill Clinton. It is a vote against bigotry. It's a vote against fundamentalism. It's a vote against the right-to-life movement. It's a vote against the radical right. This is truly the first battle in a great culture war. And if this President is impeached, it will be a great victory for the forces of evil – evil – genuine evil.

A prominent feminist in attendance warned, "We are looking at theocrats. We have to mobilize like we mobilized against the war in Vietnam, like we mobilized against slavery. This is about race! This is about crack cocaine in the neighborhoods!" And a bishop at the rally declared that "I think of the millions and millions of people who will suffer and die because the Republicans want to get President Clinton for personal sin."

When one cannot be sure of one's audience, fears of religion may be expressed in a more guarded manner. There is a refreshing difference in philosopher Thomas Nagel's honest admission,

I am talking about . . . the fear of religion itself. I speak from experience, being strongly subject to this fear myself: I want atheism to be true and am made uneasy by the fact that some of the most intelligent and well-informed people I know are religious believers. It isn't just that I don't believe in God and, naturally, hope that I'm right in my belief. It's that I hope there is no God! I don't want there to be a God; I don't want the universe to be like that. My guess is that this cosmic authority problem is not a rare condition and that it is responsible for much of the scientism and reductionism of our time. One of the tendencies it supports is the ludicrous overuse of evolutionary biology to explain everything about life, including everything about the human mind. Darwin enabled modern secular culture to heave a great collective sigh of relief by apparently providing a way to eliminate purpose, meaning, and design as fundamental features of the world.[17]

It may be that some of the hostility directed at religion these days is because of cultural baggage that the term has acquired over the years that is not intrinsic. If so, having a more essential understanding of the term may help to defuse some of the tension around religion. Dispelling certain exaggerations and confusions on this subject may help, especially among those who have little personal experience of religion. On the other hand, understanding our term may also help us in making necessary judgments on religions in a world in which we rediscover them to be basic.

The Source of Our Confusion

The first step toward clarity is to see how we became confused over the meaning of religion, for the confusion is not intrinsic to the word. There is a story behind it.

Every encyclopedia of religion or introductory textbook in the field begins with remarks on the diversity of religions. Authors note that there are just too many differences between our familiar religions to find the common element. Notice the assumption with which these scholars are beginning. They assume that the way to go about defining things is to look at particular cases and try to find

the constant features, the essential elements, that provide a definition. In the case of religion, it seems, the phenomena are just too
diverse.[18] The assumption is that we must define a *thing*, called "religion." The words for such things are nouns, which are expected to
correspond, or to refer, to the thing they denote. We call this a real
or referential definition.

There is another kind, called a nominal definition, which is only
the definition of a *word*. (I say "only" because we seem to think that
this is taking the easy way, avoiding difficulties we may meet in the
real world of things.) One approach to nominal definitions is to distinguish a word from its nearest neighbors. An increased recognition of this approach is part of the "linguistic turn" in philosophy,
the recognition that between us and whatever-is-out-there are the
languages which fix things for our consideration.

This book will offer nominal definitions of religion and religious
(as well as of science and other things). It should not be considered to
be the easy way, for it is the only way. Earlier attempts also started as
nominal definitions, but quickly strayed, with confusing results.

Return to our example: The scholars were beginning with the
phenomena, with the actual religions that would give us clues about
defining the concept of religion. But how did they know that the
examples they used were actually religions? They assumed they were
because we use the word "religion" for them all.

So they did not, in fact, start with the phenomena but with linguistic usage. And before scrutinizing that usage they moved on to
consider some beliefs, rituals, and organizations associated with
those examples. Almost immediately the books will admit that there
seem to be no universal features among the things we are calling
religions. But how else could one proceed, we wonder? At this point
it is common to shrug off the matter of consistency and to plunge
ahead with the discussion. So they never got back to the point of
wondering whether we were right in our linguistic usage.

The other way of proceeding with definition is to ask how
"religion" relates to neighboring words, or words that are used in
other, but similar ways. According to the approach associated with
Ferdinand de Saussure it is not the relations of words to things that

allows them to signify, but their relations to other words. How does religion relate to superstition, spirituality, philosophy, ritual, mysticism, belief, or magic, for instance? Not how do these things relate to each other, but how are the words used in meaningful discourse? This is one way of making a nominal definition.[19]

Religion presents a peculiar, perhaps unique, difficulty for referential definitions. It is the difficulty of identifying religious phenomena for purposes of objective *reference*. Religion is not the same kind of thing as tree or quark. The intangible nature of so much that we will call religious seems central to the notion. That makes a difference. We know what trees are. Cultures might differ on which things to call trees and which to call bushes, but they will all have a word that we could confidently translate as "tree." Quarks are more problematic. Physicists think that their equations indicate something discrete and irreducible, for which they are using the term "quark." They currently think it is a thing and not a collection of things. But in cases like these, real or referential definitions would be appropriate and perhaps unproblematic.

Religion is not part of "nature" in that way. (We will suggest a nominal definition of nature in chapter 6.) Scholars realize that cultures differ markedly in the general area that we identify as religion. Some cultures include things that seem to be related to the subject that our culture does not share, and for which we do not have a word. Take the Indian concept of "caste" for instance. If we translate that as "class" it might miss the religious context. But if we use the English term "religion" about a range of Indian practices (including caste) we may likewise confuse things. Indians doubtless have words that they use in this area, for which we would find no English equivalents. The obvious answer would be to respect cultural diversity, even to the point of admitting that we do not entirely understand each other. For to understand others fully we would have to begin by learning whole languages, and not just certain words.

In short, the problem with defining religion by correspondence to its referent is that we cannot be sure we have nailed down that referent. *A real definition would have to prove that all beliefs and practices that were called religious really are religious.* But nature is no guide here, and cultures differ. Proving that something is *really* religious actually means proving that religion is the right word for it under the rules of our language. Not language-in-general, for there is no such thing, but in a particular language like English.

How Confusion Developed

This brings us to the crucial point of this chapter. There is good reason for thinking that some of the things we have been calling religions may not be religions according to a consistent English definition. This is an odd claim that will require a detour into history.

As Europeans began trading in Asia and elsewhere during the sixteenth and seventeenth centuries they became aware of the rituals and beliefs of the peoples they met. Some, like Columbus, at first concluded that these peoples had no religions, but only magic.[20] Others saw more to it than that and called their practices "religious." But they did not immediately aggregate the practices into "religions." That would have implied a coherence among the practices that Western observers did not detect. So they found religion to be useful as an adjective but not as a noun. In comparison with Christianity, Judaism, and "Mahometanism," which they understood to be textually constructed, there was not enough unity among Indian, Chinese, or Siamese beliefs, for example, to justify calling them full-scale religions. They did not immediately start calling them Hinduism, Buddhism, or Confucianism, which would have implied more respect than they felt.

In later centuries, the Western missionaries and scholars who heard these travelers' tales thought that at least their leading thinkers were worthy of respect. They called them "sages," the "learned Brahmins," and such, comparing them with ancient Greek philosophers (rather than with Jewish or Christian religious figures). The scholars and missionaries certainly distinguished them from the idolaters around them, whom they simply termed the "heathen." But until about 1800 authors grouped the curious beliefs and practices of the East only according to region and race, and not as religious systems. There was a widespread assumption that these apparently incoherent beliefs and rituals were the decayed remnants of an original monotheism, the natural religion of all mankind, mentioned in the Hebrew Scriptures.[21] As historian David Pailin puts it, "Outside discussions of Christianity, Judaism and Islam, religions tend to be treated [by early scholars] as nationally or geographically defined entities which are largely indistinguishable from the society, politics and even culture of their adherents."[22]

It might have been wiser to maintain this understanding of things, rather than to postulate "world religions" covering those vast areas. But in the early nineteenth century scholars began to construct textual religions out of these materials, to match what they were familiar with in the West. The English word "religion" (and similar words in other European languages) were stretched to fit this new view in academic parlance.

For instance, the term "Boudhism" and "the Boudhou religion" first appeared in an English book in 1801. By the 1820s scholars had begun to assemble such a religion out of the various traditions they were finding in Asia. While the bits and pieces were real, and religious, the reified religion, involving Asian philosophies, was a projection of the Western imagination. Indeed, by 1860 Buddhism had ceased to exist primarily in the East, but rather in the Eastern institutes and libraries of Europe! Western scholars had decided that this religion was in such a decadent state in Asia that they would have to save it. They thought they were recovering Buddhism's original form or essence, declaring that Asians no longer understood their own religion. As historian Philip Almond puts it, being "defined, classified, and interpreted through its own textuality . . . the Buddhism that existed 'out there' was beginning to be judged by a West that *alone* knew what Buddhism was, is and ought to be."[23]

The scholars may have been right about the incoherence of the elements they were discovering. But this was taken as evidence that primitive monotheism had decayed into fragments which it was up to them to reassemble. They even talked Asian scholars into joining the effort to create a textual framework for this Buddhism.[24]

Something similar happened to "Hinduism," a term that was first used in English in 1829 to refer to a single religion. Nowadays, scholars take the view that Hinduism is more properly thought of as a civilization that accommodates numerous and fairly distinct religions. That is, Hinduism is not a religion, though the various Indian cults are religious. It is said that the differences between "Hindus" are as great as those between Jews, Christians, and Muslims.[25] But the temptation to think of it as one of the "world religions" even affects Indian law today.

There are so many religious communities in the Indian subcontinent that it falls to their secular courts to mediate between them. Judges find themselves thinking in terms of Western religious concepts as they tamper with indigenous practices. In an important 1966 case regarding "untouchables," the Indian Supreme Court revealed difficulties introduced from Western sources. It was already customary to categorize Sikhs, Jains, and Buddhists as Hindus socially and culturally, though not religiously. Now the justices found that they could not find a workable test for who is a Hindu "religiously." They observed that being Hindu was more like an ethnicity or a culture, but that did not keep them from declaring that the defendants' rejection of untouchables was "founded on superstition, ignorance, and complete misunderstanding of the true teachings of the Hindu religion"—which they had just said they could not define. To add injury to insult, they rejected the defendants' protest that they were not Hindus religiously and therefore not bound by the laws governing that classification.[26] In short, the Indian judicial elite had begun to think of Hinduism in light of an alien scholarship that had recreated something that was never there, a textually constructed and doctrinal religion like those of the West.

Even earlier than this reification of Buddhism and Hinduism, Jesuit missionaries to China manufactured something called "Confucianism," by summing up the activities of Chinese scholars then engaged in a kind of intellectual restorationism. Later scholars found it natural to think of this as a religion.[27] The Chinese may protest that this is a misunderstanding. It has been said that whether Confucianism is a religion is a question that the West has never been able to answer and the Chinese never able to ask.[28] Chinese scholars have only recently coined a term that we could translate "religion," which literally means "the teaching of the sects." They would not use that term for their own wish to create "a bond between all creatures without doctrines, without creeds, and without dogmas." So our insistence that this effort be given the name "Taoism" is ironic.[29]

Generally speaking, people lack names for their religions until a late stage in their cultural development. One does not need a brand name for what is self-evident. The names are often coined by foreigners, who find the practices or the beliefs curious. Shinto is a Chinese word for Japanese traditions. The Greeks gave Judaism its name, and Christians were first called that by Jews.[30]

Comparative religion scholar Jonathan Z. Smith identifies the 1870s as the high point of the effort to identify a universal religious impulse. Several encyclopedic works appeared then, offering taxonomies of world religions for scholarly purposes. It comes as no surprise that Smith finds that Judaism, Christianity, and Islam always stood out, seeming different from the rest.[31] That difference was not sufficiently recognized among the Victorian scholars. But Werner Cohn, Timothy Fitzgerald, and many others have observed that only Western languages have unambiguous words for religion, used in self-description.[32]

Or at least they used to be unambiguous. But the temptation is great to use our word "religion" to make things seem familiar. There was an unconscious imperialism by which the West colonized the practices and worldviews of others under concepts that best described our own. This justifies scholars like Edward Said who hold that any representation of one culture in the terms of another cannot be true, and that the distinction of representation and misrepresentation is only a matter of degree.[33]

Since these early scholarly moves, we have found that Asian "religions" stretch our term. Most often, this is an issue with the so-called "non-theistic religions" like Theravada Buddhism. In the last century we have grown so used to calling them religions that we may feel it would be impolite to say that those peoples do not really have a religion after all. Our reluctance is a hindrance to consistent definition.

It is common for authors to declare that theism is not essential to religion because Confucianism, for example, does not appear to be theistic. Almost immediately the same writer will admit that there is some question as to whether Confucianism is a religion "in our sense of the word." Often the problem is not resolved. To raise the question of whether religion is universal would make us feel provincial. But if we stretch our term to cover what the Chinese do, we end up with a word that does not communicate.

Possible Reactions to Our Confusion

Of course words can change. We should not insist on fossilizing a particular usage. But in fact, this is a word that has not changed. Virtually every description of Asian "religions" expresses some awkwardness in using the English word in that context. Some words do change, so completely that the problem disappears. The English word "let" has exactly reversed its use since the sixteenth century, from meaning to hinder to meaning to allow. No one complains that we cannot define "let" as a result. So why do they complain of the difficulties in defining religion? Because it is a tough word which is resisting what we have been doing to it.

Words change slowly. The human body may have changed more in the last hundred years than this word has done. The fact that our ideas keep changing does not indicate that the words we use for them have changed. Indeed, ideas could not change in any coherent way if the words we used were slipping and sliding. Intellectual change depends on something remaining stable, and that thing is our vocabulary. Today the term "spirituality" is being used, by way of expressing disillusionment with organized religion.

Sociologist Robert Bellah has traced what he calls a "religious evolution."[34] He argues that the characteristic organization, scope, and functions of religions have changed in the course of Western history. This does not, however, signify a change in our term. Indeed his longitudinal analysis depends on our being able to use the same term throughout, rather than needing new terms at each juncture. To argue that religion served different functions at different times makes a merely functional definition impossible.

When English men and women first began reading about Chinese culture, they already had the word "religion" and used it confidently. They could even make jokes about its abuse, as when Henry Fielding has the blimpish Parson Thwackum in *Tom Jones* (1749) make himself ridiculous by saying, "When I mention religion, I mean the Christian religion; and not only the Christian religion, but the Protestant religion; and not only the Protestant religion, but the Church of England." By then, cultured opinion was beginning to sense that there might be a problem in this area.

But as Murray Wax points out, the man in the street can still use religion fairly precisely, without confusion or apology. So what we have now is a scholar's definition and an ordinary definition:

> When we reflect on the fact that *religion* is a term easily and intelligibly employed in popular English speech, functioning unproblematically as a folk category of discourse, both highbrow and lowbrow, it surely is perplexing that scholars have found the term "notoriously difficult to define" and have emerged with "a bewildering variety of definitions."[35]

When scholars insist that religion is a Western term which may not fit other traditions very well, they should draw the logical conclusion, which is that we need to find another word for those other traditions.

Scholars have offered various responses in light of the situation. Jonathan Z. Smith thinks that "religion is not a native term; it is a term created by scholars for their intellectual purposes and therefore is theirs to define." He means, presumably, not native to the peoples that he studies. Obviously it is a native English term and already has a standard use or definition. His proposal would work if religion were only something to study. As Smith recognizes, a science of comparative religion needs analytic terms and concepts that are universal and referential:

> It [religion] is a second-order generic concept that plays the same role in establishing a disciplinary horizon that a concept such as "language" plays in linguistics or "culture" plays in anthropology.

There can be no disciplined study of religion without such a horizon.[36]

But the "science of religion" still awaits such a definition, which will find itself at odds with native English usage.

The scholar of comparative religion, Wilfred ·Cantwell Smith, was one of the first in the West to respond to this problem. Since he did not think that "religion" was applicable to non-Western cultures, he proposed that we should discard the term in favor of the terms "traditions" and "faiths."[37] Presumably he only meant that scholars, for their limited purposes, should discard it. Cantwell Smith emphasized that the names we use for Confucianism, Taoism, Hinduism, and so forth represent Western reifications of diverse cultural systems. He complained that this was imperialistic as well as confusing. Still, he knew that a science of religion would require unambiguous terms.

But "faith" and "traditions" may also prove to be Western terms and subject to the same charge of imperialism. His dichotomy does at least suggest that the study of religion *need* not take the form of a comparative science. There could be two lines of study, viewing things from the outside or the inside. The traditions could be the subject of cultural studies (viewed from the outside) while the faiths could be studied by theologians (from the inside).

Some scholars are more clearly in agreement with our present contention. Richard King, in *Orientalism and Religion*, states this as plainly as possible:

> We should be aware, therefore, that the central explanatory category of religious studies, namely the notion of "religion" itself, is a Christian theological category. Like the terms "mystical" and "mysticism," "religion" is a culturally specific social construction with a particular genealogy of its own. In applying this category to the study of non-Western cultures, one should be aware of the theological origins of the term. Indeed for scholars like Balagangadhara it is highly questionable to even assume that there are things as "religions" outside a Christian-influenced context.[38]

One popular response to the definitional problem has been to take a page from the works of philosopher Ludwig Wittgenstein. When Wittgenstein was defining "game," for use in his phrase "language-game," he used the analogy of "family resemblances" between cases. Approximating a definition in this way often seems good enough for practical purposes. So this approach has been widely taken up by scholars with reference to our problem.[39] However, this approach has problems of its own.

William P. Alston offers the most complete attempt to carry this project through, in his article on "Religion" in the *Encyclopedia of Philosophy*.[40] He begins by assuming some examples of recognized religions, without wondering what implicit definition he is using to identify them. That is, he trusts current usage, assuming that Buddhism is a religion because we are used to calling it that. After several pages on the difficulties in reaching an agreed definition he suggests that we can at least agree that religions will involve many (though not necessarily all) of the following "Characteristic features of Religion": belief in supernatural beings, a sacred/profane distinction, ritual acts, moral codes, certain feelings, communication with gods, world views, comprehensive organization of personal life, and a social group bound together by the foregoing. Alston does not insist that every religion have all the above, but if they have a good number of them he thinks we can be confident we have a case of religion. Anthropologist Anthony F. C. Wallace agrees that there are "about thirteen behavior categories" involved in religion which help us to recognize it.[41]

There are problems with such an approach. Are some of these elements essential while others are only incidental? That would seem to be required in a definition, as opposed to a characterization. How many of these elements are necessary in order to qualify? Could two such religions not share a single one of these characteristics? Are some religions more religious than others?

There are two further difficulties. One is that Wittgenstein violated his own principles in seeking this "real" definition of game; he generally favored nominal definitions and could have pursued that approach in this case. I deal with this question in an appendix to this chapter. The other difficulty is that Wittgenstein developed the concept of language-game in *opposition* to the hegemony of scientific discourse. So it would be ironic if scholars tried to use that definitional approach in an effort to ground a comparative science of religion.

Mark C. Taylor has shown how things still look to some in the world of scholarship. He introduces a new handbook of terms used in religious studies by wondering,

> What if religion has no such essential identity? What if religion is not a universal phenomenon? What if religion has not always existed or has never existed? . . . Far from existing prior to and independent of any inquiry, the very phenomenon of religion is constituted by local discursive practices. . . . Some critics claim that appearances to the contrary notwithstanding, religion is a *modern Western invention.*[42]

We will try to face up to these possibilities without flinching.

The Way Ahead

The fact that scholars recognize confusion in the use of "religion" means that the term is resilient enough to be giving us trouble. Our uneasiness in using the term for nontheistic "religions" does not mean the term is useless. Rather, it suggests that we pretty well know what it means in ordinary English. This book is an effort to show how to find the common sense of the term. Of course, as more people meet scholars and take courses from them and read their works, there is a chance that we could lose a perfectly good word by stretching it.

In short, we have argued that it is a mistake to think that one can define religion by looking at those things we may be currently calling religions. Referential definitions work for more tangible things, where everybody is truly in agreement on cases. But in this matter we need a definition in order to decide whether something is religious by our way of thinking. Our only option, therefore, is to define the term with reference to other terms. That way, scholars will not stray so far from our more general usage.

Second, it is possible that defining the adjective form may be the place to start. Religious *institutions* inevitably carry baggage that will clutter a definition. We can easily derive the noun from the adjective, for the noun essentially signifies the institutionalization of the religious. So we might better approach the problem through the adjective (religious) or even adverb (religiously). Cantwell Smith himself remarked on this possibility, but did not point out that it implied the need for a nominal definition, since adjectives and adverbs are more obviously terms and not things.[43]

Third, we must brace ourselves for the objection that we may end up with a definition that only fits English. Again, there is no other option. No one speaks Language; we speak particular languages like English. We do not even think in Language, as opposed to particular languages. This has been known for a long time, but habits are hard to break. We are constantly reminded to respect diversity, and it is time to take that seriously. By showing respect for our English word "religion," we are showing no disrespect to other cultures. They have their own words, and they may even have their own experiences in this area. Creating a neutral language for these subjects is as "imperialistic" as mistranslating their doctrines into ours.

We will make no judgments in this book about whether any particular tradition is religious or not. That is for specialists to argue over, following the English usage that we will attempt to lay out. It is possible that even specialists on Eastern traditions will not agree with each other in such an effort. Meanwhile we should be ready to acknowledge our Jewish and Christian cultural heritage in this matter of terminology. Our languages themselves privilege certain understandings; it is not a personal bias.

A problem does arise if the word or concept of religion is not universal. We must wonder whether the experience we think of as religious exists in a culture that lacks our word for it. Nominalists take seriously the way language constrains or determines thought. But it does not follow that an experience is unreal because other cultures do not have a word that translates exactly. It may be true that experiences shrivel for lack of adequate cultural expression. We hear of experiences that other cultures recognize linguistically, of which we are deprived or experience in a narrower range. We may have only a latent appreciation of what their languages open up to them. Likewise, some societies may have only a latent experience of what we call religion.

Students of religion may object to thinking that the term fits only our own culture and historical experience. They would object even more to a naïve assumption that all these "religions" are similar. They, more than anyone, understand the awkwardness in calling "Hinduism" a religion. This book will not decide whether Confucianism is a worldview, ideology, philosophy, or religion. That is for others to decide, on the basis of English terms used properly, conventionally.[44] Perhaps it is becoming a religion, under Western influences. After we come to understand ourselves better, we can apply our terms to these areas without superiority or apology.

Appendix
Did Wittgenstein Make a Mistake in Defining Game?

It seems odd that Wittgenstein, who is famous for teaching that "the meaning of a word is its use in the language,"[45] did not employ that insight when considering the term "game" in his famous discussion of language-games. That was where he popularized the idea of definition according to "family resemblances." Given the frequency with which this approach is used in attempts to define religion, it deserves some attention.

In Wittgenstein's definition of "game," so basic to his notion of philosophy itself, he attempted a real or referential, rather than a nominal, definition. That is, rather than show the word's difference from its linguistic neighbors, he began by trying to relate word to thing. Admitting defeat, he proposed that we settle for "family resemblances" among the *designata*, in order to approximate a definition of game (and language-game). Remember that his term "resemblance" shows how things relate by similarity, not by difference, as in referential relations.

Wittgenstein's larger problem at the time was to show that the idea of a metalanguage that could mediate all questions was unrealistic. It was not possible, as he had once thought, to show the essential nature of language *per se*. So he used the metaphor of language-game to indicate the limitations on our different discourses, and their autonomy. But in *PI* §65 Wittgenstein imagines a possible objection, by someone who says "you talk about all sorts of language games, but have nowhere said what the essence of a language game, and hence of language, is: what is common to all these activities, and what makes them into language or parts of language."

Thereupon (§66) he asks readers to imagine all the games they know and try to think, "What is common to them all?" He admits that one might appeal to the linguistic evidence, that "There *must* be something common, or they would not be called games." But Wittgenstein demands that one "*look and see* whether there is anything common to all" (his emphasis). "To repeat: don't think, but look!" He mentions a variety of instances, meant to show differences between what we call games and the lack of any *necessary* common elements.

Norman Malcolm describes Wittgenstein's usual method of definition—of describing the language-game that uses the term—as "comparing and contrasting its use with the use of other words."[46] Had Wittgenstein taken that approach here, and asked how the word "game" is used differently from neighboring terms or concepts, he might have found that its use could be closely specified by difference. For example, games are activities, as contrasted with "idleness." They involve enough in the way of rules that the game is different from just "fooling around." They are not "work," nor "rituals," nor the serious "business" of life.

We begin to see boundaries closing around the term. By contrasting it with the way we use other terms, we become able to test our sense of the term by applying it to unfamiliar cases. This is done by thinking, not looking. Wittgenstein said, in reference to games (§69), that "we do not know the boundaries because none have been drawn." But the neighboring terms are the boundaries. So we need not proceed by accuracy in reference; our criterion in definition is our sense of the mastery of a rule-bound behavior. This is what gives us the confidence to use the word flexibly, to make jokes and contradictions like "he's just treating this job as a game."

Philosophers discuss just what problems Wittgenstein was addressing here.[47] But students of religion need to recognize the problems involved in using the "family resemblance approach" in defining religion. Wittgenstein's point in using the concept of game was to heighten the contrast between language-"games" and the serious language of science, which must bear the weight of theories and explanations. Language-games (like all games) have their own rules, he thought, and need not reflect a super-game (or metalanguage). The point was that while such systems might have resemblances to each other they also have their own individuality or personality.

Religious scholars who try to define religion by family resemblance hope that it will support a discipline (if not a "science") of comparative religion. This would go far beyond the study of the "forms of life" Wittgenstein talked about. The latter would be more like anthropologist Clifford Geertz's "thick description." Perhaps a more proper use of the concept of language-game within religious studies is that proposed by theologian George Lindbeck, discussed in chapter 8. He used it to indicate the incommensurability of religions rather than the resemblances.[48]

CHAPTER TWO

Defining "Religious" and "Religion"

Paul W. Pryser, writing on the psychology of religion, announces, "I myself regard the problem of defining religion insoluble."[1] Bernard Spilka and his associates in the same field, declare, "We therefore agree with Yinger (1967) that 'any definition of religion is likely to be satisfactory only to its author.'"[2] Winston L. King begins his *Introduction to Religion* by admitting that "the real difficulty, however, has to do with definition." He does not pretend to solve it.[3] Ninian Smart starts his *New Encyclopedia Britannica* entry on "Religion: The Study and Classification of," with "an acceptable definition of religion itself is difficult to attain," and he falls back on a search for "family resemblances."[4] Benson Saler does the same after an introductory chapter called "Abjuring a Definition and Other Matters," in a book entitled *Conceptualizing Religion*.[5]

None of this keeps scholars from proceeding with their studies of various aspects of the subject. University religion departments seem to be the only ones that cannot define their subject. Judges, legislators, and educators who must deal with the practical concerns of a wider public may learn that they cannot rely on the experts. So there is trouble in our legal culture, where religion is disappearing into the concepts of conscience and privacy; trouble in our political and journalistic culture, where religion is increasingly associated with a puzzling collection of "cultural" issues; trouble in those sciences which would like to study religion but cannot find the handle on the subject; and trouble in our popular culture, where we hear people saying that their morning coffee is sacred.

A word of uncertain meaning is not useful. And when a word decays, the experience it describes can decay too. Although the experience is perfectly real, we cease to make much sense of it, and so it disappears from our common life and culture.

Paradoxically, the fact that scholars realize that they are having trouble shows that the word *does* have a meaning, which lurks in their minds and gives them pause. My hope is not to offer a new definition for religion, but to restore a sense of what the term meant before it was stretched in the ways described in chapter 1. This will involve some discussion of what is wrong with other approaches, like the most notable recent attempt, by Paul J. Griffiths in an article "On the Future of the Study of Religion."[6] Griffiths does not recognize this as a linguistic matter, but treats it as "ontological" classification into natural and "artifactual" categories (corresponding to the referential and nominal terms I use). For he thinks this is necessary if we are to remain within the "science" of religious studies, as presently conceived. We will see why this approach is doomed.

This chapter (1) rehearses the reasons for a nominal (semantic), rather than a real (referential) definition and (2) offers assurance that this does not abandon a sense of the "reality" of religion. We will see that (3) a generic rather than a normative definition is necessary in order to reach agreement. That is, we will be interested in what religion is, rather than what it should be, which is a theological question and not part of our more semantic exercise. Then we will (4) argue for starting with the adjective "religious" before moving on to the noun "religion" and (5) face the embarrassing fact that there is no hope for a culture-free definition of an English word. We will consider (6) the question of substantive versus functional definitions. Then we will (7) offer the *structure* of any successful definition. Not

 to keep you in suspense, *we call something religious if it is a certain kind of response to a certain kind of power.* We can put more flesh on this skeletal frame, by characterizing the kind of response and the kind of power, both of which seem to be beyond anything else in our experience. We will notice that this structure already stands behind the most widely acknowledged definitions. Although we arrive at the definition by a different route than those used by Rudolf Otto, Paul Tillich or Clifford Geertz, it is encouraging to find that theirs share that general structure. Then we can consider (8) how religion is distinguished from some neighboring terms. Finally, we will briefly see (9) how this definition could affect the treatment of religion within scholarship. This last discussion is in terms of the study of history, which is the scholarly field with the least esoteric methods.

In the chapters to follow—on how religion would appear in the contexts of education, law, politics, the physical and human sciences, and theology—I will not be saying what a particular "religion" might make of these topics, because ours will be an analytical definition, a statement of how to recognize our concept of religion. Particular instances of religion probably vary in their approach to education, law, and the rest. Rather, we will try to see what difference any religious perspective will make to subjects, even when they are assumed to be secular.

Different Kinds of Definitions

(1) There is an important difference between the kinds of definitions usual in science and in the humanities. Science must generally work from real or referential definitions, while the humanities may use nominal or semantic definitions. That is, scientists must be sure there is something "out there" to be studied, because their studies must be open to confirmation or disconfirmation by others. Many things can be defined either way, but referential definitions work best for tangible things that we are not likely to mistake. Religion obviously gives us a problem here.

For example, social scientists may measure different kinds of activity—like church membership or church attendance—to quantify the incidence of "religion." But there is a deeper question, namely, what makes church attendance religious. That is a "hermeneutic" question, a question not about the cause of the activity but about its meaning to participants. Scholars in the humanities mostly do studies that investigate how human subjects have seen things. So they may "bracket," or ignore, the more objective and impersonal reality of things and focus instead on the sense people made of them.

Religion seems appropriate to a hermeneutic approach, which is a search for the meaning we find in experience. Church attendance, for instance, is religious because of the understanding of the participants. This directs our attention to language, which embodies our meanings. We will see in the following chapters that scientists have trouble pinning religion down because its objective reality is so notoriously problematical. In fact, this difficulty in objectifying the religious will turn out to be part of our essential understanding of it.[7]

(2) Already it may appear that we are dropping any question of religion's reality. The term "real," however, is not popular with philosophers when used as a metaphysical compliment. They prefer to say that things can be real for certain purposes, rather than real in general.[8] In any case, objective reality is not the only kind. Linguistic reality may be just as hard to escape. It is best to take real to mean irreducible—that something is *sui generis*. If we cannot make sense of experience without a concept, it has proven to be an essential and real part of our "world."[9] Our point is that it is not only referential or physicalist definitions that witness to inescapable realities.

Even in the hierarchy of the sciences it is clear that each level of analysis (each science) discusses things that would be rendered meaningless by reduction to the terms of a purportedly lower level. The concept of animal could be reduced to concepts of atoms, but it would lose its essential meaning of a living, unified, and independent being. The concept of democracy could be reduced to individual psychology and from there to neurobiology and eventually to physics. But at each level one would lose something real.[10] So we say that things are *real to each other* at the various levels of analysis (roughly, the levels of the different sciences).

The study of religion can follow either the scientific or the hermeneutic approach, using real or nominal definitions. Sociologists can study how religion was faring, from some operational definition like church attendance. Meanwhile historians can study how people were being religious—what they seemed to think was their religious duty. But we have already seen that scholars doubt those real definitions of religion needed for their sociological or other scientific purposes. They would always have to prove that what they count as religious really was religious. So their real definition has to move on to a hermeneutic one.

For an example of the difficulties of real definition, note those of philosopher John Hick in *An Interpretation of Religion*. He starts by admitting the "immense range of definitions" which scholars think "apply" to the religions they study. The term "apply" suggests that the word is to be understood by its correspondence with a thing. Hick soon admits the difficulty of deciding what is "authentic as opposed to merely nominal religiousness." This is a question that cannot be resolved by science; only theology offers to deal with the matter of authenticity. Hick eventually declares that he will arbitrarily focus on "belief in the transcendent, although this is not the essence of religion—for, as I have just suggested, there is no such [defining] essence."[11]

So it appears that the problem of the reality of religion is more acute for those who insist on a real definition than on those who use a nominal one. For nominal definitions place one in the very heart of the real worlds of law, education, and culture.

(3) Nominal definitions may be either normative or generic. Normative ones involve value judgment while generic ones do not. As Hick recognized, some cases of religion may be considered to be more authentic than others. Science does not recognize differences of this sort; things are *x* or *not x*. But in culture or subjectivity there might be a question about whether x "deserved" to be considered religious.

Happily, a nominal definition of religious can defer questions of authenticity. We can define the word generically and then use it later within the context of normative judgments. Once defined generically, we can go on to speak coherently of religious pretenses, religious surrogates, and so on. This is fortunate, because normative definitions are more difficult than generic ones. For example, one might think that defining Protestant Christianity would be easier than defining religion. But in fact it is harder; indeed it cannot be done to everyone's satisfaction. Whether speaking theologically or simply historically, scholars may not agree on what qualifies as *true* Protestantism. A generic definition of religion will actually be easier to formulate than a normative one, and that is what we will aim for.

(4) Defining the adjective "religious" rather than the noun "religion" will emphasize the advantages of nominal definition. Adjectives are obviously words; they do not refer to things but only describe those things. Defining religion or "a religion" (noun) involves much more than asking whether one's church attendance was "religious" (adjective). The statement "his church attendance was not at all religious" makes perfect sense. A global definition fitting all putative religions, with all aspects of their organization, doctrine and ritual, would be impossibly cumbersome. So our eventual definition of "religion" can await the prior judgment of "religious." We can then move from the adjective to the noun, since a religion amounts to an aggregation of "religious" elements.

To repeat, the trouble with trying to define religion before we have defined religious is that religions seem to be complex social-cultural institutions, involving liturgies, rituals, laws, symbols, organizations, doctrines, and the like. But since there are also rituals, laws, and symbols that do not appear to be religious, we need a criterion for labeling some "religious." That criterion will be, effectively, our definition. So we need to start with the adjective and then proceed to the institutionalization of these things in what we can call "religion" or "a religion."

Approaching a Nominal Definition

Approaching definition through language use puts a premium on our more unconscious linguistic behavior. Our casual use of words is a surer guide to usage than more formal and conscious usage. And we are probably less self-conscious about our adjectives than our nouns. When William James, in *The Varieties of Religious Experience*, discussed the difficulty of defining religion, he complained that "there is religious fear, religious love, religious awe, religious joy, and so forth." He despaired of discovering one specific and essential kind of religious emotion or object or act. So "it would indeed be foolish to set up an abstract definition of religion's essence."[12] James had the key in his hand, as he showed by using the adjective form in his title. Since he was interested in religious experience rather than in "religion," he might have skipped the frustrating effort to find that referential object, act, or emotion. James wanted to be true to usage, but he settled for a sense that appeared convincing, so that his audience agreed long enough for him to unfold his reflections on the subject. But his best move at that point would have been to discuss why particular experiences were termed "religious" and others not.

The way toward nominal definition is not to find elements or functions unique to religion. Not all beliefs are religious beliefs, not all rituals are religious rituals, not all symbols are religious symbols, and not all faiths are religious faiths.[13] Perhaps not all mysticisms, myths, or cosmologies are religious. When we find ourselves deciding (implicitly) which are the "religious" ones and which are not, we are on the track of our definition.

But how can we test our more or less implicit nominal definitions if not by accurate reference to a thing somewhere? As philosopher John Searle puts it, nominal definition is not even a generalization from the behavior of a linguistic group. It is rather a sense "of my mastery of a rule-governed skill." So the question is whether we, as native speakers, are satisfied that the definition is true to the way the word is normally used[14]—that is, whether we will confuse other native speakers or not.

(5) By "we" I mean twenty-first-century English-speakers. This is a major stumbling block. We don't want to be "ethnocentric." But, after all, we are defining an English word. No one speaks Language; we speak particular languages like English. This explains why Danièle Hervieu-Léger's recent efforts to define the French cognate, "religion," may seem to English readers to be informed by a slightly different usage.[15] (This need not raise criticisms of her work or of ours.)

Though other languages have cognates to the English "religion," the meanings of those terms probably vary slightly, and this is determined by social and cultural use, not by their putative common origin. The probable Latin roots of our word are often mentioned as if that would be determinative. In fact, only native Latin speakers would be guided by that sense!

Scholars often point out the parochialism of "Western" definitions of religion, but announcing such awareness does not overcome the problem. We should admit that our word may not confine all human experience. I do not mean that our definition of religion will describe only ourselves; we may speak about other peoples in our terms, while admitting that they may understand themselves rather differently. Likewise, they have their own words for these topics, which may involve different aspects of the subject and not translate into our terms exactly. This is the diversity we talk so much about.

The prominent student of comparative religion, Wilfred Cantwell Smith, often complained of the Western parochialism of our word. His recommendation was to scrap the term "religion" (at least within scholarship) because it did not describe Asian cultures, and to use the two words "tradition" and "faith" instead. In his frustration he sometimes threatened to settle for defining the adjective "religious."[16] We will see what would have happened had he carried out that threat.

Anthropologist Melford Spiro is one who recognized the need for a semantic definition. He was not concerned with the accusation of ethnocentrism. Since religion is a "creation of definition" (as opposed to discovery) we need not be "obsessed with universality." He warned readers not to assume that all societies have a religion. Rather, one should be true to linguistic usage: "Since 'religion' is a term with historically rooted [i.e., cultural, rather than natural or scientific] meanings, a definition must satisfy not only the criterion of cross-cultural applicability but also the criterion of intra-cultural [linguistic] intuitivity." So he thought nominal satisfaction must come first, which is our position.[17]

One might object that a nominal definition, being culture-specific, will indicate that only those cultures with the equivalent term could have the experience. If other cultures do not have the word religion or the concept, would that mean it is not entirely real? Universality is commonly taken to be a test of reality. It does not follow, however, that peoples who have no such term could have no such experience. True, they would not be able to think about it, or talk about it, if it were not recognized within their culture. But one would want to see how easily they could learn and use our term. Missionaries often report the excitement people express when they hear an unfamiliar message bring latent understandings to consciousness. Similarly, Westerners sometimes welcome Eastern concepts as making sense of their own feelings.

Anthropologist Clifford Geertz is notable for having wrestled with the issue of defining religion in the context of cultures. The common reference to religions as "meaning systems" derives from his classic treatment of "Religion as a Cultural System."[18] According to Geertz,

> a religion is (1) a system of symbols which acts to (2) establish powerful, pervasive, and long-lasting moods and motivations in men by (3) formulating conceptions of a general order of existence and (4) clothing these conceptions with such an aura of factuality that (5) the moods and motivations seem uniquely realistic.[19]

Geertz is offering a referential definition, but the reference is to a culture and not some transcendent reality. He specifies that he is defining "a religion," and not "religion" or "religious." He goes further, telling us how to decide which symbol systems are authentically religious, based on the fact that culture is shared behavior. Defining religion culturally suggests normative judgment, following the distinction between communal agreement and individual idiosyncrasy, heresy or superstition. Superstition suggests a mistake. By it, we normally mean the odd beliefs of people we do not respect. The same normative objections appear in the assumption that because churchgoers now arrive with absolutely no theological knowledge—or interest—there is nothing we need to call "religious" in their attendance.[20] The point is that we will need to discover religion before going on to judge it, and we therefore need a generic definition preceding any normative one. But later we will find other use for Geertz's efforts.

The Trouble with Functional Definitions

Geertz, like all social scientists, is alert to the functions that religions may serve. Their interest in studying religions is to find the purposes religious activities have within society and culture. This leads us to consider whether a nominal and generic definition is more likely to be functional than substantive.

(6) Functional definitions are popular because of the bewildering variety of religious ideas and practices. Scholars search beneath these for commonality of function, by way of defining the area of religion. Finding similar functions would be a way of finding the religious essence, and of avoiding normative judgments. This is congenial to the scientific approach. Thus anthropologists, for example, are apt to define religion in terms of its putative function of social bonding.

Problems arise immediately with functional definitions. For example, religious groups have often been dysfunctional, disruptive forces, splitting societies between established religions and opposition sects.[21] Beyond that, students of religious ritual have sometimes concluded that these have no end beyond themselves. They are like play, except that one cannot lose.[22] In any event, it is not clear that religions serve the same functions in every society, or that the functions remain the same through time. Any of these objections mean that while functions doubtless characterize some religions at some times, they are not essential and defining.

There are even deeper problems. It is a mistake to assume that functional definitions will be value free. "Function" implies some need of human or social existence. If such a function were judged to be essential, the adequacy of a religion in meeting such a need would invite normative judgments. Indeed, religion would have to be defined normatively.

But the biggest problem with functional definitions is that they are not specific. That is, they are apt to place religion into larger categories along with the other things that serve the same function. If the essential purpose of religion were social bonding, for example, it might be included along with other things that helped toward that end. This confuses the issue; should one extend the term "religion" loosely to everything in that category, or are we differentiating the religious element from its functional equivalents by some implicit definition of the religious?

The point is that a definition should identify unique aspects of the definiendum, and functional definitions do not. Think of the definition of "religions" as "meaning systems." Are all meaning systems religious? If not, how are scholars differentiating the religious from the nonreligious (parts of the) meaning systems? That tacit definition will not be functional, but rather what we call a "substantive" one. Of course, religion can have many functions—explanatory, expressive, ethical, existential. We are only saying that these functions are not its defining characteristics.

Geertz indicated what he thought made a particular meaning system religious. Its concepts are "of a general order of existence," which induce moods and motivations imbued with "power" and "unique realism." In short, he treats religious symbols as a culture's ultimate symbols—the symbols that govern other symbols. He seems to be defining "a religion" by something like an ultimate, absolute, or transcendent quality.

Here we are on the track of a nonfunctional definition. Ordinarily we contrast functional definitions with substantive ones, and we think of religion's substance in terms of a body of agreed doctrines. Scholars reject such a notion. But the substance of this nonfunctional definition is not elements of belief or action, but its analytical terms. Specifically, it is that quality of ultimacy that Geertz mentioned that seems destined to be part of our analytic (and generic and nominal) definition.

Geertz did not present the analytical element of ultimacy as the defining characteristic of religion, and he may not have recognized its contribution to his definition. But the fact that it was only implicit shows how basic it is to his understanding of religion. Paul Tillich recognized it more clearly in his definition of religion as one's "ultimate concern," which has been so useful. What made anything religious, Tillich thought, was its position as ultimate—the final term in one's existential orientation. The mark of religion, for him, was in that quality, rather than in any particular doctrines.

Tillich's definition is often taken to be functional. That would mean that he is saying that whatever "functions as" one's ultimate concern becomes one's religion. Grammatically, however, the ultimate (furthest or absolute) is *sui generis*. So it would be tautological to say that one's ultimate concern "functioned as" one's religion, or that one's religion "functioned as" one's ultimate concern. It would be absurd to suggest that something else (less than ultimate) might have performed that function.

As a theologian Tillich had problems with his own formulation. He complained that many people had concerns—like their nation or worldly success—that they put in the position of being ultimate, which were not *truly* ultimate. He called them "idolatrous."[23] We may think of idolatry as "religious," but Tillich was too much the theologian for that. (We will note his resolution of this issue in chapter 8).

The thing to note here is that Tillich came to his definition via a different route than we are taking. While we are glad to have his company, we note an inconsistency when he tries to qualify it in doctrinal terms. The fact that Tillich came to his definition inconsistently actually makes it more useful to our argument. It shows a certain inadvertence in adopting it, which is always useful in identifying casual (nominal) understandings. The fact that the public has found this formulation especially useful suggests that we are on the track of common English usage.

The Structure of a Definition

Ultimacy seems to be the analytical element we are looking for. The fact that it is an element in so many definitions of religion suggests its importance. It is confirming that there are several paths to it. Ultimacy escapes the charge of being a functional definition, with all their shortcomings. This analytical element, not being doctrinally specific, escapes the charge of being normative.

If we can find what seems ultimate to someone, we will know that we are talking of his "religion." But can we give this definition more substance? Is there a particular category that is being qualified as ultimate? What could be the most obvious object of such an overriding concern or devotion? While it is common to recognize ultimacy as the defining characteristic of the religious, it is not so clear whether we have in mind an ultimate concern, ultimate obligation, ultimate meaning, transcendent order, basic reality, or absolute power.

(7) Here is where another tradition of scholarship may come to our aid. Philosophers and religious scholars of a phenomenological bent may help us identify our ultimate category. Phenomenologists emphasize, not "reality," but more modestly "what appears"—the significant organization of our awareness. And as Tillich observed, "For phenomenology, language provides access to the intuition of essences." Accordingly, phenomenologists pay attention to language and nominal understandings. It is a hermeneutical approach, which we have argued is suited to the subject of religion.[24]

Within religious studies, the phenomenological approach is associated with philosopher Rudolf Otto's classic description of religion as the sense of awesome, uncanny, and alien power. Something has got to seem ultimate or basic—behind or above or under everything else. To Otto the best term to use in capturing our sense of "the ultimate" was that of a mysterious and transcendent *power*.[25]

The important thing for us is not just what Otto thought or why he thought it. The important thing is the very wide scholarly agreement in support of Otto on this point. Hans Kippenberg has noted that the main approaches to religious studies—whether evolutionary (Tylor, Marett) or sociological (Durkheim, Weber)—have likewise found the basis of religion in "an original experience of extraordinary power" and the "ambivalent psychological reactions" to it.[26] Indeed, if one goes back through the classic theories of religion—by Hume, Schleiermacher, Spencer, Frazer, Söderblom, James, Jung, Wallace, and even Tillich and Geertz—one finds that "power" enters all their definitions at some point.[27] It is significant that it is not always uppermost in the scholar's mind but that they found it impossible to avoid. Max Weber is often said to have avoided a definition of religion, but his derivation of religion from magic suggests that he also assumed that its origins were in a concern with power.[28] Biologist Alister Hardy's Religious Experience Research Unit at Oxford collected thousands of reports from the public in the 1970s, and he attests that "power" was in them all, in one way or another.[29]

The very fact that allusions to power seem almost incidental to the scholars' definitions makes them all the more significant in identifying common usage. It is as though some scholars barely recognized that power was the substantive category involved, as concerned as they were with the *characterization* of that power. Their recognition of religion's association with power seems to have come from their European languages, and it was natural to their thinking. In their inclusion of power they are not exhibiting academic expertise so much as showing their mastery of a common cultural idiom.

So we find remarkable convergence in using religion to mean a kind of response to a kind of power. Put in the form of a nominal definition, *"religion" in our word for a certain kind of response to a certain kind of power, the response and the power both understood as beyond anything else in our experience.*

We finally have a toehold on a consistent nominal, generic, and analytic (nonfunctional) definition, in the quality of ultimacy and the category of power. We did not derive this from Tillich, Otto, and Geertz, but it would be a weakness to have to ignore them. I do not aspire to an original definition, which would make it suspect, but have found that, in fact, their various definitions have a common structure. There may be nothing else in common between their interests or methods, but their understandings of religion all combine the elements of (1) response to (2) something of a (3) unique and transcendent kind. For Tillich, it is (1) concern for (2) something unspecified and personal, which is seen as (3) ultimate. For Otto and the ethnographers it is (1) awe of, or entreaty of, a (2) power which is deemed to be (3) beyond anything ordinary. For Geertz, it is (1) motivations and moods established by (2) important cultural symbols of a (3) unique realism and power. Incidentally, Paul Griffiths, who we mentioned as seeking a referential definition, finally offers a definition close to our nominal terms: "the visible patterns of action by which we respond to God as distinct from the created order."[30] Philosopher Charles Taylor has recently echoed our pattern, combining awareness and response in defining religion as "belief in transcendent reality, on the one hand, and the connected aspiration to a transformation which goes beyond ordinary human flourishing on the other."[31]

Answering Objections

Talal Asad, a scholar who denies the possibility of a universal definition of religion, notes that Geertz's attempt "has a specific Christian history."[32] The same might be said of the definitions by Otto and Tillich. This is not a fault. Asad is sensitive to the difficulties of translating different cultures into English terms, but we do not propose to do that. Other cultures may see things differently without being a threat to our understandings. We may note, however, that Otto's philosophy of religion has been successfully translated into other European languages and that Tillich learned to translate his own thinking into lucid English.

The accusation of being too Christian or too Western is very common. But it is weakened by the fact that the dream of an objectivist "view from nowhere in particular" (Thomas Nagel's phrase) is everywhere under attack. It may be that hints of Jewish and Christian monotheism can be sensed behind the English term as commonly defined. After all, the language has grown up in the company of those influences.

But there is the added fact that it is perfectly reasonable to assume that a power to which one responds is what we call personal. This cannot help raising the issue of theism. Alister Hardy noticed that "person, not sensation, is the basic element," or object, in the accounts his subjects gave of their religious experiences.[33]

As mentioned in chapter 1, the self-reports of "spirituality" do not stress ethical or existential imperatives. Rather they point to feelings and to aesthetic structuring of these feelings. Religion goes beyond that, implying that the power is of such grandeur as to demand a response, involving an ethical element. Thus our "merely" nominal and analytic definition is not vacuous.

A concern with power might seem more characteristic of earlier periods of history and bygone understandings of religion. Some have suggested that concerns over meaning in life, rather than power, have become ultimate in recent thought. Sociologists Thomas Luckmann and Robert Bellah thought that by the 1960s the West, and perhaps the rest of the world, was moving into a period in which personal identity, self-actualization, or "personal transcendence" would become our ultimate concern, under growing conditions of dehumanization, stress, and anxiety.[34] But to date, power has never been absent from a common understanding of the religious. For instance, we use a different word—philosophy—for thinking that is *only* concerned with meanings or identity. For "religion," the element of response that is part of English usage suggests an engagement with power, rather than simply contemplation. Similarly, religious "belief" must imply a kind of commitment, beyond mere consideration. Tillich called the religious response "concern," which suggests more than mere interest. Religious "faith" likewise means more than assent. Geertz acknowledged that religion must make a difference when he made "powerful motivations" part of his definition.

So the "particular response" in our definition is something like faith, trust, and worship, and the particular power is somehow personal, divine, supernatural. Those who think of "salvation" as a function uniquely associated with religion should note that it means power—over death or other evil powers. Even in Gnosticism, where salvation is more a matter of illumination or knowledge, salvation is still understood as investing one with the divine nature. It is the power to escape finitude. Some forms of Gnosticism, therefore, could count as religious by our definition.

Perhaps we need not formulate our definition more closely than that. One is still free to argue over particular cases. Whether the type of response or the character of the power seem adequate to characterize something as "religious" will always be matters of judgment. I am only claiming that this is the structure of acceptable definitions. But loose as it may seem, it is not vacuous, and it considerably limits the range of possible understandings. The following chapters will show the difference it makes to common questions.

Asian Spiritualities

Before we test our understanding of the term against its linguistic neighbors, we might revisit the problem of "Asian religions." Asad rightly objected when Western concepts are imposed on the East. But the reverse also happens. Scholarly confusion in the West starts when someone objects, "But you can't define religion as belief in x because there are Asian religions that don't contain x." Usually this involved theism and the so-called "nontheistic religions." There is a circularity here. The statement reveals that one is already committed to an implicit definition of religion while pretending to be searching for a definition. Somehow, one has already decided that "Confucianism," say, is a religion, perhaps because we commonly hear it called that. In the previous chapter we considered the possibility that this was a scholarly mistake that the language has always resisted. The test would be if a native speaker of both English and Mandarin, for instance, thought the English term "religion" was appropriate to both "Confucian" philosophy and the cultic life of the same Chinese people.[35] Only a truly bilingual person could say. Martin Southwold has caught the confusion by hinting that Buddhists are religious even though Buddhism is not.[36] This could be meaningful under our definition, where the emphasis is placed on the adjective before the noun.

Western projection has created confusion for the Japanese as well. Helen Hardacre describes the puzzle of how to categorize Shinto. Before the nineteenth-century Meiji reforms the Japanese had no word for a "sphere of life that could be called 'religious,' as opposed to the rest of one's existence." Their Western-style constitution in 1889, however, dutifully granted freedom of religion. Authorities then declared that Shinto was not a religion, so that it could be enforced by the state. The 1947 constitution again included religious freedom, and defining "religion" is still causing difficulties. Treaties with Western states have forced the Japanese to find an equivalent term, and not surprisingly they studied Christianity as prototypical. Though they are more familiar with "Buddhism," they did not look in that direction for their definition. Yet Hardacre observes that there is some question whether they fully understand our term: "The best philosophical minds understood Christianity as a system of thought, in relation to the state, and as moral philosophy." Japanese intellectuals accordingly deny that Shinto is a religion because they think it superstitious. They reserve religion as an honorific term for something on a more elevated philosophical plane.[37] So we see here something of the untranslatable character of the Western term.

It is one thing to recognize that Asian cultures have sophisticated worldviews and ethical codes, aiming at harmony with cosmic law.[38] It is another thing to insist that these are religions. We may be embarrassed to conclude that they are not, as if denying them our word somehow diminished them. But we have long recognized problems in using our term to describe those cultures, especially as we learn more about them. We should ask what our awkwardness tells us about *our* word. What it tells us is that, after a century of confusion, English speakers still feel some oddness in using the word when it does not refer to something like submission to supernatural powers or beings. No doubt persons in those cultures have terms for themselves that they cannot apply to us, perhaps to their regret.

One might object that I am violating common English usage in questioning whether Buddhism, say, is a religion, when it is so regularly called that. But all definitions have this two-edged quality, starting from usage but also correcting usage. Perhaps some forms of Buddhism are religious and some are not. Surely our continuing and universally recognized awkwardness in calling some forms of Buddhism "religious" justifies the clarification we are attempting here.

Testing a Nominal Definition

(8) The test of our nominal definition is in how the word "religion" looks beside neighboring words or concepts and in whether the dif-

ferences seem consistent. Spirituality, mysticism, magic, philosophy, traditional, superstitious, fundamentalist, fanatical, mythic, ritualistic, faith, and worldview come to mind. There is an example of using this method in Supreme Court Justice William Brennan's stipulation that "it is prayer which distinguishes religious phenomena from all those which resemble them or lie near to them, from the moral sense, for instance, or aesthetic feeling."[39]

"Spirituality" has come into more common use recently, and its use suggests a difference of emphasis. Reinforcing our discussion in chapter 1, two recent studies have found that those who termed themselves "spiritual" rather than "religious" thought that the former suggested a more individual and less institutional commitment. Nevertheless, they indicated much the same "connection or relationship to a Higher power of some kind" as did subjects who identified themselves primarily as "religious."[40] There seemed to be less sense that this spirituality will make unwelcome demands, so the word may suggest something more like appreciation. In short, it may prove to be an aesthetic rather than a religious category. Spirituality might have too little moral weight to be religion and too little intellectual content to be philosophy.

Aesthetic experience has been distinguished from religious experience even when dealing with similar phenomena. Michael Paffard thinks that his empirical researches indicate that "aesthetic experience involves perception and contemplation of objects in and for themselves." Religion, by contrast, involves feeling "a mysterious power or presence, a 'something beyond everything.'"[41] In this understanding, aesthetic experience could be a means to religious ends. Religion, however, could not properly be thought of as a means to aesthetic ends, for its ultimacy makes it an end in itself. As Earle Coleman puts it, the goal of art is to restore us to wholeness, while the goal of religion is to unite us to the whole.[42]

We have said that religion contains spirituality among other elements or associations. What seems to have happened is that in the West, spirituality has declared its independence from religion. Those who use it most freely prefer that it not be too closely defined. The overdefinition of institutional religion was one of the reasons it is being rejected, if we believe the polling results reported in chapter 1. They do not want to see it harden into sectarianism.

If neuroscience really were to reduce certified instances of spirituality to measurable energies and specific brain location, it would be in danger of reification and reduction. For it would presumably be possible to induce it at will, as drug effects are produced. The contrast with religion in this respect would become even more noticeable. If religion involves moral and existential commitments as well as feelings of commitment, it is hard to imagine such effects being induced.

"Faith" has likewise become a substitute for "religion" among those who want to give the latter term a rest. We have seen faith as part of our notion of religion, characterizing the implied response.[43] But it also serves a more simply cognitive function, when used to mean one's basic intellectual and personal orientation, the source of one's values and hopes. As such we have become used to talking of a scientist's faith.

The English word "worldview" is commonly employed in translating the concepts of Asian cultures, as are terms like "cosmic consciousness," "illumination," and "enlightenment." Where such a worldview makes no demands, it would be closer to what we call philosophy. If it suggested a regulation of life in tune with a less than personal universe, it might be termed an ethic. Worldviews might indeed be part of a religion. This does not argue they are better for doing so, for we are not treating "religious" as an honorific.

Mysticism, of course, has a long association with religion in the West.[44] Evelyn Underhill's *Mysticism* classically defines it as the sense that "the spirit of man, itself essentially divine, is capable of immediate communion with God, the One Reality." Or it is "an impassioned desire to transcend the sense-world, in order that the self may be joined by love to the one eternal and ultimate Object of love."[45] The pull of Love, which Underhill finds in mystics generally, might be the kind of response that would bring it within our definition of religion.

Scholars will continue to elaborate this definition on the basis of empirical study, but that is unlikely to change English usage. As academic culture becomes ever more complex, it distances itself from our common culture and from the institutions we will be dealing with in later chapters. But R. C. Zaehner may suggest a change in popular culture in *Mysticism: Sacred and Profane*. There he reports that his own mystical experience started with what seemed a purely "natural" awakening. So he describes a "nature mysticism" that differs from the religious variety in inspiring no "sanctification of character."[46] It would seem, therefore, that mysticism and religion might sometimes be related, but that sometimes mysticism is closer to simple spirituality.

"Sacred" conventionally describes things that mediate between humans and the transcendent source of religious experience. They are the things that carry religious power or partake of the transcendent. Rituals and myths are cultural forms of the sacred. Religion uses them, but they are not the thing itself.

Of the terms of opprobrium—like "fanatical," "fundamentalist," "traditional," "repressive," "escapist," "obsessive,"—only "superstitious"—could be considered synonymous with "religion." With regard to the others, religions could only be particular instances of these things, since not all obsessions, for example, are religious. One would still have to decide how the religious variety differed from others.

There are, in addition to all these, obviously metaphorical uses of the term "religion," as when one calls Marxism or baseball or Coca-Cola religions. They are generally used ironically, and are only effective as metaphors when the irony is recognized.

Last Concerns

One of the common mistakes with regard to religion is to call it an "explanation of the unknown."[47] David Hume encouraged this semantic error by speaking of a search for "unknown causes" as the source of religious notions.[48] There is a solecism in speaking of an explanation of the unknown, for if one has an explanation, then the cause is not "unknown." One's explanations constitute one's knowledge. Of course the explanation may be wrong. But one would never say that science consists of "explanations of the unknown." That would simply imply a doubt that science had got it right. It would suggest a pretension to knowledge, which is what people mean in applying it to religion. But when religion offers explanations, one is no longer in an *unknown* world.

In all this discussion it has not been necessary to consider religion's etymological roots. Nominal definition is sometimes pursued by an etymological search. But taking things back to Latin is now pointless. Thomas Aquinas listed the three derivations of the word over which scholars still argue. But whether the Latin *religio* came from *religare* (to bind back, tie up, or rebind), *relegere* (to reread, review, or rehearse), or *reeligere* (to seek again), we cannot assume that this governs subsequent English development.[49]

Despite the fact that we have concentrated on the word rather than the experience of religion, we cannot ignore the fascinating question of the origins of a religious sense. In recent scholarship, the "intellectualist" view that religion is ordinarily the product of induction from experience, as Hume and others have held, is usually denied, as we will discuss in chapter 7. From his anthropological perspective, Geertz thought that the world does not furnish *evidence* for one's religious beliefs, but is taken as an illustration of them.[50] Sociologist Peter Berger expresses a similar point by saying that "at the heart of the religious phenomenon is pre-reflexive, pre-theoretical experience."[51]

Difficulty in expressing the religious is a common and perhaps necessary feature of such prereflexive experience. Words may fail to express what is typically associated with the ultimacy of the experience of death, birth, overwhelming beauty, tragedy, or size (whether cosmic or microscopic). In analyzing English-language accounts of "transcendental experience," Paffard found that his respondents were most likely to mention its emotional weighting—of awe (112), joy (105), fear (83), enchantment (47), calm (44), or trance (43).[52]

Such problems in expression are familiar to mystics. Paul Ricoeur observes that "'ultimate concern' would remain mute if it does not receive the power of a word of interpretation, ceaselessly renewed by signs and symbols which have educated and formed this concern over the centuries."[53] But, of course, it may indeed remain mute. For as defined here, religion can represent a heuristic moment of fresh intuition or insight. Transcendence is that which leaps a logical gap. It is for this reason that rationality is its enemy, since the latter limits us to what we can reach by logical steps.

Finally, we must decide whether we need a different word for second-hand religious "experience." Berger talks of "second-hand experiences of transcendence." He thinks that most people's religion is probably of this kind, but that it should not thereby be discounted: "One of the most important *raisons d'être* of religious institutions is their capacity to sustain this kind of experience."[54] It is enough if there is something within us that resonates to reports of first-hand experience. Those who find certain accounts of revelations, visions, visitations, and providences to be credible often appear to build stable and rational religious understandings on them. And most of us build a second-hand rationality on the reports from others.

Scholarly Use of the Term

(9) Before looking at the practical understandings of religion that will take up later chapters, we may briefly see how scholarship might use our definition, taking the example of history. If historians insisted on a "real" definition of religion they would be discussing how that religion affected their subjects. The hermeneutical historian, on the other hand, would be interested in how their subjects found religious meaning in their worlds.

There is a big difference here. The first group may only try to find what religion "stood for" in a particular instance, or what some religious movement "really meant," in other terms. In other words, religion's reality is thought to be of a different sort than its believers supposed. Cultural historians, by contrast, might try to discover the religious aspects within culture, even where their subjects would not have used the term. For example, there is a big difference between asking what part "religion" played in the development of American nationalism, and asking how American nationalism exhibited a religious character. The first question assumes that we all recognize religion when we see it, but are really interested in something else, while the second is seeking to discover religion where it had not been suspected. Similarly, there is a difference between asking what was really behind the "religious revival" of the 1950s, and asking whether American foreign policy then had a religious character. In the first instance one is looking for some deeper meaning behind religion, while in the latter one is looking for the deeper religious meaning of our political culture.

Those who study "religious history" often treat religion as a code to be broken in search of something else. A hermeneutic approach treats *culture* as a code and might ask whether religion offers a key to that code. Thus, rather than reducing religion to a deeper level of analysis, cultural historians might see religion *as* that deeper level. In recognition of this difference, philosophers have contrasted the use of religious language with the religious use of language.[55] The former reports a secular activity, while the latter activity undermines secularism.

A hermeneutical approach to religion could go to the very heart of cultural history. What could be more central to our histories than the ultimate concerns of our subjects? There is no reason to abandon the older fields of church history and religious history, centering on recognizably religious institutions, doctrines and leaders. But there will be a greater sense of discovery when we stumble into an ultimate dimension in the lives of scientists, conquerors, composers, constitution framers, explorers, statesmen, architects, educators, and revolutionaries. It should not have to be labeled religion for one to find it so. And we can thereby restore a more adequate sense of religion's role in human life.

All this is not to say that religion is necessarily the deepest level of one's motivation or awareness. Historians often suspect that they are dealing with a merely conventional or instrumental religiosity. Does such a piety deserve the name religion, by our definition? Psychologists Gordon Allport and Michael Ross introduced the distinction of "intrinsic" and "extrinsic" to remind us of the difference we all sense, between those who are truly in the grip of the religious and those who only use its symbols for ulterior ends.[56] A definition that claims to represent common usage must acknowledge the fact that "religious" is regularly used of personal professions and actions which are less than authentic. What should historians do with persons who are caught in religious pretense or hypocrisy? It seems that we should provide an addendum to our definition, declaring that a merely extrinsic religion is an *imitation* of what we have defined as religious. Our generic definition would still be useful in these normative discussions, by providing a baseline against which to measure deviations.

Even if one readily accepted our definition of religious and religion there would be judgments on the authenticity of particular experiences. No doubt the experience that Otto and others described is not nearly as widespread as conventional religious allegiance. Even those who report having experienced the real thing may not claim to live in it always. How should we think about second-hand religion?

One may admit the problem without calling the original religious experience into question. For religious awareness may color the whole of life for those who experience it, and even for those who only hear about it. In Peter Berger's words,

> it is the very purpose of any religious tradition to preserve for generations of ordinary people not only the memory of the great founding events, but the possibility of replicating them in a much lower key. Many of us have obtained comfort, insight, and even a modest measure of spiritual transport from participation in the worship of an ordinary congregation of fellow believers. With all due respect to the virtuosi, I have long maintained that those of us who can only play a mediocre violin should pay attention to the intimations of transcendence that can be found in everyday experience.[57]

Semantically, there is nothing wrong with speaking of false religion; it only means "something that could be mistaken for religion." Indeed, it assumes the reality of the experience. Yet this distinction between intrinsic and extrinsic religion is an admission of how hard it is to get away from real, normative, and functional approaches, for all three seem to be creeping back into our considerations. But I have not claimed that our word does not describe institutionalized religions, that have functions, and are more or less worthy of the name. I only mean to say that these are not essential, defining characteristics of the word. Both intrinsic and extrinsic modes can claim the name, in their different ways.

To sum up, we have offered as the normal understanding of religious, that it is the word used to signify a particular kind of response to a particular kind of power. When people sense anomalies within their experience—things that defy "natural" description—they find themselves using a language which may evoke the "supernatural." A religious sense need not always be intense, but its tendency will always be to relativize ordinary reality. The kind of response involved might be termed faith or dependence, and the kind of power will be something beyond what we have nominally defined as the "natural." Religion represents the ultimate challenge to our normal lives and thinking.

We have come a very roundabout way to get back to a fairly commonsense definition. That definition is not intended to be original, but is meant to represent our common understanding. What we have tried to accomplish is the elimination of several kinds of confusion. We have argued that Western religious traditions are more exceptional than we might have thought, without being overcome with embarrassment by that fact. The main test of the value of greater clarity is in the chapters to follow. There we will see how various issues look in the light of a consistent understanding of religion. We will see how many of the puzzles regarding religion in relation to education, law, politics, science, psychology, arise from contaminated definitions.

CHAPTER THREE

Why Religion and Education Challenge Each Other

Ordinarily we think that making something part of our educational curriculum is a way of indicating its importance. Studying religion might be considered to be a way of showing respect. But our common definition of "religion" and an operative definition of "study" make things different in this case. In fact, we will see that religion in the way we use the term and the practice of schools call each other into question. It begins to justify those who sense that what we normally think of as education is directly challenging to religion.

In considering the term religion in the context of our educational thought and practice, the point should not be to offer my own sense of a proper relation, but to reveal what the word most naturally suggests along that line. So I hope to avoid personal advocacy, seeking instead the integrity of what is admittedly a Western concept of religion. Others may better advocate their preferences once we have made this clear.

Our definition showed the term religion to indicate the response of faith to a transcendent power. So religion involves practice or belief, or we could say that it exists *in* practice and belief. The natural engagement with religious awareness is something like worship and commitment. To study, by contrast, means to distance oneself, to find a larger perspective in which to understand or redefine the subject. Studying something translates it into terms more familiar and seemingly more basic. Such study will naturally question religion rather than letting it question us.

Something of this was understood by a member of the department of religion at my university. An expert in Chinese religion, she explained to colleagues that

> Buddhism must be *experienced*. What Buddha did to arrive at what we now call Buddhism was to just sit under a tree. So how do you teach something that is to be perceived, conceived of and actually *practiced*, such as quiet sitting under a tree?
>
> You do it by teaching performatively, meaning that students must physically participate in the religious practices. If a specialist in chemistry had never gone to the chemistry labs, what would we say of his expertise? It's incomplete, right? So students who have the theoretical part of Buddhism but who've never sat in any meditation, never tried a single asana to see what happens to their consciousness, never tried the effects of the mudras or never drawn a single mandala, . . . their experience, their knowledge, is incomplete.

A third to a half of her course consists of something like a religious laboratory. She teaches breathing exercises, meditation techniques, and how to think with love and compassion.

This skirts some legal limitations in U.S. law, which we will take up later. The Supreme Court, for example, recognized that Bible reading without comment can be an actual exercise of religion, unlike teaching *about* religion.[1] Our universities, despite their secularist rules, may feel that Buddhism is so far from a real religious option for American students that we can allow what would be prohibited in teaching a majority faith. They may think my colleague is teaching "meditational tools," or having her students study their feelings by sampling pieties. But she was right to point out our schools' attenuated sense of religion. "Religion can't be cut off," she insisted, "because it imbues everything we do: the way we read books, the way we communicate, the way we go to school, the way we eat food— everything is permeated with our spirituality."[2]

This is not just true of Eastern traditions. Those outside of a religious tradition are apt to treat them as something to think about; for those within, it is a way of thinking. That is, religion thinks it is the widest perspective, and it does not recognize more inclusive ones. This is how one discovers one's religion, by noting what goes unquestioned. Questions of purpose in life, the significance of events, the moral use of things, the grace of life, seem naturally religious. A really secular rationality is more guarded, concerned mainly to seek verification of such matters within some other, perhaps unrecognized perspective.

Another way of putting this is that religion is not ordinary knowledge so much as an awareness of the limits on ordinary knowledge. To be religious makes one more aware of the ordinary. Though we may think of any particular religion as doctrinal propositions, we use the adjective "religious" for that which calls the familiar into question. This is why religion has trouble expressing itself. It is not *like* anything else, so one has to use metaphors. From all this it follows that studying *about* religion is bound to be viewed with suspicion by religion itself.

But Is Education Necessarily Religious?

That is one side of the issue of religion and education. But we must also ask whether all education is necessarily religious in the sense of resting on ultimate intellectual commitments. Do all educational programs necessarily have a prerational basis, something like a faith? Those who have most actively thought and written about "faith" recently have popularized the sense of its being *one's basic intellectual and personal orientation, the source of one's values and hopes.* Later, we will discuss the view that even science can be based on a faith of this sort. So we may have to learn to live with a cultural tension between different faiths, some that are recognized as "religions" and excluded from the public sphere, and others that go unnoticed and may enjoy the support of official institutions.

This point is clearer if we view it from the other side. What if government schools taught *about* science, instead of just teaching science? That is, what if the primary curriculum made children mainly conscious of how science had developed through history, how it was still developing, and stressed its false leads, revolutionary breaks, and the quarrels it has inspired? Scientists would react negatively if the emphasis was on *understanding* science in these ways. Emphasizing its contingency would relativize the enterprise, tending to neglect its truth claims.

Feminist scholars have argued that the order in which scientific problems have been taken up, the questions asked, and the uses made of the knowledge would all have been different if women had been in the forefront of science.[3] Thomas Kuhn's classic *The Structure of Scientific Revolutions* remarked on how long "normal science" may proceed on the wrong track before major, revolutionary corrections occur—something formerly passed over in textbooks. Ever since Durkheim's classic work we have known that the most basic "modes of our categorical grasp of the world are inextricably embedded in religion."[4] Such understandings are reserved for advanced scholars, while children are indoctrinated in something like a naturalistic faith.

One can imagine our public schools teaching *about* secularism, seeing the secular mindset in a historical perspective. If teachers problematized secularism through a study of its history, assumptions, contradictions, and its supporting institutions and ambitions, it might make students more open to rival faiths. At the moment, state schools "teach secularism" in the sense of insinuating it rather than considering it. Meanwhile, children may be innoculated against religion by teaching it by comparative and historicizing methods.

We can either "learn" religion or "study" it. The first means learning the symbols and affirmations of a faith, as one learns the terms of a science. The difference between learning and studying is in the attitude—the humility—involved. Learning something involves our mental, personal or spiritual formation, as we submit to something beyond us. It is obviously difficult, and may even be impossible, for a pluralist democracy to be fair to all sides at this fundamental level of mental formation, if it insists on a common schooling.

There is another sense in which religion may be involved in all education. There is an important difference between teaching the narrative or doctrines of a particular religion and using religious concepts within more general arguments. Terms like purpose, person, creation, justified, evil, humane, responsibility, and a host of others seem to relate to ultimate values or concerns. It is a challenge to make sense of them in a naturalistic context, if that proves to be possible at all. So any of our education that involves understandings of the human situation or the human good will be dealing in what sound like religious concepts.

Which Rationality?

If, in Western education, rationality is expected to govern the enterprise, one must ask how it now relates to faith. Michael Polanyi's *Personal Knowledge: Towards a Post-Critical Knowledge* (1958) is relevant in showing how scientists master their knowledge. A chemist himself, Polanyi noted that research scientists do not learn the attitudes, skills, and rules that govern their enterprise as a set of principles. There are no formulas by which scientists do their work. Knowledge does not assemble itself mechanically but calls for various *personal* skills, for participation and judgment—something like that mentioned by the teacher of Buddhism. Polanyi thought that scientists are often unconscious of the skills and judgment they bring to bear on their problems and that they could not describe them exhaustively, even if asked to do so. That is why science must be taught by apprenticeship, like medical internships. Mentors show their pupils how to do things, while attempting to explain. Hence the importance of *personal* knowledge.

Nor is logic in the forefront of their most dramatic discoveries. Anything that qualifies as a true discovery involves a logical gap. Such gaps are crossed by what Polanyi can only call "illumination," which has sometimes included dreams.[5] According to Polanyi and Kuhn, the great discoveries of science—the revolutionary "conversions" as they call them—require a "heuristic passion" which helps one abandon logic momentarily in search of a new basis or new assumptions. It also helps in convincing others who are clinging to old scientific models.[6] For in such creative situations, even what counts as evidence or experimental fact may be in question—a matter of definition.

In *A Social History of Truth*, Steven Shapin showed how difficult it was to establish the values and trust that made scientific discourse and cooperation even possible in the aristocratic and classical milieu of the seventeenth century.[7] Science is grounded in a whole culture, involving a particular etiquette, morality, judgment, and even aesthetic standards. These did not come from science itself, but were borrowed to form its basis. All this reminds us of what is necessary besides simple logic, even in our most rationalized enterprise. There is some question where this discipline will come from in the future. It was recently reported in *Nature* that a third of scientists surveyed said they "had engaged in at least one [professional] practice that would probably get them into trouble" within the previous three years. The other two-thirds may have been restrained by some vestige of a religious code.[8]

So it is not just at the stage of childhood that schooling will involve a religious or ideological grounding. What is often called "the Enlightenment Project" has long been seen as quasi-religions.[9] So postmodernism has popularized the idea that Western rationalism imposes limits that seem artificial from some angles, like the requirement that all knowledge be public and impersonal. In a secularizing world, we have to work to justify concepts like sanity, wealth, beauty, love, fulfillment, purpose, and judgment. There is nothing more real in our lifeworld than these concepts, and yet naturalism, for example, has trouble accounting for them in its own terms. So, vital as they are, they have difficulty finding a place in academic discourse.[10] Religious discourses, on the other hand, find places for them all. *Ethics?*

For example, what is called "economics" has earned its status as a science by objectifying ("commodifying") everything from land and labor to currencies and kidneys. While politically, we keep orphans from being sold as slaves, it might be hard to justify this within a naturalistic science of economics. This is not far from the actual issue regarding harvesting living fetal tissue, which involves sacrificing living beings. Economics would be different if it was thought of as the study of human welfare rather than as the science of production and exchange. As such, its most pressing problems might be the condition of the poor or children, as the most truly helpless. We would not be puzzling over the place of ethical instruction in the business school, for it would be at the heart of their curriculum. And religion would not be accused of intruding itself in this area, where it "has no business."[11] In chapter 7 we will note that "disease" is not accounted for within the terms of scientific naturalism. Medical education must simply assume something that religion is better able to talk about.

What all this means is that the idea that religion represents authority while science equals self-evident rationality is unrealistic. This is where the thoughtful book *Educating for Intelligent Belief or Unbelief* misses the point. Intelligence is based on belief, not the other way around. Polanyi, who was not a religious believer, reminds his readers of the universal validity of St. Augustine's principle of *nisi credideritis, non intelligitis*: Unless you believe, you will not understand. "No intelligence, however critical or original, can operate outside such a fiduciary [faith] framework." As Polanyi notes, such a commitment underlies science itself.[12]

Augustine and others who have appealed to this principle did not mean that whatever one happens to believe is going to turn out to be justified rationally. Rather, it means that belief is what sets one on a journey of understanding. The goal will be the understanding, and not the originating belief. Belief is the intuition and confidence that first sustains the search, like the scientist's belief in the regularity of phenomena—what we call "nature." The prior belief may be refined or even transformed by that search for understanding. When St. Anselm called theology *fides quarens intellectum*—"faith in search of understanding"—he cannot have thought that this meant belief being satisfied with belief.[13]

We cannot submit our beliefs to intelligent scrutiny so long as they are beliefs. When we view them from outside they are no longer functioning as beliefs. Beliefs seem self-evident. When they no longer work that way, they become thoughts or simply ideas. If there is no transcendent rationality—what Thomas Nagel called the "view from nowhere in particular"—then individual beliefs can only be criticized within the belief system containing them. From outside, they can only be rejected, on the basis of our commitment to another. Tax-supported schools may have to decide what groups to disfranchise in this respect.

Therefore, if government schools consider religion, it will almost surely be in an effort to get children to view their beliefs from outside, and to accept them back as ideas. The U.S. Supreme Court made this explicit in *Abington School District v. Schempp* (1963), when it said that

> It might well be said that one's education is not complete without a study of comparative religion or the history of religion and its relationship to the advancement of civilization. . . . Nothing we have said here indicates that such study of the Bible or of religion, when presented objectively as part of a secular program of education, may not be effected consistently with the First Amendment.[14]

This may have struck them as a concession, but it actually meant that religion must be treated with suspicion in government schools, within a "secular" program of education. Even those who see religion in terms of its threat to our social order, such as philosopher Amy Gutmann, acknowledge that it is hard "to teach religion without teaching an attitude toward religion."[15]

Legal philosopher Mark Tushnet commented on the Court's view that study *about* the Bible did not threaten their goal of a secular agreement: "Teaching Scripture differs from teaching about the Bible because participants in the former activity open themselves to inspiration and participation . . . in ways that participants in the latter need not."[16] Secular liberalism believes that education should encourage autonomy, making individuals the final judge in all matters. Religion, as our definition suggests, does not think that is realistic. For it does not think we choose our beliefs. Our beliefs are what have formed us.

Indoctrination, which is usually discussed with reference to religion, may be understood as the effort to close minds rather than open them, to keep persons in a childish state.[17] It is most successful when other influences can be kept out. Government schools which exclude religious perspectives run the same danger. Awareness and respect for diversity is intended to avoid such dangers. But a *study* of various belief systems may not insure against superficiality, as we may distance children from their home culture. While one might nurture diversity within a school, it is not possible within an individual, since one can only accommodate one set of first principles. As for the liberation that education should provide—the opposite of indoctrination—people can only do that for themselves. Schools can only liberate us from one tradition by delivering us into the hands of another.[18]

Comparative Religion as an Example of Indoctrination

There might naturally be more concern about the relativizing effects of study with children than with later stages of education. Yet it has been easier to see in the advanced study of religion. Some of those within the field of comparative religion worry over this fact. Wilfred Cantwell Smith emphasized that scholars' assumptions dictate what they see as facts in the traditions they study, as well as how they judge them. He admitted being "haunted by the sense that method, technique, is a device for dominating. . . . If we learn the right method, we can manipulate, control, exert our superiority." Since the real goal is to understand other people and not just their ideas, Smith thought that one's "methodology" should include respect, humility, and openness. For the goal was surely to make alien faiths intelligible and not just objective.[19]

Others worry that the domination can be more tangible. Edward Said warned that placing Asian cultures within the frame of European conceptions has justified the exercise of actual power over them.[20] The field of ethnology, which initially centered on the study of "primitive" religions, developed in the wake of Western imperialism. Michel Foucault thought it still forms a part of Western power:

"Ethnology can assume its proper dimensions only within the historical sovereignty—always restrained but always present—of European thought."[21]

Scholars seem to worry more about disrespect toward foreign traditions than about the routine disparagement of Western traditions, as students bring them from home. We have reached a point at which our own religious are treated as foreign—or at least primitive—by educational establishments.

This could be seen at a symposium on religious studies held at the University of California, Santa Barbara, in 1985–1986. Some of the participants recognized the hostile implications of their study while others did not. John F. Wilson acknowledged that "there is a sense in which our study of other societies with respect to their cultural presuppositions is a continuation of the imperialistic relationship in an analytical mold." But John B. Carman noted that we often turn the weapons of study against our own religious traditions, employing a "hermeneutics of suspicion" there, while being generous toward those of others.[22]

Other participants did not see such problems. Gerald James Larson suggested the model of psychoanalysis for the field of religious studies, assuming that both were meant to free individuals from the past. James M. Robinson considered renaming the field of religious studies "Humanizing Studies," to assure dubious academic colleagues of its value. He recognized that this would reduce enrollments, since many students were drawn by the hope that the courses would deepen their religious awareness instead of distancing them from it. William Scott Green was more candid, admitting that religious studies "is perhaps the only field of study for which secularity is an absolutely necessary prerequisite." He saw his job as explaining his students' religion by translating it into nonreligious terms.[23]

One participant, Eric Sharpe, tried to explain the need to investigate religion from the inside rather than from an alien perspective. He noted that the academic study of religion judged religions "without actually submitting to the conditions of any part of it," even though "submission" is one of the defining characteristics of religion. He reminded the group that this was the reason that some scholars had adopted a phenomenological study of religion.[24]

This is likely to be seen as special pleading, putting religions beyond criticism. But philosopher Louis Dupré, who was not at the Santa Barbara symposium, explains why a strenuously neutral, phenomenological approach is especially appropriate to religious studies. Religious experience is exceptional, he says, in that its "object" seems to provide its own meaning, rather than receiving a meaning from the human subject. He calls that religion's defining characteristic. Dupré rejects the idea that religion is an *a priori* intellectual category. It is not inborn, self-evident, or a category we impose upon experience. Rather, the religious character of experience seems to be *given*, as our words "revelation" or "disclosure" suggest. We shall revisit this idea in chapter 8, where we argue that religion is one area in which there may be something like uninterpreted experience.

Dupré admits that religion cannot be sustained without symbolic expression. This symbolism is the proper subject of religious studies. The fact that the symbols change is often taken as evidence of psychological projection or of the social relativity of religious experience. But change in symbolization may only mean that the culture is changing, and not the experience itself. For symbols *must* change if the experience itself is unchanging—assuming that culture is always in flux.[25]

Some religious studies scholars are impatient with the fear of reductionism. They often associate it with the prominent anthropologist Mircea Eliade, who insisted that religions be understood in their own terms.[26] We might agree that there ought to be the possibility of studying religions under the rubric of cultural studies without privileging that approach over investigating them from within.[27] Much is lost if a hermeneutic of suspicion amounts to secularist indoctrination.[28] If a relativizing approach to religion is our only engagement with it, society will be robbed of a potent source of cultural critique.

Premature Rationalism

There is also an educational issue involved in exposing children to a secular or objectifying rationalism before they can incorporate it within a developing identity. Psychologist Bruno Bettelheim is famous for showing how much mental work the child must do before "formal" educational programs can begin to have effect.[29] He thought that the appropriate materials in this effort were folk stories, not unlike religious sources. Fairy tales have offended experts from the eighteenth century onwards, by their unsavory elements. Bettelheim showed that the child's moral and intellectual development follows a more winding path than we might assume.

Folk literature characteristically presents not lessons but models, appropriate for a time when the child's task is the construction of an identity.[30] It presents images that help children to distinguish feelings that are the source of their inner conflicts, and it gives children the confidence they need to proceed in a world they cannot yet understand. To deny something like magic at that stage will not bring realism but only discouragement. Indeed, offering information and moral lessons at that stage would tend to estrange children from their inner life. Bettleheim thought that we need not fear that the magic will prevent the development of rationality later. In fact it provides the kind of faith that underlies rationality.

Bettelheim represents a recent trend away from an older psychology that took the educated adult as its model of mental life. There is now an increasing recognition that moral development does not follow the logic of academic study. The campaign to master moral reasoning through values clarification was disappointing in its results, making teachers eager for something different.

They found it in narrative, the main element in "character education." This held that personal and moral development is not a matter of solving the problems presented by "situations," but is a matter of inhabiting certain narratives, and creating dispositions. If the goal is to teach us to take others into consideration, this is done by helping students incorporate worthy models, fictional or otherwise. Concentrating on principles of moral judgment does not seem any more likely a method than memorizing rules of morality. And if morality is a social category more than an individual matter, we need rituals, ceremonies, shared models, and stories. All this sounds more like religious socialization than the problem-solving approach which has long been our model of pedagogy. Older models have brought on our dysfunctional myth of the presocial individual, with all the bureaucratic and therapeutic elements of modern alienation.[31]

This raises the old issue of respecting the child's freedom by waiting to present anything religious until they are old enough to choose for themselves. *Religion could almost be defined as how we make our choices.* Belief is basic to choosing, as well as to thinking. It includes at least the following axioms: the world is reliable; we can understand it; there is some purpose to it, if only in human lives; we are significant; and there are powers to help us, though we may not see them. None of this is the result of scientific investigation. We may grow up to doubt some of it. But an effort to keep all this from children because it is recognized as religious would cripple the child's *intellectual* development.

Harvard psychologist Robert Coles, who has spent his life listening to children, thinks that "the entire range of children's mental life can and does connect with their religious and spiritual thinking." They use religious stories "to look inward as well as upward." The concept of God, especially, awakens questions for children; it stretches their thinking and makes philosophers out of them. Even if their image of God initally *results* from psychological projection, it is a *cause* of developing rationality.[32]

Coles does not think schools should teach religious or moral lessons directly, for the doubts raised above concerning teaching ethics by principles. But if teachers used the intuitive language of religion occasionally and naturally, they would avoid giving the impression that religion is off limits, unimportant or bad. He is inclined to think that the present refusal to take any notice of the religious interests of children "might relate to the [current] educational problems among some children. It is a tragedy intellectually as well as morally and spiritually."[33] Coles' sensitivity to the language used with children recalls what others have said about the fact that it is not the lessons alone but the entire classroom atmosphere that builds our mental and moral habits.

Diversity: Social or Individual?

The power to divorce children from their beliefs is compounded by the issue of compulsory schools. Granted that someone must make educational choices for children, is it to be parents or the state? When the financial penalty for parental choice is so great, there is a feeling that government schools ought to take religion into account in accommodating our diverse population. The problem may be that the ideal of neutrality in religion, or the celebration of diversity and multiculturalism, may become simply dismissive. Programs on cultural diversity may suggest the importance of religion but the unimportance of any particular religion. At worst, it becomes the disparagement of majority culture in an effort to correct some perceived imbalance.

Multiculturalism can become something like teaching Language without teaching any particular language. Religions are radically different. Comparatists warn against the widespread assumption that all religions teach the same thing. As religious studies scholar Jonathan Z. Smith points out, Enlightenment thinkers thought that this was a discovery, when in fact it was an assumption.[34] By contrast, one of the most notable early efforts of sociology was Max Weber's investigations into how the massive differences between the world's civilizations centered on their religions.

Scholars are aware that religions aim at radically different goals. But among secondary educators, true relativists are rare; the temptation is to teach either that religions are different paths to the same goal (pluralists) or that they are essentially the same path (inclusivists). Asserting a core philosophy contained in them all may save the reputation of religion among secularists, showing that no religion can be wrong if understood properly. But Mark Heim parodies this denial of meaningful diversity with what he calls the "Idea of Travel."

It is as if we were faced with a number of different tickets (train, boat, plane, bus), each with distinctive maps and itineraries attached. Those who favor a pluralist theory . . . could maintain that because travel of any sort involves some constant generic elements (tickets have a price; some representation of the path is needed; we will never depart if we don't show up on time) it is false and arrogant to suppose that we would miss something on one trip we might find on another or that we don't all have the same destination. There is, after all, only one world. And these trips are all ways of relating to it. . . .

It would be relentlessly (and rightly) insisted that none of the maps or itineraries provides a "literal" representation of its destination or of the trip itself. Instead we will be told it is "traveling" as a human condition, "arrival" as the subjective realization of a sense of completion, and "the Destination" as the ultimate ground of the possibility of any arrival which are truly real. Jaffna, Kyoto, Santiago de Compostela are mythical forms of "The Destination."[35]

J. A. DiNoia recounts the tale of the Buddhist scholar who studied the lives of Catholic saints, sadly concluding that they were bad Buddhists.[36]

Neil Postman and George Marsden likewise have warned that teaching comparative religion should not be for the purpose of "narrative busting."[37] They point out that elementary teachers need not imagine that their responsibility is to broaden students' minds by loosening the religious assumptions they bring from "culturally disadvantaged" homes. Diversity describes societies, not individuals.

To "learn" a religion, as my Buddhist colleague noted, entails sitting under the judgment of the religion. This may only be possible in sectarian schools. For nothing can replace kneeling in prayer in "teaching religion." It is true that if religion is felt as ultimate, it transcends culture and judgment and may truly be dangerous. But while parents might accept the possibility that their children might someday abandon a "birthright" religion, they will not think it is the school's job to wean them from it. They may doubt that religions are all equally true or valuable or relevant to our population, and that teachers who insinuate that are establishing irreligion.

The Legal Situation in the U.S.

The legal position of religion in U.S. public education would profit from greater clarity in definition—of religion, study, and belief. And we need to start with educators' distinction of the formal curriculum, the hidden curriculum, and the null curriculum. In our government schools, Protestant Christianity was once part of the formal curriculum. It was later left to the hidden curriculum, by teachers who could just not help occasionally expressing religious attitudes. Recent court rulings have been understood as making religion part of the null curriculum, not a proper subject unless handled with special care.

In justifying this exclusion a number of reasons are adduced. (1) There is the constitutional prohibition of religious establishment. (2) There is the impressionable nature of small children. (3) There is the fear that minority children will feel left out of American society, even when recognition of majority traditions falls far short of establishment. (4) There is moral suspicion of religion, which is argued in light of the historical record. And (5) there is the feeling that religion has no rational importance. Our definition of religion may prove relevant here.

On the first point, there is much debate today. Nearly all of the First Amendment religion cases tried by the Supreme Court have involved educational issues.[38] We have already noted the ruling that publicly supported schools may teach *about* religion but must not *teach religion* in the sense of urging belief. As "part of a secular program of education," religion must be treated as an element of human culture.

But there is more to the First Amendment than the establishment prohibition: "Congress shall make no law respecting an establishment of religion, or prohibiting the free exercise thereof; or abridging the freedom of speech. . . ." Limiting government involvement in religion is for the sake of safeguarding free exercise, since the clauses have the same purpose of safeguarding free exercise, of minorities on one hand and majorities on the other. Courts show a growing recognition that government must be neutral among religions. This has been judicially construed to mean neutrality also between religion and irreligion, so that state power does not compromise any of these positions.[39]

Some citizens object that public schools are our most central intellectual and ideological institutions. So they claim that leaving religion out undermines the basis of our common culture. Secularism becomes ideological when it is established as a cultural base. These parents may wonder whether teaching *about* religion would only raise questions about it and be worse than nothing. We have argued that these are not unreasonable concerns.

On the second reason for exclusion, the Supreme Court has suggested, in *Lee v. Weisman* (1992), that impressionable age extends at least into the middle school years. Different principles have been applied in cases primarily involving older persons.

Thirdly, courts have ruled that the First Amendment must imply a right of minorities not to feel excluded. They suggest that schools do this by leaving religion out of what we might call the "life" or the ethos of the school as well as out of the formal curriculum, in such matters as release time programs and commencement exercises. In *McCollum v. Board of Education* (1948) the Court additionally declared that schools have the job of generating nationalism in the population. Religious differences would interfere with that. So even in a release time religious education program, away from the school setting,

> The children belonging to these non-participating sects will thus have inculcated in them a feeling of separatism when the school should be the training ground for habits of community. . . . In no activity of the State is it more vital to keep out divisive forces than in its schools.[40]

Thus the court established what sociologists call "civil religion," which we will discuss in chapter 5.

In *Abingdon v. Schempp* Justice Brennan worried that even the refusal to participate in a release time religious education program would violate students' freedom of religious exercise, by forcing them to profess their disbelief.[41] Actually, refusal could be for any number of reasons besides disbelief. But Brennan registered an official nervousness about any appearance of religion in public life.

Since that Cold War-era ruling, American society has begun to realize that diversity is the very point of the freedoms of speech, press, and religion protected by the Constitution. But Supreme Court rulings continue to cite the dangers of peer pressure with relation to moment-of-silence proposals and commencement prayers.[42] This sensitivity shows a recognition that children are not fully rational agents and that Justices had begun thinking more generally of the ethos of the school. In one case, those who objected to letting student religious groups meet on school grounds warned that "the State has structured an environment in which students holding mainstream views may be able to coerce adherents of minority religions to attend club meetings."[43] They meant to say "influence," but the exaggeration shows the threat that religion, even when promoted by fellow students and not state officials, poses to some minds. The implication of the Court's civil religion is that children should always feel part of a majority.

The fourth reason for excluding religion is in seeing religion simply as a negative influence. In the landmark decision of *Lemon v. Kurtzman* (1971) the Court observed that "political debate and division, however vigorous or even partisan, are normal and healthy," but that "division along religious lines was one of the principal evils against which the First Amendment was intended to protect."[44] That decision continued to refer to unspecified dangers of religion in nearly every paragraph.

There was a time when historians emphasized the constructive impact of religious institutions and values in the West. They pointed out that state power was initially curbed by religious resistance; that aristocratic dominance was eventually tempered by religious values; that peace, learning, and racial and class inclusion were promoted by Christian religion, in the teeth of opposition which might also be Christian. But that approach lasted long enough to generate an academic reaction, which is now dominant. An atmosphere of suspicion on these subject pervades textbooks that may not mention the older views.[45] To attempt anything like a moral balance sheet would be rejected as special pleading. Both of these historical views have abundant basis in fact, while judgments might differ according to whether one was considering religious ideals or practices.

The fifth critique, the denial of the intellectual significance of religion, depends on whether one assumes the naturalist or rationalist foundationalism we have discussed earlier. But many important questions, like the uses of our knowledge, will not have answers in those terms. What we call secularism borrows many terms from our religious heritage for which it cannot give an independent justification, starting with the concepts of the human discussed earlier. Thus the argument that religion is unworthy of our schools' time might be turned around, into an argument that secularist schools cannot do justice to the important issues religion raises.

It seems to be time to revisit these various arguments, in light of more current understandings of social diversity, individual identity, and of philosophical objections to an old-fashioned rationalism. We may conclude that religion cannot be handled effectively in compulsory public schools. All Western European countries offer state aid to religious schools, respecting peoples' rights to be themselves as well as being nationalists and democrats.[46]

Examples

Lest readers think too much is being made of hypothetical threats, there is the troubling example of judicial and journalistic prejudice in the case of *Hawkins County School Board v. Mozert* (1983). This involved the authority of government schools to force students to study texts that offended what were probably majority beliefs. The textual material did not represent alternative "facts" but simply rival beliefs. The case raised the issue of who decides what is taught in the schools—parents, teachers, school boards, democratic majorities, educational authorities, publishers, journalists, pressure groups, or judges.

When a group of parents asked that their children be excused from studying a reader specializing in currently fashionable themes—science fantasy, occultism, and witchcraft (but no stories involving Christianity)—a court ruled that students did not have the right to absent themselves from lessons they or their parents found offensive. The suggested assignments involved the requirement that children write their own incantations. The court thought this was acceptable, while requiring children to write prayers would not have been. Journalists, following the line taken by People for the American Way, presented the case as fundamentalist parents trying to dictate the curriculum for the other students, which fit a media paradigm in such matters. So parents who asked that their children be allowed to read alternative materials were termed "censors," when the actual censorship was done by publishers who had purged any reference to Christianity. School officials were presented in the national media as the guardians of "liberty."

After the school board and some local ministers and judges had looked through the texts they dismissed the objections. In school prayer decisions the vulnerability of impressionable children had sometimes been an unanswerable objection, but in this case the court declared that "mere exposure" to irreligious ideas did not constitute a burden on the children's beliefs. Judges found a compelling state interest in educating all children uniformly, and they told the parents that they needed to understand different people and their beliefs. Ironically, they had just shown that they did not even recognize the plaintiff's beliefs as religious, let alone worthy of respect. It might be noted that some of the parents had more academic credentials than the authorities ruling on their case.

Students who refused to read the texts were suspended, their parents were arrested, and some lost their jobs. The school board committed scarce funds to a legal effort to force children to read those texts or nothing. For by now they were trying to teach something other than reading—obedience to bureaucratic power. The

American Civil Liberties Union broke a long standing policy in favor of individual rights in order to back this demand for uniformity. The president of People for the American Way expressed pride in having contributed to this "victory for religious pluralism," which he privately admitted was the opposite of the truth. He was pleased that the most respected national newspapers and magazines followed his characterization of it as "Scopes II."[47]

Of course, the parents were reminded that they could always pay to send their children to private schools.[48] It has been ironically suggested that if adamantly secularist parents objected to a religious school atmosphere, they could always pay for private education where secularist views would go unchallenged.[49]

What we see here is that religion is the one area in which Americans' commitment to individual freedom falters. Courts which cannot allow even release time religious instruction for those who choose it have required students to attend lessons in sex education and values clarification over religious objections.[50] This has nothing to do with superior factuality, but might be viewed as an ideological more than an educational matter.

The power involved in compulsory education implies power over religion. Our courts have some sense of children's special vulnerability, but they have been selective. The Justices who dissented from the Supreme Court's decision in *Board of Education v. Mergens* (1990) to allow religious clubs to meet on school grounds, warned that

> when the government, through mandatory attendance laws, brings students together in a highly controlled environment every day for the better part of their waking hours and regulates virtually every aspect of their existence during that time, we should not be so quick to dismiss the problems of peer pressure as if the school environment had nothing to do with creating and fostering it.[51]

Astonishingly, they were only thinking of pressure on nonreligious students. The Justices used terms like "most dangerous" and "substantial risks" in describing the "threat" that extracurricular religious clubs might pose. But if a student's secularity is threatened by a momentary commencement ritual, how can many years of total immersion in a secular curriculum and the stares of peers not threaten a student's religious identity?

The one time the Supreme Court balanced their concern for impressionable secular children with a concern for impressionable religious ones was in *Wisconsin v. Yoder* (1972). They did so by giving Amish defendants the right to their own schools and their own school-leaving age. For the court recognized that their alternative was emigration. It concluded that the Amish had a right to emphasize "a life of 'goodness,' rather than intellect; wisdom rather than technical knowledge; community welfare rather than competition; and separation from, rather than integration with, contemporary worldly society."[52]

That decision still troubles those constitutional scholars who think the state must be not just neutral but secular. Justice Douglas dissented from *Yoder* over the question of whether the wishes of the children had been considered or only those of the parents. The real question, however, was whether the wishes of the state should override them both. Such a mindset suggests that only school diversity will do justice to the religious integrity of families. Victorian liberals like J. S. Mill as well as radicals like Marx recognized this. They opposed government monopoly in education, fearing the influence of state churches. Now that liberal ideology is the new establishment, it opposes the educational freedom it used to champion. There were other issues involved in *Mozert* which were political and not definitional. I describe the plaintiffs as victims, not to advocate particular policies but to show the kind of problems we have created.

Secular Humanism

In protesting situations like these religious spokesmen have attacked what they call "secular humanism," which they characterize as our new established religion. That is an issue that might be resolved by our definition. Religious spokesmen point out that this is not their phrase but was coined by Justice Hugo Black who included "Secular Humanism" in a list of nontheistic "religions" in the Supreme Court ruling on *Torcaso v. Watkins* (1961). That was a free exercise case, and Black's purpose was to stretch the definition of religion beyond the original intent of the First Amendment.[53] But seen in light of the establishment prohibition, Black and his successors are accused of promoting a federally established secularism.

The issue reached the headlines in 1986 when a federal judge in Alabama reviewed the objections of parents to the secular tendency of some textbooks. After expert testimony on the philosophical and religious character of humanism he removed some of the books until the schools could find other texts to balance them. Secularists treated the ruling as if he had imposed texts of his own choosing. One Harvard law professor called him "the Ayatollah Khomeini of the federal judiciary . . . a constitutional outlaw in robes, a Torquemada of the twentieth century. His judicial opinions deserve no respect. They are simple bigotry under cover of law." A court of appeals overruled the judge, on the basis of their own views on what is offensive.[54]

The defendants' retort to the religious plaintiffs was that they did not know what they meant by secular humanism and wished someone would define it.[55] But there had been several public offers to define humanism, starting with the "Humanist Manifesto" of 1933, which did liken it to a religion. Then in 1981 *Free Inquiry* published "A Secular Humanist Declaration," above the signatures of fifty-eight persons from eight countries. It dropped the earlier religious rhetoric from a fear that the position might be legally vulnerable under the establishment prohibition. And it defined the humanist position primarily in terms of its opposition to religion. The ten principles listed are free inquiry, "reason," secularist ethics, science and technology, evolution, political freedom, education, moral education, religious skepticism, and separation of church and state. Recognizing that recent totalitarian regimes have been secular, the signers began by saying that they only promoted that form of secular humanism that was "explicitly committed to democracy." They went on to characterize those evil regimes as quasi-religious. The longest section of the 1981 Declaration is the one advocating "Religious Skepticism."

Secular humanism is not hard to define. It involves the claim that we can know nothing that is not the result of human experience (empiricism) or reflection (rationalism); that we are motivated essentially by rational choice (rather than conceptions of virtue); that the unit of analysis is the individual (rather than the society); that the highest value therefore is tolerance (more than justice); and that everything about our biology and culture should be understood in terms of evolution.

The reason that the secular public is puzzled by the concept of secular humanism is that they seldom hear it questioned. It seems self-evident. And whoever discovered water, it wasn't a fish. Fundamentalists might be in a better position than philosophers to see this as the ideology of a particular class at a particular time and place. This is why teaching about religion will not really give us a rounded view of our society until it is balanced by teaching *about* secularism.

In 1934, when John Dewey's *A Common Faith* appeared, the climate was different. Dewey wanted to present humanism as a religion in order to promote it in American society. It required him to redefine religion. Like his contemporaries, he understood religion primarily as dogmatic propositions. But he held that if religion were allowed to "develop" further it would turn into humanism. Pragmatically, he thought it was helpful to think of religion (on a functional definition) as whatever helps people to "adjust" more successfully to the world. The balance of the book is an attack on American religion, despite his irenic title.[56] Positively, his religious humanism meant affirming human values and community in the face of nature's indifference.

This humanism or secular humanism is not religious by our definition. It does not expect to meet with Rudolf Otto's *mysterium tremendum et fascinans*. And yet, studying Dewey's educational program, Catholic historian Christopher Dawson thought that a religion of sorts did pervade it:

> Dewey, in spite of his secularism, had a conception of education which was almost purely religious. Education [in Dewey's view] is not concerned with intellectual values, its end is not to com-

municate knowledge or to train scholars in the liberal arts. It exists simply to serve democracy; and democracy is not a form of government, it is a spiritual community, based on "the participation of every human being in the formation of social values." Thus every child is a potential member of the democratic church, and it is the function of education to actualize his membership and to widen his powers of participation. . . . It is inspired by a faith in democracy and a democratic "mystique" which is religious rather than political in spirit. Words like "community," "progress," "life," and "youth," etc., but above all "democracy" itself, have acquired a kind of numinous character which gives them an emotional or evocative power and puts them above rational criticism.[57]

Still, we cannot think that humanism is religious enough to be subject to the establishment prohibition. Courts should rule in accordance with the language of the governed. We take religion to deny the secular humanist's orthodoxy that we are bounded by a self-existing universe and must make the best of it.[58] So the courts were justified in rejecting the claim that secular humanism is an establishment of what we call religion.

Nevertheless, educational philosopher Warren Nord has shown that the educational establishment of a secularist ideology still has a legal problem. The Supreme Court has ruled that the government must observe neutrality between religion and nonreligion, as well as between different religions.[59] We have seen the public spokesmen for secular humanism acknowledge that their position is antagonistic to religion. So public schools are constrained not to teach secularism to the exclusion of religious views. Rather, they should be tasked to teach *about* secularism, thereby relativizing it as they do religion. However, few teachers would have the training to do it, or would even see the point. For many of them, secularism is self-evident. They would not recognize that its talk of human personality or democratic values bristles with assumptions that secularist naturalism would not find meaningful.

An example from my own experience reveals the difficulties. I gave a class of college students an examination question asking them to discuss the effects of the last century's science upon rationalism.

Good answers would have described how evolutionary biology, the discovery of the unconscious, Marxist sociology of knowledge, and quantum theory's uncertainty principle all tend to destroy the notion that our minds were designed to give us truth. Since I had not belabored the point in class, the students were unprepared, and they twisted the question into one about religion versus science. They are so used to thinking of religion as the only impediment to intellectual development that they could not see the way that science has destroyed rationalism. The question revealed that secularism is too big for them to see.

The Current Situation

Having seen the reasons that might be used to keep religion out of the public curriculum, we may finally ask whether religion has anything to offer to education. Historian George Marsden found his experience on the faculties of Calvin College and the University of California at Berkeley to be relevant to this question. Calvin hardly compares in stature to one of the world's greatest universities, but Marsden found students at the former

> on average to be excited about a wider range of intellectual interests and to relate these to ethical and social questions that would shape their vocations. They were more likely to see some coherence in their education and to view it as preparation for a vocation and not simply for a career. . . . Most of its students come from the same denomination, Christian Reformed. Nonetheless, such apparent homogeneity produces surprising diversities. Rather than, as in a secular university, where almost every discussion has to go back to irreconcilable first principles, people can debate issues at a much higher level. They might agree on first, second, or third principles, but have strong and creative debates after that.[60]

Marsden thinks it is small wonder that most university students today have abandoned the liberal arts, which were expected to address life's questions, and have resigned themselves to training in job skills. Attempts to address ultimate questions in the secular classroom may either be dismissed as fruitless or stopped before treading on forbidden ground.

This shrinking of the curriculum is reaching downward into the primary grades. Since the 1960s government schools have become less comfortable with a socializing role, or with nurturing bodies and spirits as well as minds. The insistence on common schools used to be justified by teaching a common culture. Now the common schools themselves insist that there is no such thing, and they may take steps to eradicate it. The one thing that educators can agree on is that it should not include religion, which historically nurtured all the philosophies and arts they once taught.

Education professor Nel Noddings thinks that confusion here is at the heart of our public schools' problems. She notes that teachers caught in legal crossfire hide behind an ideal of bureaucratized knowledge. Discussing morals (or their religious associations) is simply not their "expertise." But ignoring them makes ordinary instruction in other fields more difficult. She concludes that religious schools are often more effective, not because they *teach* religion, but because they *are* religious. They alone try to retain the holistic view of life that was John Dewey's goal.[61]

Religious schools may have this holistic ethos even without directly teaching religious doctrine. *Lemon v. Kurtzman* noted that Catholic schools have a religious "atmosphere" in all instruction, due more to the teachers than to the textbooks.[62] As Coles noted, such an atmosphere is conveyed by a language that has not been purged of religious overtones. And as Noddings points out, schools cannot operate without rules of behavior. Moral education, which is doubtless more effective as part of the hidden curriculum, should not be relegated to the null curriculum.

Warren Nord resists the idea that secular and religious elements should be offered in different schools in order to respect the liberties of our citizens. He thinks that a comprehensive education must include serious consideration of religion. Since First Amendment jurisprudence requires fairness toward both religious and nonreligious perspectives, we cannot be satisfied with private religious schools for those who can afford them, but must offer balance within the public schools for those who cannot afford them. He also thinks that one cannot be just to religion if it is only treated when the subject comes up naturally. He concludes that public schooling should require courses in religion.[63]

By contrast, I have been arguing that courses *about* religion may not suffice for those who think that religion deserves more than cool respect. Learning religion involves the whole person and not just the mind. The proposals for moments of silence or "nonsectarian" prayers were not absurd. They showed a more adequate idea of what constitutes education. Student chapel might once have served a vital educational purpose if it reminded students of the limits of their knowledge and the need for wisdom in applying what they learned. Beyond this, one will not understand our world unless our schools also teach *about* secularism, as we have said.

Cultural Contributions of Religious Education

There are important cultural contributions for which we might look to religion—cultural criticism and cultural creativity. Historically, religions have sometimes been culturally dominant and sometimes marginal. When dominant, they are expected to create intellectual systems or syntheses. When marginal, they offer cultural critiques. George Marsden observes that cultural critique is the most obvious use of religious perspectives in scholarship today.[64] Interestingly, this reflects our definition of religion, as that which questions more ordinary experience. Our definition would suggest that the critical mode is always closer to the essential meaning of religion, which points beyond normal experience. When religion is marginal, a religious mentality will be more alert to the assumptions of the dominant secularist culture than are those who are entirely submerged in it.

On the other side of the coin, some argue that something like religion is necessary to encourage creative or divergent thinking. This is a point we will see Einstein making in chapter 6. Whereas logic tightens our thinking, religious awareness may promote mental flexibility. In his book *Creativity: the Magic Synthesis*, Silvano

Arieti observes that "religion, like art, resorts to mechanisms of the primary process or to earlier mechanisms of the secondary process, to . . . support the newly acquired abstract insights."[65] Historians have long argued that the origins of cosmic speculation and of the systematization of ideas was in a religious context.[66]

Whether it can ever outgrow that connection is a question. Even science needs inspiration from outside itself, as Einstein says. For science must look outside itself with any questions about the projects to take on, the things we want to know, the proper use of that knowledge. Religion can help keep such questions open.

Universal state education was a dream of the nineteenth century, when governments tried to generate a nationalism that would overcome class divisions. There was something almost religious about making the nation a focus of devotion. Public schools had a social, political, and economic, as much as an intellectual, purpose. Their enemy was religious division.[67] That tension is still apparent within educational systems. It is not necessarily to be regretted. There is value in disagreement and perhaps in institutional separation if, indeed, the full truth is still beyond us.

Philosopher Pierre Hadot has pointed out that in ancient Greece all academic subjects—logic, physics, and ethics—were supposed to be lived out, practiced as spiritual exercises. "Philosophy" meant the love of wisdom, rather than arguments over wisdom. Hadot noted that this was what Wittgenstein tried to do in his later writing— make philosophy more than the study of philosophy, recognizing it as a "form of life."[68] Such philosophical life was done in community, and involved service to society.

Philosophy changed into an academic study in the nineteenth century, as part of the expansion of universities. This seems the more natural understanding of philosophy and of education to us today. But our educational institutions would seem equally curious to earlier ages. They might offer more political, cultural, and social leadership if they could reconsider whether our wariness of religion is at the heart of our educational problems.[69]

CHAPTER FOUR

Religion and the Law

Since laws take the form of words, confusion over the meaning of "religious" or "religion" can cause not only individual unhappiness but social discontent as well. Secular states have succeeded churches in deciding the acceptable forms of religion and what religious activities are permitted to us, in their efforts to keep the peace. On the other hand, religion has always seemed a major rival to the authority of the state. Given the state's ever expanding powers, this calls for special clarity. In trying to relate our English term "religion" to specific examples of our jurisprudence, I aim to be true to our common sense of the term rather than to personal preferences in this area.

Take the following examples of recent uncertainties: some legal scholars think that if judges must define religion in rendering a decision they risk "establishing" a particular understanding of religion, contrary to our First Amendment prohibition.[1] Others assume that a secular conscience should share the constitutional protections that religious consciences have been granted, so that our laws do not privilege religion.[2] There has been puzzlement over whether the "secular humanism" that Justice Hugo Black introduced into legal terminology has become America's established religion.[3] And some have wondered whether choosing an abortion may qualify as an exercise of religious freedom.[4] There is also the issue of whether one can claim anything whatever to be one's religion, in hopes of being granted First Amendment exemption from certain laws. These are a few of the confusions that a nominal definition of religion may resolve.

Definition is not an arbitrary matter. Languages are social, not individual, and we are only understood by observing common usage. A judge who tried to legislate a new definition would indeed be guilty of establishing his views. And while we are free to believe what we like, whether our beliefs are "religious" is for our culture to decide. We must play by the rules of the language we speak, which is why we cannot declare that our beliefs are purple.

The common complaint that our courts need help in dealing with religious questions points to the notorious difficulty of defining the term. "There is no accepted definition of 'religion' for constitutional purposes, and no satisfactory definition is likely to be conceived," declares Phillip E. Johnson.[5] Kent Greenawalt thinks that no definition "will capture all and only the beliefs, practices, and organizations that are regarded as religious in modern culture." He and others think that Wittgenstein's notion of "family resemblances" offers the safest approach, following by analogy with indisputable examples.[6] Winnifred Fallers Sullivan advises courts to seek the help of scholars in religious studies to help in this matter, but this is advice that we have seen reason to question.[7]

We have taken the position that nominal definitions avoid the charge of proceeding by fiat. If it were really true that we could not agree on a definition, then a court would have to prescribe one by an exercise of power. But since we have defined the term without regard to its legal implications, courts can feel justified in using that definition when deciding cases. Watching the legal mind grapple with distinctions will begin to show us the merits of our definition.

In this chapter there will be more pointed criticisms of some vagaries in definition. We are dealing here with particular actions and not with larger social trends. I do not intend to advocate a particular religious viewpoint, but greater consistency in following our common language.

An Example of Confusion

We may start with a notable case in which the U.S. Supreme Court tried to address this issue. In 1965 when the Court was deciding *U.S. v. Seeger,* a case of conscientious objection to military service, it felt that certain statutory definitions of religion were problematical. (Religious objection was the only statutorily recognized justification for avoiding combat service.) So the Court looked for help from outside, and quoted "eminent theologians" of that day: erstwhile Lutheran Paul Tillich, controversial Anglican bishop John A. T. Robinson, and Dr. David Saville Muzzey of the Ethical Culture Movement, as well as a draft report from the Vatican II ecumenical council.[8]

This did verge on "establishing" those theologians' views of religion as the law of the land. Theologians are involved in prescribing *proper* understandings of their subject. They may not be guided simply by ordinary usage, as courts should be, but may seek to mold usage. But whom should the Court have consulted if not these? The power to decide what is proper religion and what is arrant nonsense has taken the place of the question of what is orthodox and what is heresy, in terms of its seriousness.

A court's act in defining religion does indeed run the risk of "establishing" its particular sense of religion and interfering with the "free exercise" of those who operate from another understanding. It is clear that, in the United States, the Supreme Court has the *power* to define religion. But the *source* of their definition will be a critical factor in public acceptance of their decisions. The public in a democracy should not feel that laws are being enforced according to an arbitrary understanding of their terms.

That being the case, where should the Court have turned for definitions that would have the needed authority? There are dictionary definitions, which are important because they try to reflect common usage. On the other hand, it may be precisely those who have eccentric views on religion who will need the law's protection. Or, the Court might feel bound by the meanings of terms as they were understood by those who wrote the First Amendment—say James Madison or his contemporaries.

There are various academic possibilities as well. Theological definitions are the work of experts operating within particular confessional groups. Courts would want to be sure that these were general or "generic" definitions, that did not favor a particular religious tradition or theological agenda. There are other academics—anthropologists, sociologists, historians, philosophers, and psychologists—who study religious behavior. They may be sympathetic to religion, but they operate outside any particular tradition in their academic capacity. So these fields are not seeking to *impose* a definition, in the manner of the more aggressive theologians, but to derive a definition from use.

We may postulate further possibilities. One might let "the people," or their elected representatives, decide on a political definition of religion by an exercise of power, voting down those whom they think are superstitious. But this is the very thing that the establishment prohibition was meant to prevent. Finally, we might assume that only the individual can define religion in a manner wholly satisfactory to that person.

In the case before us the Court chose to consult reformist theologians. The reason that the justices saw the need to rethink the definition of religion was that earlier decisions had already moved away from stipulating a belief in God or a supreme being. Such a definition would have been "normative"—implying that theistic beliefs were acceptable and others were not. Not wishing to be too narrow in its treatment of religion—as the country itself became more diverse— the Court shied away from specifying the content involved in religious belief. Still, there had to be some way to decide which beliefs are "religious," and the Court found help in Paul Tillich's notion of "ultimate concern." This seemed the sort of generic and functional definition that might show that a defendant's ideas could be protected as religious even if they were atheistic when judged by the old standard of belief in God.

The Court should be given credit for trying to preserve our heritage of rights in a changing culture. But it could have given more attention to the understanding of the Founders, who were surprisingly clearheaded on this subject. By the time that the First Amendment was penned, the process of institutional secularization had begun.[9] In chapter 9 we will see that secularization does not necessarily refer to a decline of religious belief but initially points to the separation of various areas of life and thought from religious direction. So initially, secularization tends to reduce religion from *practice* to mere *belief.* It may actually encourage the emergence of a more *conscious* faith. We may be surprised to think that religion had not always been a matter of explicit beliefs. But for many people, then and now, religion seems more like an *implicit* trust in certain practices.

Thomas Jefferson had already reached that understanding, of religion as explicit beliefs, when he penned the *Bill Establishing Religious Freedom* for Virginia.[10] This view was apparently common among the upper classes or intellectual elites of British and American society by his day. Madison, however, hinted at a broader definition in the *Virginia Declaration of Rights*, when he spoke of religion as "the duty which we owe to our Creator and the manner of discharging it."[11] That implies actions as well as beliefs. Samuel Johnson's famous *Dictionary* (1755) straddled that same divide when he defined religion as "(1) Virtue, as founded upon reverence of God, and expectation of future rewards and punishments. (2) A system of divine faith and worship." So the time of our First Amendment was a time in which religion involved action or response as well as belief or awareness.

For most early societies, and for many elements in American society even today, religion is as much a matter of actions as of beliefs. Things would be easier for the Court today if religion only meant beliefs, since it is only by our actions that we disturb others. The Court could leave "mere opinions" alone, and be confident that legal restrictions would never touch the heart of a "faith." But the Court would have to ignore the wording of the First Amendment to do that, since it speaks of the "exercise" of religion and its "establishment." That implies actions. It is hard to imagine establishing a belief, except by compulsory education. Practices are what one can establish.

Commentators on the First Amendment sometimes assume that it guarantees freedom of belief or of conscience. But hard cases have forced the Court to recognize that religious *actions* need protection as well.[12] The Court has been slower to realize just how diverse this makes us. Diversity does not only refer to articulate conscientious objectors. Courts should also consider groups that are not likely to pursue their concerns to the Supreme Court. There are many in our midst who have inherited religious cultures which were already "out of date" in the time of the Founding Fathers, but which may outlast the culture of Jefferson's Enlightenment.

At the time when the First Amendment was being drafted the term "conscience" was used freely in those debates, as more or less synonymous with religion. What is interesting, however, is that in the end it was kept out of the document.[13] Laura Underkuffler-Freund has shown that writers then used "conscience" in an effort to dignify religion, by highlighting its "rational" character as against mere superstition. But she argues that since religion and conscience were virtually synonyms *then*, we are *now* free to interpret them both in the more secular sense which conscience has acquired. Surely it is more logical to conclude that we should treat them as people did then, both meaning religious.

Quite aside from the fact that the writers she cites were not present at the constitutional debates, she has shown a drift of the meaning of "conscience" since then, into something less like religion. "Conscience" has changed, whereas "religion" has not. She hoped, by equating the terms, to substitute freedom of thought for freedom of religious exercise. This would save courts today the trouble of distinguishing religion from philosophy, which she declares to be impossible.[14] But we do not speak of the free exercise of philosophy, which shows that we still make a distinction.

Why We Privilege Religion

We already have an answer to the puzzle of why the Founders privileged religion above other "comparable activities." There is nothing comparable to an "ultimate concern." It would be like saying that government should not privilege *life* above comparable activities. There is nothing comparable to life. So secular persons have no need for protection analogous to the protection of religious belief. A secular person has no interest above that of life itself, which is already a primary end of the state. But for religious persons, religious demands may rank higher than life itself, so that when they are threatened we may consider the need for special protections.

Philosopher Richard Rorty was one of those who wondered why religious conscience is honored above a secular conscience in conscientious objector cases.[15] Why should the Court work so hard to interpret objections as religious, even over the protests of the defendants? But as Rorty would agree, personal autonomy is a defining feature of secularism or atheism. A secular conscience would not acknowledge any authority outside oneself, or outside the human community. That is why the community can democratically ask such persons to change—its wisdom being superior to the individual's.

Many legal scholars think that original intent is only one of the relevant criteria in interpretation. I am only arguing that we can make sense of the unique standing that religion has enjoyed in American law, for any who are puzzled by that fact. Religious persons do not feel they can adopt just any manner of life they choose. They may be wrong, but that is not the point. The law's respect is not for religion per se, but for religious *persons*. The rights of religion, so called, are the rights of religious persons. Those persons should have the freedom to follow practices that may seem absurd, wrong, or puzzling. For to ask them to go against their religion would be analogous to enslaving them.

Treating religious and nonreligious persons with equal respect means treating them *differently*. In the words of Bette Novitt Evans, "Religious accommodation is not to be justified because religion merits special privileges but because doing so is necessary to achieve equal respect."[16] This is a challenge to the bureaucratic, rationalizing mentality.

Searching for Consistency

In concentrating on the problems that courts in the United States have had in defining the subject for us, we do not mean that other nations do not have analogous difficulties. After all, dealing with transcendent concerns will be the greatest challenge any culture and any legal system will face.[17] Judges in India act as theologians, deciding what is superstitious and deciding issues between powerful religions in a country where nonreligion is unthinkable. They have determined that the state must arbitrate between religions while each religion must "confine itself to its legitimate sphere of facing the eternal riddle of the universe" and not interfere with "the material life of the community."[18] That has not yet become the attitude of U.S. courts.

Our state arose not to dominate but to represent its citizens, and it has tried to respect their religious identities. The first real challenge the federal state had to its tacit understanding of religion was in *Davis v. Beason* (1890), when the court told Mormons that their practice of polygamy was not really a religious tenet. They thought this was obvious from the fact that it went against "the laws of all civilized and Christian countries" and would "shock the moral judgment of the community."[19] In short, religion was what the Court and the country found more or less self-evident, the consensus of "civilization."

During the next century the state became more sensitive to cultural variety, and religion was recognized as a problem. We may return to the case of *U.S. v. Seeger* (1965). The Court was looking for a definition that would leave the content or dogmas of a religion aside, and determine what was religious on some other basis. Tillich's formula, of an "ultimate concern" was offered as a neutral way of deciding whether an unfamiliar belief might qualify. They ruled that whatever counted as one's ultimate or most serious concern should be protected as an exercise of religion. The Court's assumption was that functional definitions were more acceptable than "content-based" definitions because they are not normative.[20] Identifying religions by their common functions would not get into questions of what doctrines are more acceptable to the state.

There are two things wrong with the Court's thinking here. In the first place, functional definitions are not *sui generis*. They make religions part of a larger category—along with whatever else shares the same function. So the definition fails to discriminate, as definitions should do. Second, it turns out that functional definitions can be normative after all.[21] We should take up each of these points again.

The court avoided considering content from a fear of establishing a particular creed. But there is another important distinction than the function/content one. The Court assumed that all substantive or content definitions referred to specific beliefs. But there are definitions which are analytical; they distinguish the "content" in the sense of the elements of the *concept* "religion." These elements amount to the structure of a definition, as we called it earlier. An analytical definition might assert that religious signifies ultimate concern, without even specifying that this will involve a supreme being. In chapter 2 we found the structure of our definition of religion to include the response of faith, say, and its object, something uncanny or beyond the ordinary. Neither is specific to only some religions, but they are part of our nominal usage.

The thing that makes analytical definitions more appropriate than functional ones here is that they see things in terms unique to them. While functional definitions see things as part of a class of those things that can perform a function, a successful analytic definition has a unique denotation. If courts could make functional substitutions (secular conscience, philosophy, worldview) there would be no need to invoke a freedom of religion.

The second problem with functional definitions is that they can be normative, too. Tillich thought that some people had concerns—like their nation or worldly success—that they put in the position of being ultimate, which were not *truly* ultimate and were therefore not religious but only "idolatrous." That is speaking normatively. Idolatries are religions too, whether Tillich the theologian approved of them or not. Justices do not want to have to be theologians, deciding which of our ultimate concerns deserve protection and which are superstitious.

Other semantic mistakes were made in the *Seeger* ruling, which would be compounded in later decisions. The Court noted that the statute in question, the Universal Military Training and Service Act of 1948, declared that "a merely personal moral code" would not merit a religious exemption. The Court claimed, appealing to Tillich's formula, that a moral belief can "occupy in the life of its possessor a place parallel to that filled by the God of those admittedly qualifying for the exemption."[22] Legal scholar Jesse Choper has pointed out that purely ethical or moral beliefs are not, in fact, comparable to the beliefs of those who claim that their actions are subject to ultimate or "extratemporal consequences." This is not to claim that religious beliefs are more true or moral than others, just different— but significantly different.[23] This is in line with our definition.

Defendant Seeger claimed that he had "a religious faith in a purely ethical creed." The Court took this as his way of expressing an "ultimate concern." But they went on to declare that they would accept "all sincere religious beliefs which are based upon a power or being, or upon a faith [sic], to which all else is subordinate or upon which all else is ultimately dependent." And thus they created a generic and analytical definition of religion to go along with their functional one. Seeger's "ethical creed" did not exactly qualify as "a power or being or faith." More editing might have revealed their confusion.

Another defendant in the *Seeger* case (Jakobson) characterized his religion as "attitudes," the violation of which did not seem to involve any consequences to him. A lower court had ruled against him, arguing that one of the statute's tests was whether such attitudes or beliefs were "externally compelled" as opposed to being "internally derived." The Supreme Court overturned that ruling, declaring that distinction an "impermissible classification" under the Due Process Clause of the Fifth Amendment. In other words, they faulted the lower court for favoring one religious position over another.

That, again, missed a defining distinction. Religion is nominally understood to be compelling. By our semantic definition religion involves power or "a Power" outside the believer. (The *Seeger* decision itself uses the term "power" eight times in wrestling with the notion of religion.) Even Jefferson, who took a rationalist's approach to religion, recognized the essential element of compulsion, which we refer to as a necessity of response. His *Bill Establishing Religious Freedom* began by declaring that he was "well aware that the opinions and belief of men depend not on their own will, but follow involuntarily the evidence proposed to their own minds."[24] Thus he recognized that religion is a compulsion rather than a choice.[25] One's religion is, by definition, that which is not in one's control. By contrast, a personal moral code, as Congress had recognized, is more likely to be "internally derived."

The sense that religion defines one's being in this way is illustrated in an exchange over conscientious objection from the time of the composition of the Bill of Rights. One congressman pointed out that there was no point in issuing weapons to persons whose religion made them rather die than fire them.[26] Seeger might not have passed that test.

Justice William Douglas thought that the *Seeger* majority had not been forthright. He thought they should have invalidated the statute for specifying a supreme being and thereby singling out one type of religion for protection. Douglas was thinking back to the *Torcaso v. Watkins* ruling of 1961, which stated that not all religions are theistic. His colleagues had dodged the issue by claiming that Congress was already trying to liberalize the notion of religion by using the phrase "Supreme Being" instead of "God." Now, the Court was only liberalizing further, allowing anything that purportedly functioned as religion to offer an exemption from military service.[27]

Actually Congress had done a creditable job of defining religion in the Universal Military Training and Service Act at issue. They held that religious objections derived from "belief in an individual's relation to a Supreme Being involving duties beyond a human relationship but not essentially political, sociological or philosophical views or a merely personal moral code." Thus, they tried to distinguish the word from neighboring terms as nominal definitions do. Congress was here echoing Justice Charles Evans Hughes' dissent in *U.S. v. Macintosh* (1931) which took religion to mean "belief in a relation to God involving duties superior to those arising from any human relation." He in turn was guided by the ruling in *Davis v. Beason* (1890), which said that "the term 'religion' has reference to one's view of his relations to his Creator, and to the obligations they impose of reverence for his being and character, and of obedience to his will."[28]

There is nothing very original in these definitions, or ours, or the many others one finds in law review articles that circle around the same terms, making religion "the subordination of the individual will to the unchallengeable dictates of an extra-human, transcendent force or reality."[29] But in the confusing period around 1965, the Supreme Court felt drawn further afield.

Growing Confusions

In 1970 the Court further broadened the meaning of religion in *Welsh v. U.S.*, in which the facts were very close to those of *Seeger*. Justice Douglas and others were still troubled by the hint of religious establishment that he thought was implied in Congress's conscientious exemption from military service. There were two ways to deal with the issue: nullify the statute as an unconstitutional establishment (and perhaps do away with this traditional right) or define religion so widely that it lost any independent meaning (thereby expanding the right). In *Welsh* the Court chose the latter, and were accused by Justice John Harlan, who did not approve of a religious exemption, of "groping to preserve the conscientious objector status at all cost."

Plaintiff Elliott Welsh denied that his objection was religious, but the four prevailing justices thought he was not the best judge of that matter. His political and personal moral views—specifically excluded by statute from the exemption—were taken as religious by the Court's new criterion. For the Court's discussion now turned on how "strong" or "deep" the belief was. In other words, for this Court religious just meant *intense*. As in a functional definition, religion is here seen as one instance of a more common characteristic.

One must ask, though, what is an intense belief? A belief held by an intense person? That would be a psychological rather than a religious characteristic. Religion, on this understanding, is not a type of belief but a level of belief. In the *Welsh* ruling, the exemption which was originally justified only because of religious imperatives is now denied to "those whose beliefs are not deeply held and those whose objection to war does not rest at all upon moral, ethical, or religious principle but instead rests solely upon considerations of policy, pragmatism, or expediency."[30] This contradicted the statute's wording quite directly. The original, religious basis for the exemption would have allowed it to someone who might not have minded the prospect of killing and was only restrained by religion. Such a person would fail the Court's new test of emotional revulsion.

Justice Harlan revealed the erosion of the notion of religion. "Having chosen to exempt," he wrote, we "cannot draw the line between theistic or nontheistic religious beliefs on the one hand and secular beliefs on the other." To keep from transgressing the establishment prohibition, he thought, the exemption had to be extended to all beliefs of a certain "intensity of moral conviction." Again, we see an assumption that the First Amendment was to preserve belief or conscience. Since the Amendment protects *religion*, however, the logical conclusion was that the statutory exemption should be offered to all religions, not all beliefs. Harlan further assumed that the religious exemption was an historical relic, from a time when ethics and morals were taught mostly by religious institutions. He implied that ethics is now the province mostly of secular philosophy. Again, we see the assumption that religion is being replaced by functional equivalents and that it is not *sui generis*.

The exasperation of a minority on the Court was shown in Justice Byron White's dissent. He and two colleagues pointed out that the court's concern over establishment was misplaced; the issue in Congress' law was free exercise. Seen in that light, they thought Congress had done a good job in accommodating free exercise, while the Court was embarrassing itself by its strained and arbitrary redefinitions.

Two years later, in *Wisconsin v. Yoder*, the Court showed some realization that they had ventured too far. To justify another exception they now tried *narrowing* the definition of religion. In distinguishing the Amish from the likes of Thoreau they pointed out that his famous nonconformity was "philosophical and personal rather than religious." Amish objections to state socialization arose not from "subjective evaluation" but were "traditional," not "merely a matter of personal preference."[31] Here the Court began to recapture a sense of religion's difference from philosophy.

Further Corollaries

It appears that there is still no settled definition guiding U.S. courts in the area of religion. Our definition of religion as signifying the response of faith or obedience to absolute power, could be a help in several ways. For instance, authors who speak of "ultimate concerns" (in the plural) are missing the point.[32] By definition, only one thing can be considered ultimate, meaning last or furthest. To say that someone had several ultimate concerns is a way of saying that they have no personal core. Such a person is free to decide which of his concerns will override the others in a particular instance. Being in control this way, arbitrating various concerns, is the defining characteristic of secular autonomy. Such persons are not *governed by* an ultimate concern.

Another semantic mistake is to think that "religious freedom" is primarily the freedom to choose one's religious beliefs. This view is urged by those who engage in the "deprogramming" of "cult members." They claim that religion deserves legal protection only when it has been freely chosen, and not when it has somehow been imposed.[33] This is philosophically and psychologically unrealistic. One *discovers* one's beliefs. That is what makes them beliefs rather than ideas or opinions, which we can more easily choose and change. Ideas or opinions are argued *on the basis* of our beliefs. This is the challenge of religion to a liberal philosophy which assumes the rational autonomy of the "unencumbered individual."[34] It would seem odd to say that we "chose" our parents' religion.[35]

The more coherent understanding of religious freedom makes it the freedom to follow one's religion, and not the freedom to adopt it in the first place. This is not to say that people may not find themselves leaving an earlier religious identity and finding another. But that would probably be a less common meaning of the phrase.

This difference of understanding can be seen in philosopher Ronald Dworkin's argument for abortion as an exercise of religious freedom. The notion that the freedom of religious exercise could be used to permit abortion shows a confusion, according to our definition. Insofar as religions represent ultimate commitments they do not permit things; they command them. The final term in one's thinking—an ultimate concern—takes the form of an obligation. Granting *permission* to do something suggests that something *else* will become determinative—some personal preference.

The only way that abortion could be considered a religious exercise is if the religion *required* the abortion of a particular child or of all children. Either would be tantamount to child sacrifice, which was rhetorically rejected in the first free exercise case decided by the Supreme Court, *Reynolds v. U.S.* in 1878.[36] Dworkin himself mentions the ruling of *Gillette v. U.S.* (1971) that rejected selective conscientious objection to particular wars. The Court rightly sensed that such selective objections were not "religious ones."[37] Analogously, choosing to abort a particular child cannot be a religious act.

The outcry against a religion that demanded abortion as a religious duty would be tremendous. To *permit* abortion would mean that an ultimate concern was giving way to some lesser consideration—health, career, family finances, a less-than-optimal baby. But religion does not invite other concerns to take over; the choice would have ceased to be religious.

The question of whether Satanism or witchcraft would qualify as religion in our courts may depend on cases. The state's obligation to protect its citizens might well limit them. For insofar as they consist in exercising power over others, their antisocial character might keep them in trouble. Freedom of religious exercise is always limited by like freedoms for others.

Besides the difficulties we have noted in spotting the religious identity of individuals, there are issues in identifying organizations as religious. Churches and such involve so much organizational machinery that the core religious impulse may not seem uppermost. Some may appear focused on promoting their survival as institutions rather than on obedience to their mission. So legislatures may be justified in discriminating their religious activities from their organizational ones. The Internal Revenue Service, for example, has long experience in distinguishing the core activities from peripheral ones.[38] Our focus on religious awareness and response as the core meaning of the term might provide some guidance.

Nor should we forget that, for many people, religion is primarily a corporate matter, a group identity. America's legal tradition has reflected a Protestant culture which thinks in individual terms, so that it seemed that only persons could be religious. Bette Novitt Evans urges that the law protects religious "identity" in its social dimension, as well as individual activity and belief. She regrets the Court's decision in *Lyng v. Northwest Cemetery Protective Association* (1988), which sacrificed a tribe's sacred burial site to the benefit of a logging company. The decision made a form of religious worship impossible, with no argument of a compelling state interest.[39]

In some such cases, the courts have considered the "centrality" of different beliefs to a particular religion. But they would like to avoid becoming theologians in deciding such matters. Still, despite what we have said about religion dealing in commandments rather than suggestions, we recognize that the core activities and beliefs can sometimes be distinguished from more practical concerns. Courts are likely to make individuals decide this for themselves. When one's religious activities are limited by the need to preserve a similar freedom for others, the individual must deal with the situation. At one extreme, they may emigrate. At the other extreme they may treat their own accommodation of others as an exercise of religious charity, compromising one religious duty by the exercise of another.

This reminds us of the inescapable fact that the First Amendment does in fact establish a particular kind of religion. Acceptable religion in our system must be satisfied with spiritual sanctions, and not use social sanctions or official power to sanction its doctrine and discipline. It must be voluntary and tolerant of other faiths, whether grudgingly or not. These seem to be the inevitable rules of our pluralist condition. There are religions in the world today that would have trouble with these constraints, a situation we will consider in the next chapter.

A Permanent Tension?

The relation of religion and law cannot be resolved without friction. For they represent two kinds of power, the state and something that may stand in judgment against it. The growth of the modern state has been at the expense of "intermediate" institutions like gilds, towns, families, and churches. The beneficiary of the state's domination over all these institutions was supposed to be the individual, as the state's courts freed them from the dominance of those institutions. Since they were local and the state was remote, this new freedom initially seemed quite real.

The unforeseen consequence was that individuals lost the protection of those institutions against an all powerful state. The possibility of totalitarianism emerged quickly—four years into the French Revolution—treating individuals as resources for the state to use. Modern "alienation" developed, when individuals could not relate to the symbols or rules of states that claimed to be synonymous with society. As a reaction to this situation, "communitarian" political philosophies have developed to encourage rebuilding those intermediate institutions. Some of them may call on religious traditions to offer an alternative sense of solidarity.[40]

There has been some response by our courts, in a more generous, "accommodationist" stance toward religion. It is not universally applauded, and it must strain against the widening regulatory role of the bureaucratic state. In recent years accommodationists have raised objections to the "compelling state interest" invoked in requiring haircuts or autopsies against religious objections, for instance. They have asked why government ignores virtually every Native American religious challenge in land-use cases. They have pointed out how the *Lyng* and *Employment Division v. Smith II* (1990) cases, which dismissed the need for the state to show a compelling interest, demonstrate that government respect for religious liberty is only a part of our national mythology.[41] The focus of the current conflict is on *Smith II*, the case involving exemptions for making religious use of peyote.

The roots of this conflict go back to cases involving education. In *Everson v. Board of Education* (1947), Justice Hugo Black propounded the view that the First Amendment was framed in order to protect the state from religion. As background he emphasized that

> the centuries immediately before and contemporaneous with the colonization of America had been filled with turmoil, civil strife, and persecutions, generated in large part by established sects determined to maintain their absolute political and religious supremacy. . . . Men and women had been fined, cast in jail, cruelly tortured and killed.[42]

Actually, historians are just as likely to argue that the First Amendment was to protect religion from the state, that is, from federally established churches. But since *Everson* the assumption has often been that the free exercise protection is *for* religion, especially minority religion, while the establishment prohibition is *against* religion, at least majority religion.[43]

The important precedent of *Lemon v. Kurtzman* (1971) is in this tradition of casting religion as the most obviously disruptive force in society:

> Ordinarily political debate and division, however vigorous or even partisan, are normal and healthy manifestations of our democratic system of government, but political division among religious lines was one of the principal evils against which the First Amendment was intended to protect.[44]

A secularist perspective considers religion to be irrational, regressive, and disruptive, something that can only be tolerated if confined to the private sphere.[45]

The idea that the two "clauses" of the First Amendment had different purposes has produced inconsistent, irreconcilable bodies of case law. For example, it seemed to require separate definitions of religion for the two clauses. There would be a broad and generous functional definition to support individual liberty claims, and a narrow substantive definition to curb the churches. The first would protect unfamiliar minority religions; the second would not interfere with government social and educational programs that might seem ideological.[46] Any apparent unfairness could be justified by the fears of religion we have just noted.

Recently, it has been argued that the two clauses are sides of the same coin. They both have to do with protecting the free exercise of religion against state interference.[47] In effect, they balance the religious rights of some against the religious rights of others. The establishment prohibition was not aimed at independent churches but at the possibility of a federal and tax-supported church. In any event, it is a mistake for judges to think that their job is to make America secular. For some, separationism has become an end in itself. Recently, judges who want to accommodate religion in public life have been reduced to calling it tradition or culture. This was the point of *Lynch v. Donnelly* (1984), which declared certain December symbols to have been secularized and therefore in compliance.[48]

The Myth of Religious Exemptions

One of our myths has been that any heavy-handedness by the state could be balanced by judicial protection against laws that "burden" religious persons or force their consciences. It was widely stated that there could be religious exemptions, either legislative or judicial, from generally applicable laws. Textbooks mentioned the "Sherbert Rule," under which an "incidental burden on the free exercise of religion" must be justified by a "compelling state interest," if the religious activity poses no "substantial threat to public safety, peace or order."[49]

The decision in *Employment Division v. Smith II* (1990) took issue with this view. First, it pointed out that such exemptions were always rare. But it was still a surprise when the Court dismissed the Sherbert Rule. The new rule was that there would be no exemptions from laws of general applicability simply because of religious considerations. *Smith II* denied that exemptions had ever been made outside of unemployment compensation cases.

Smith II was about unemployment compensation too, after the firing of Native Americans for having taken part in peyote rituals.

The Court proudly observed that two years earlier it had refused to stop a logging road that also had "devastating effects on traditional Indian religious practices."[50] If this was a concern, it said, one should look to legislative exemptions rather than some supposed right to judicial exemptions. So it is up to states to provide statutory exemptions with their laws.[51]

The disingenuousness of the decision is often commented on. The Court knew that legislative exemptions would be unlikely for minorities and would have trouble in courts on establishment grounds.[52] Of course, the two types could coexist, with legislative exemptions to accommodate groups while courts accommodated individuals, when it was possible to do so.

The *Smith II* majority took the First Amendment to mean that Congress shall make no law *intending to* prohibit the free exercise of religion. Justice Antonin Scalia's opinion even calls this reading a "permissible reading of the text."[53] Why it is better than the literal reading is not explained.[54] The Sherbert Court thought that the Constitution recognized that laws might have the inadvertent effect of interfering with religious conscience and that courts could help out here. Scalia expresses fears of a general "anarchy" if people think they have a *right* to free exercise exemptions.[55] He credits the fact that Sherbert had not led to such a general breakdown of government to the Court's stinginess in granting such exemptions. There would be no end to it, he writes, if all laws had to be scrutinized for religious burdens, even listing eleven areas in which such claims might be made. Justice Sandra Day O'Connor thought the list actually proved that the government was perfectly capable of being sensitive to religious practice. Interestingly, the dissenters against the decision were the justices with the most experience on the Court, who should have known whether they would be overwhelmed by such appeals.

One would think that all that is necessary is that religious exemptions should not create inducements to religion. By our definition, religious people are not choosing to be different. It's just who they are.

Congress responded to *Smith II* with a Religious Freedom Restoration Act (1993) which tried to prohibit the federal government from substantially burdening a person's exercise of religion, "even if the burden results from a rule of general applicability." That law was declared unconstitutional as it applies to the states, by *City of Boerne v. Flores*, 520 U.S. 507 (1997). The Court said that Congress had overstepped its powers in extending the *substantive* rights in the Constitution. Some saw this as the end of the judicial or legislative exemptions for religion, but a differently constituted and unanimous court resurrected the RFRA in *Gonzales v. O Centro*, 546 U.S. 418 (2006). That decision made clear that the scrutiny of laws for religious burdens still applied to federal laws, though not to state laws. States must look after themselves.

Incidentally, the *Smith II* decision did avoid some of the mistakes made in *Seeger* and *Welsh*, in respect to definitions of religion. It specifically acknowledged the constitution's protection of religious actions as well as beliefs. And it recognized that any action whatsoever can be religious if understood as such. That is implicit in the Court's declaration that the First Amendment prevented states from prohibiting "acts or abstentions only when they are engaged in for religious reasons."[56]

Tension is understandable in the relations between incommensurable powers, and is a reminder of the relativizing effect that religion can have on human institutions. But Congress and the Court could probably agree on a definition of religion which would echo their earlier ones, while stopping short of the wayward conclusions of *Welsh*. The criticisms made in this chapter could be answered by combining the formulas that clashed in *Seeger*: The protections guaranteed to religion are offered to those with a sincere belief in, or relation to, a power or being to which all else is subordinate, but excluding essentially political, social, or philosophical opinions or a moral code involving no transcendent consequences. Or, in the words of some earlier Supreme Court decisions, our laws guarantee the rights of religion "to those who, by training or belief, bear responsibility to a power or authority higher than any worldly one, which would lead to the disregard of elementary self-interest."[57] Some such definition would be truer to common usage and restore integrity to the First Amendment religious clause.

Efforts at definition should not be dictated by practical considerations, lest the public suspect their integrity. If the Court were to settle on its earlier, more conventional definitions of religion it would tend to narrow the protections for free exercise in a few areas. For our courts have recently used the cover of "religion" to enlarge a right of privacy.[58] Correspondingly, such a definition would also narrow the scope of the establishment prohibition. That would make it hard to accuse the government of establishing secularist ideologies. On the other hand, it might be easier to allow ceremonial observances of a "civil religion" that some think provides an essential foundation for the Constitution itself (see chapter 5).

CHAPTER FIVE

Religion and Political Variety

The fact that, as we understand it, religion always makes demands means that it raises political questions for us. This is because religion's demands characteristically strike us as absolute or ultimate, so that negotiating them may seem impossible. The current debate on "religion in politics" has to do with something much tamer, like political etiquette. Within that debate, religion has already been defined as what is acceptable in pluralistic democracies. We will address that debate later, but to see how a more general understanding of religion might be an issue we need to glance at a greater variety of political systems. After all, they lurk in the background of the debate over democracy and give it urgency. Such threatening terms as theocracy, state church, religious nationalism, civil religion and culture wars appear in these discussions.

Only after surveying the whole field can we see how religion may be thought of within our accustomed politics. And then the purpose will not be to say how we would like such issues to be resolved but how our definition might clarify the issues. Our goal, then, is not to find the "proper place" of religion within a democratic politics that is taken for granted. That would be natural for theologians and political philosophers who assumed that there need not be friction.

We cannot assume that, in our task of clarifying the terms and the issues.

Governments today do routinely rule on what constitutes proper religion and what is not permitted, as has happened throughout history. They no longer use the term heresy, but may treat things that way, with lethal sanctions like those enforced against Falun Gong in China today. Religion is too powerful simply to be ignored, and political philosophers will want to help prescribe its proper scope. Our interest is broader, defining religion per se, in order to see all possible relations.

Politics is the deliberate ordering of group life, including the public negotiation of social differences. Nothing is intrinsically political or unpolitical; anything, including religious worship, can be governed by political deliberation. Nor is anything intrinsically secular, and government itself has often been thought of as part of a religious sphere, as we will show in chapter 9. So we should expect some awkwardness between them, some tension in their relations. Politics and religion represent incommensurable powers which are likely to challenge each other. While one mobilizes human power, the other responds to supernatural powers.

In the course of history religions have helped create political communities, and helped destroy them. They have promoted nationalism, and they have transcended nationalism. They have encouraged social change and resisted it; preached political participation and counseled passivity; organized external aggression and mediated peace. They have promoted particular policies and called for limits on the politicization of life. During the recent collapse of communist regimes churches provided an independent forum for public discussion in the virtual absence of government. Histories that are organized around the development of the state see these activities as distractions from a story that they think should be secular.

This secular bias is encouraged by history's many examples of religious crimes. While these are dwarfed by the scale of recent ideological atrocities, one can understand the commonplace assumption that "religion . . . is incompatible with any democratic theory of the modern state."[1] Others might object that religion has been involved in numerous political campaigns which are generally looked on with favor. Religious groups have taken leadership in the abolition of slavery and of child labor. In the United States they have tried to prohibit alcohol, capital punishment, and the exploitation of migrant labor. They have been involved in civil rights, human rights, and pro-life agitation, as well as conscientious objection, pacifism, and political asylum. Religion was even a vital source of the drive toward religious toleration.

The puzzling thing is that there were religious persons on the other side of all these campaigns as well. It does not negate that abolitionist accomplishment to recall that religion was also used to justify slavery. It only reminds us that religion is not a particular set of ideas, but relates to experiences of, or to a language of, transcendence. For religion directs our attention to a unique power to which persons may respond.

Survey of the Field

In line with our definition, if religion means obedience to an authority felt as transcendent, we might expect theocracy to be its characteristic form. Theocracy (the rule of God or divine representatives) or theonomy (the rule of divine law) would seem to eliminate politics, if politics meant human deliberation. Human decision suggests compromises rather than the assurance that we associate with religion.

In practice, institutionalized religions have learned to live with a variety of arrangements. Some have settled for an alliance (or "union") of church and state. That is quite different from theocracy. An alliance of church and state places politicians in conversation with religious officials. Americans use the phrase carelessly to indicate any influence that religious ideas or rhetoric might exercise on politics or administration. But a real church-state union is a situation in which religious officials also have jobs in the state by right—where an archbishop might double as minister of health or education; where courts could invoke scriptures when the law was ambiguous; where the chief executive had saving rituals to perform; and where the economy was governed by the rules of charity. In such a situation, religion exercises power as well as influence. It is a form of government we have not seen in the West for three hundred years.[2]

More typical today is a religious nationalism that is causing widespread concern. The end of a Cold War between secular liberalism and militant secularism has given way to tension between religious nationalism and liberalism. Each side sees the other as the true terrorists. Liberal regimes are accused of using economic and even military power to impose their secular political forms, under the cover of human rights. These are denounced as corrosive of indigenous freedom and government, which Western states may see only as traditional means of oppression.

But it is a mistake to think that today's religious nationalism is the last gasp of traditionalism. Modernity has helped create these new religious forces, which may accept and make use of the modern nation-state. In Japan, for example, the modernizing destruction of rural cultures ended local cults but inspired a national cult. It has only been in the last century that Shinto grew up to challenge the elite efforts to create a Western-style politics. Today, Japanese politicians are trying to revise the constitutional separation of religion and state—imposed by a triumphant West—by redefining their civil religion in such a way that they can feel free to enforce it.[3] The West tends to universalize its "modernity," but in Japan some feel that the importation of democracy, capitalism, and political rationalism has failed to provide a satisfying legitimation for the state.[4] The West is also puzzled to find Muslims thinking of Western politics as Christian. But the latter see westernization and secularization as religious in nature, given their Christian origins.[5] It is a point not stressed in our schools, so we have largely forgotten the origins of individualism, democracy, and equality within the Jewish and Christian tradition.

We will later consider the concept of "civil religion," which embodies the view that no society could do without a religious sanction for the sacrifices it requires. For the present, we suggest that even modernized societies seem to need a sense of their place in history, of a transcendent destiny. Modernization theory itself was such a quasi-religious myth, seeing history *sub specie aeterni-*

tatis. Otherwise we exercise power without purpose, and see politics simply as the means of managing prosperity.[6] When politics is seen as involving transcendence, it is natural for others to accuse the Western, developed world of a "religious" imperialism. They see the assumption that westernization is universal and inevitable as a religious belief, embodying the spirit of history.

Muslim and Hindu religious nationalisms are not simply the archaic remnants of former cultures but often involve modern states. They look for a more convincing justification of power than the West's devotion to individual rights. Western rights and contracts cannot create the justification that governments need to exercise powers of life and death. The secular nationalisms of Nehru in India, Nasser in Egypt, and Shah Pahlavi in Iran all failed to recreate the order and self-confidence needed in the aftermath of colonialism.

Even the violence of these regimes may be seen as efforts to create order, not disorder. Similar things happened so long ago in the West that we have forgotten the revolutionary and violent origins of our systems. In any event, the new regimes can sometimes show more progress toward stability than secular ones left by colonialism.[7] The upshot is that they may accuse secularism, not religion, of being incoherent and chaotic. They see the West's insistence on secularist versions of human rights as disruptive.

All this makes a contrast with the assumption within academic debates on religion in politics, that sees secularization as mediating. But there is a sizeable section of the American population that also thinks that an aggressive secularism is disrupting our domestic politics and that secularized intellectuals are blind to this. Beyond this, "demographic trends coupled with conservative estimates of conversions and defections envision over 80 percent of the world's population will continue to be affiliated to religions two hundred years into the future."[8]

There is, then, a global religious challenge to Western assumptions about the secular state system.[9] Some think we would be wise to find a new dimension in our diplomacy with some of these areas. We tend to deal with foreign women's movements, labor organizations, journalists, and other secular aspects of a democracy, but not with the religious communities closer to power—because of our Supreme Courts's *Lemon* test against government involvement with religion *within* the United States![10] Edward Littwak observes that Western diplomats make mistakes by assuming that religious factors only mask ethnic or economic interests. He suggests that religions may help in bringing peoples together and providing the basis of trust. This may be true between countries, but even more so *within* countries that must overcome regional or other suspicions. Religious leaders might be useful in reconciling domestic parties to international settlements, or reconciling citizens to difficult agreements. People will concede to God what they would scarcely concede to former enemies. Many in the two-thirds world who are suspicious of the utilitarian, self-interested language of free-market capitalism, might find common ground within their religions. Luttwak suggests maintaining "religion attachés" in such countries, trying to work with or through religion rather than around or against it.[11]

It is possible to overemphasize the idea that religion is characteristically violent. Figures like Gandhi, Martin Luther King Jr., Desmond Tutu, the Dalai Lama, and Pope John Paul II remind us that nonviolent tactics, so surprising in our violent world, are generally religious in motivation. Since World War II, the Nobel Peace Prize has increasingly gone to religious figures.[12] Churches provided sanctuary for the groups engaged in political struggles in South Africa and Eastern Europe. Religious figures are sometimes able to mediate between secular groups as well as between religious ones.

In short, we cannot assume that religious conflicts can only be resolved by greater secularization. All religions include notions of sympathy. These might be expanded, and what may be needed are indigenous theologians in place of foreign peacekeepers.[13] The effectiveness of religious leaders always seems proportional to their independence from secular support. At times when secular politics has raised suspicions, nations may feel the need of religious involvement in their affairs. Many Americans apparently think this of their country also, as we shall see.

In many non-Western countries, politics has always involved what we call "culture wars," where religion may frame the issues.[14]

India is a country suffused with religion, having seen the birth of several world religions (those of the Hindus, Sikhs, Jains, and Buddhists) and having found room for the rest (Jews, Christians, Parsis, and Muslims). Their secular state finds its usefulness, not in transforming Indians into Westerners, but in keeping the peace between faiths that hope to conduct their own affairs. Their own concepts of toleration are derived more from Gandhi's Indian traditionalism than from the secularism of Nehru.

Nehru's attempts to institute modernity seemed to mock believers for their piety, and provided nothing that could take its place as a social bond.[15] He tried to define India in terms of its secular future rather than its religious past. A newly emerging Hindu nationalism is evidence of disappointment with his Western models, and it finds its support among the rising elites—young professionals who may be more "religious" than their parents. This is true of Islamic nationalism as well. Peasants and the elderly are not the backbone of the new order; universities and technical institutes lead the way.[16]

The function of the new religious nationalism is initially to create the "nation"—understood as a people, not just a state. So it is like what we call "civil religion" in the United States. The West never produced a major religion. Rather, it produced political ideologies, which seem to be disappearing today. But among the most resilient of these is what we term civil religion.

Civil Religion

By our definition of religion, American "civil religion" probably fails to qualify. It better fits Clifford Geertz's definition of ideology: "The function of ideology is to make an autonomous politics possible by providing the authoritative concepts that render it meaningful, the suasive images by means of which it can be sensibly grasped."[17] Geertz calls both religion and ideology "cultural systems," but he understands the latter to refer more to a political context than to religion's transcendent elements. He defined religious symbols as those that governed not only politics but all other symbols, defining reality itself.

Robert Bellah, whose 1967 article "Civil Religion in America" first introduced the concept of American civil religion, defines it not as national self-worship but as "a genuine apprehension of universal and transcendent religious reality as seen in or, one could almost say, as revealed through the experience of the American people."[18] In calling it a religion, Bellah was claiming that "at its best" it could express prophetic and transcendent judgment over the nation, as in the works of its greatest theologian, Abraham Lincoln. Thus civil religion set America in the transcendent context of "world history" and asked challenging questions about its responsibilities. This could be as meaningful to the political left as to the right.[19]

Civil religion may exhibit some of the usual trappings of religion. Social scientists have commented on the apparent necessity of ritual in politics—in industrialized and pluralistic societies as well as in tribal situations.[20] Legal philosopher Sanford Levinson describes a "constitutional faith" that guides our officials, and perhaps also those who teach the law. As a testimony to such faith, the U.S. Constitution requires an oath of the president and all state and federal officials, legislators as well as judges. The same sentence forbids any specifically religious test for appointment to office, showing that the American cult is an exclusive one. If senators were to ask judicial appointees whether their personal religious views would ever influence their decisions, it is understood that a positive response would be a disqualification. So there is, in our political life, the establishment of a particular religious attitude.

Civil religion is a reaction to the deficiencies of liberalism. Liberalism's rational and contractual aspects encourage the idea that one will not be asked to make costly sacrifices to the political order. Where would the justification for such sacrifice come from? Civil religion amounts to the recognition that liberal constitutionalism rests on a hidden emotional base. Its national mission and creed, its prophets and martyrs, its rituals and shrines, and sacred history and holidays, provide that base. Whether these amount to a religion by our definition may depend on the individual.

National life also rests upon a character structure that must be nurtured somehow. John Adams commented that "our constitution was made only for a moral and a religious people. It is wholly inadequate to the government of any other." Dwight Eisenhower was only being more candid when he was reported as having said that "our government makes no sense unless it is founded on a deeply felt religious faith—and I don't care what it is."[21] This makes a contrast with liberalism, which trusts that a good society is most likely to result from following self-interest within procedural constraints.

Scholars use the concept of civil religion to remind us that while individuals can do without religion, societies cannot. As political systems seek to justify force, they touch on ultimacy. Naturally, such a civil commitment does not get along well with other religions. The most sectarian of America's churches openly oppose the symbols of our civic piety. And the civil religion resists church activity within the political arena.[22] All this was foreshadowed in Rousseau's original discussion of "civil religion." Rousseau blamed conventional religions for the fall of "natural man," but hoped for a kind of political regeneration. So he urged strict enforcement of the civil religion by punishing such "heresies" as Christianity.[23]

Totalitarianism, Theocracy, and Cults

Beyond any of these possibilities stands totalitarianism, which involves devotion to the state or to the people, as represented by the leader. It is similar to religious theocracy or cults in that leaders are not restrained by the rules they impose on others, since they speak for God. Anything such a state does is justified ipso facto, for there is no higher good than the will of the people, or of God. Our worst fears of religion are also realized in totalitarianism, where this cultic behavior combines with the powers of a modern state.

Surprisingly, in the West it was the traditional rivalry between church and state that restrained such idolization of the state. In that long running contest, the church was ahead of the state in creating a rule of law. On the other hand, pockets of ecstatic religion sometimes became involved in government in a way not conducive to political life, offering our first examples of totalitarianism.

The most notable instance of this was the rule of John of Leyden (Jan Bockelson) in Münster, Germany from 1534 to 1535. The key factor was John's ability to dominate sacred texts by his inspired interpretation, or by direct revelation. Like a totalitarian leader, he alone could provide the authoritative readings. Even more important were his visions, by which he claimed to embody God's mind and power. So his reign became a terror, in which all offenses were punished by death, and no meetings were allowed between unrelated persons. Finally Leyden's enemies, led by the local Roman Catholic bishop, defeated him and restored the previous law.[24] Again, we see religion on both sides of the issue. While there have been numerous religious cults which might aspire to rule whole societies, Münster presents the only notable example of such a millennial regime, brief as it was.

Theocracy, which claims to be the rule of God, is a different thing from theonomy, which is the rule of divine law rather than divine agents. This is a more familiar thing in recorded history. The difference is that theonomy at least includes the restraints of a codified law, to which rulers as well as ruled may be held. Principled opposition can be inspired by alternative interpretations of that law, whereas in theocracy there is no such recourse. It is acknowledged that in the West, the rule of law originated in the Church rather than in the emerging secular monarchies, and helped to tame the latter.[25]

Much discussion now focuses on whether the Islamic commitment to divine law can be reconciled with a truly political situation, understood as human deliberation. The focus is now on Nigeria, one state that has a close balance between Muslim and Christian populations, in which *shari'a* and democracy seem to be learning to respect each other.[26]

Liberalism and Religion

Of more immediate relevance to us than the foregoing is the position of religion in liberal regimes. Liberalism tends to view things from the standpoint of the individual. Therefore our laws tend to view religion as an individual matter. And the question such regimes have is whether persons who feel responsible to an authority above earthly powers can operate within secular rules, that respect a variety of viewpoints.

In the case of the United States, the Founders recognized the ultimacy of religious belief and tried to insure safeguards for its exercise. There has been growing puzzlement over why only *religious* conscience and belief was singled out in the First Amendment, and an assumption that it was only a sign of that generation's cultural limitations. But we argued in chapter 4 that the generation of the Founders understood that religion is not really a choice, but more like a compulsion and the core of one's identity. In this they followed John Locke, who understood that "to believe this or that to be true, does not depend on our will."[27] Both Madison and Jefferson accordingly argued for religious liberty on the assumption that beliefs are not a matter of choice. As Jefferson put it in *A Bill Establishing Religious Freedom*, "the opinions and belief of men depend not on their own will, but follow involuntarily the evidence proposed to their own minds."[28] The implication was that it would be a violation of one's person to be forced to act against one's deepest conviction. This is what constituted "liberty."

This sense has sometimes been lost in American political and legal culture. In *Wallace v. Jaffree* (1985) the Supreme Court took the view that "religious beliefs worthy of respect are the product of free and voluntary choice by the faithful."[29] Deciding which religions were "worthy of respect" skirted the prohibition on the government's (i.e., the court's) establishment. Oddly, they even cited Madison for this view, supposing that he was arguing for freedom of religious *choice*. But Madison had said that all men have "an *equal* title to the free exercise of Religion according to the dictates of conscience."[30] So he understood religion to dictate. (His reference to "conscience" rather than to "religion" only meant something more personal than the dictates of a church.) Clearly, the Founders thought of religious freedom as the liberty to *follow* one's religion. Freedom to *choose* one's religion would have seemed oxymoronic.

Philosopher Robert Audi argues that the very idea of democracy implies that people should act autonomously, or rationally, rather than under compulsion.[31] But since beliefs are basic to one's *rationality*, there are limits to this view. If religious questions are at issue, choosing on the basis of some other rationality is like choosing one's ultimate commitment—a semantic mistake. That is the mark of the autonomous, secular individual, what philosopher Michael Sandel has called "the unencumbered self." Sandel doubts its viability, for in his view

> a life without obligations that are freely acted and faithfully observed is a life in bondage to chaos, a life without meaning. Freedom is found in obedience to the normative. . . . Having decided upon the ordering of our loyalties, our loyalties order us. After choosing our obligations, we discover they have chosen us."[32]

So for Sandel, the most obvious aspects of personal identity involve group obligations that we did not choose, including nation, family, religion, ethnicity. To be sure, these may be outgrown but they should not be coerced. The individualist assumption of the "unencumbered self" is the opposite of religious faith as we have discussed it.

The great political paradox is that such autonomous, secular persons may freely be asked to change, in line with political decisions. This does no violence to any ultimate claims, since they recognize none. Only if a change would absolutely violate one's person could there be a question of the kind of right accorded to religion by the First Amendment. Short of life itself there is nothing like that personal core for the secular individual. The idea of a "secular conscience" has developed since Madison's time, to describe strongly held beliefs. But it is not understood to limit personal autonomy, as in acknowledging an authority outside the self.

Respect and Tolerance

In defining liberal democracy, it is usual to emphasize respect between citizens. If democracy respects religion, it is not because religion is worthy of respect, but because people are worthy of respect. Religion is respected not because it is useful, or harmless, but because our "liberties" are what governments exist to protect.[33]

So within liberalism, religion has rights because it is attached to persons, and persons have rights. For example, Madison thought that the duties of religion were prior in time and obligation to "the claims of Civil Society." As a natural right, freedom of religion was intrinsic and only limited by a like freedom for others.[34]

But does religion itself exhibit such respect? Philosophers John Rawls, Bruce Ackerman, Thomas Nagel, and Robert Audi fear that religious arguments within politics may violate such respect. Religious arguments may be presented absolutely, or in such a way that others feel left out. These philosophers question whether views that *cannot* be shared or even understood should be raised at all in democratic debate.[35] Such views would be like hate speech, expressed for the very purpose of putting others down.

But Rawls, who was no apologist for religion, realized that the religious population can also feel left out. Liberty of conscience, he observed, is not a *concession*, something only tolerated in a just political system. To the contrary, for this liberal, liberty of conscience is the very purpose of government:

> The maintenance of public order is understood as a necessary condition for everyone's achieving his ends whatever they are (provided they lie within certain limits) and for fulfilling his interpretation of his moral and religious obligations. . . . Liberty of conscience . . . is not derived from practical necessities or reasons of state[,] . . . skepticism in philosophy or indifference to religion.

Rather, religious freedom follows from his central principle of equal liberty or "justice." Granted, religion does not justify more than liberty over oneself, he says; it does not justify restricting the same liberty for others. But it does extend to the expression of one's religious views in public debate.[36] Forcing citizens to translate their views into a secular terminology or else remain silent would be a violation of equal justice.

This contrasts with the view we see expressed by some Supreme Court justices. Justice Black, the intellectual leader of the Warren Court, held that aiding parochial schools to the extent of providing textbooks would cause "discord, disharmony, hatred, and strife among our people, and that any government that supplies these aids is to that extent a tyranny."[37] Imagining the dangers Black described, it is no wonder that liberal philosophers want to guard against religious participation in politics. This contrasts with Jefferson and Madison's concern to guard against the power of the state. What is more, they could not have imagined the enormous growth in the power of the state since their time.[38]

One may take different attitudes toward the presence of religious viewpoints within democratic politics. If one takes the view that politics is basically interest-group bargaining or "identity politics," it would be agreed that religious voters can take their chances with competing groups. That approach frankly admits that voting is not constrained by arguments anyway. Unless the proposal would actually impose religious duties on unwilling citizens, it should be enough that voting procedures were fair.

Liberalism, by contrast, is concerned to avoid conflict. It wants people to feel that their rights are being acknowledged. Equal justice seems to require that the "public reason" of political debate makes sense to everybody so that everyone feels included. If people do not agree with the eventual decision, at least they will feel they understand it. The problems come when such debates involve arguments that come from closed or "comprehensive" moral or religious systems. Unfortunately, it is often just such systems that express citizens' real identities, as Rawls recognized.

Recently, the notion of "deliberative democracy" has attempted to overcome some of the criticisms of a narrow liberalism which focused only on formal argument. Deliberative democracy sees the goal of politics as not only passing legislation but also as building community and agreement. So they encourage a broader debate, in which people try harder to understand each other's deepest commitments, including moral and religious views. Then, if we do not necessarily hold the ideas that prevail, at least we can imagine holding them. And even if we do not respect each others' arguments, at least we may credit them for trying to make their case.[39]

As part of the respect that is foundational to democracy, there is much talk today of tolerance. It is often assumed that this is fundamentally secular, like relativism. But there are also religious roots to tolerance. Human fallibility and humility are familiar within religious discourse. It was along these lines that Madison derived the virtue of tolerance from religious arguments, just as he derived the notions of freedom and equality from religious sources.[40] Many religious organizations these days operate by the same habits of forbearance and compromise that philosophers want for democratic politics. There may be a narrower range of opinions to tolerate but the principle is familiar.

In the democratic microcosm of campus politics, speech codes can take the form of condemning any form of proselytizing for one's beliefs, in the name of tolerance. There is an irony in the fact that this amounts to proselytizing for tolerance! Understood properly, toleration means allowing for proselytizing, not censoring it. For proselytizing implies the freedom of one's audience, rather than seeking to coerce it.[41]

We also hear some declare they will tolerate anything but intolerance. That gets things exactly backwards. It would mean that they do not tolerate persons that do not tolerate all opinions. Tolerance of all ideas is not a moral position, but is intellectual relativism. Tolerating persons is the virtue. One feels there is a lack of confidence in the kind of intellectual exchange that ought to characterize university discussion when we show this desire to censor positions in advance.

Religious Arguments

This debate over religious participation raises the question of what constitutes a religious argument. We may begin with some reassurances. In Western countries, religious denominations normally govern themselves internally by an open politics which requires tolerance of differences and negotiating skills. Of course, these denominations are free to divide, which nations cannot do, but they are often known for uniting. We talk too loosely of churches being able to dictate to their adherents. In 1986, Ireland, with its special constitutional relationship to the Roman Catholic Church, held a vote on the legality of divorce. The issue would never have come to a vote if the Roman Catholic Church truly controlled the state. The electorate had the final say, and the fact that the vote upheld a ban on divorce did not mean that the Roman Catholic Church rules, but that a majority politically expressed the same position as the Church.

As a crude example of a religious argument, we might imagine hearing that some economic reform should be passed because "the New Testament teaches that we should have all goods in common" (referring to Acts 2:44). Although such a claim would only have its full effect among those of a certain religious belief, it could be aired in hopes of influencing or attracting others, who might not have thought they shared views with Christians. If the effect of the measure were not to establish a religion, voters could still act on the basis of their own economic or ethical motives, and there might be religious voters opposed to it.

Liberals and deliberative democrats hold that secular ideas are more "accessible" than religious ones. They believe they are shared or at least understood by everyone, so that they have the potential to bind together our pluralistic societies. In chapter 8 we will argue that a secular awareness is indeed logically prior to a religious one—that a secular mentality provides the mental context for a *discovery* of the religious. While religious persons may have occasional contact with the divine, they also understand a more ordinary reality.

But it is another thing to argue that religious people should be satisfied with secular reasons, just because they understand them. They may feel they have outgrown them. They may think their religious views take more into account and offer a larger sense of what the universe demands of us. What we owe to others or to our environment may seem richer in a religious perspective than in a secular one.

But we then come to the issue of coercive legislation. If democracy is more than simply the rule of a majority, it should hesitate to allow even a majority to force the consciences of others. Short of that, however, it need not prohibit legislation which some voters supported out of respect for their religious views, if passed in the usual way. Legal scholars recognize that religious consciences are sometimes forced or "burdened" by supposedly neutral laws. Equity might allow secular persons to be burdened with laws that they suspected were passed by religious voters. When one school district banned school dances, a court ruled that unconstitutional because it *suspected* that the objection stemmed from religion.[42] Actually it should not matter what the motive of voters was if the effect is not to force others to be religious. Prohibiting dancing falls well short of that.

It is obvious that religious persons may have difficulty arguing with the unconvinced. Arguments involve basic assumptions or beliefs as well as evidence and logic, and there are basic secular beliefs as well as religious ones. It is ideal if there is enough agreement that we do not have to vote to know the public will. But when there is no consensus and we must vote, it does not mean discussion is useless. Democracy involves getting to know and trust each other, building "social capital." So it is better to have the discussion, especially if it was civil. Any group will feel alienated if they are told they must listen while others do the talking. And since religious persons may vote, it will be enlightening to hear the reasons they give for their vote, whether or not it convinces anyone.

Religious propositions, asserting the evil of gambling or defining "humane" or "life," for example, may awaken similar conviction in others. Political views may not take the form of theoretical propositions. They are often expressed in narratives or metaphors. Politicians regularly win votes with loaded words, personal anecdotes, and even facial expressions. Catholic theologian David Hollenbach, S.J., points out that Catholic social thought

> rests on a conviction that the classical symbols and doctrines of Christianity can uncover meaning in personal and social existence that common sense and uncontroversial science [Rawls' favorite phrase] fail to see. So it invites those outside the church to place their self-understanding at risk by what [Catholic theologian David] Tracy calls conversation with such classics. At the same time, the believer's self-understanding is also placed at risk.[43]

The image of religious fundamentalists that runs through the philosophical discussion of democratic debate is that they only parrot a literal sense of their texts. It is more realistic to assume that they are speaking out of their experience—as interpreted by their scriptures. Thus they are much like others, who see their experience within a narrative. While we may imagine religious positions as uncompromising and self-righteous, humility can be a natural accompaniment of religious experience. Of course, hostility will become natural as those viewpoints are ignored or ruled out of order.

Philosopher Richard Rorty objected to those who think that announcing that their reasons are religious will give them greater weight. He thinks such persons should be prepared to meet with indifference:

> All liberal theory has to show is that moral decisions that are to be enforced by a pluralist and democratic state's monopoly of violence are best made by public discussion in which voices claiming to be God's, or reason's, or science's, are put on a par with everybody else's. . . . The arguments that take place [in the public square] are best thought of as neither religious nor nonreligious.[44]

Exactly. We should see which ideas turn out to be persuasive, without labeling some to be ruled out in advance.

Again, democracy does not require that we respect people's views, but that we respect the people. This is why we should let religious views be expressed, even though some will not know what to make of them. Some may be persuasive, and when religion taps into more basic mental processes than rationalist assertions, that may show up in the ballot box.

While religion may be uncomfortable with compromise, it is not always drawn to absolutist positions. In fact, religions are sometimes criticized for encouraging self-doubt. God might be thought omniscient without his followers being so. They understand that many religious imperatives—like charity for instance—are not answers so much as an invitation to think. All the liberal virtues, like tolerance, respect, and self-doubt, have their place in various religions.[45] And our political discussions would be poorer without such irreducibly religious symbols as sacrifice, charity, repentance, and forgiveness. If secularist philosophers were to eliminate all religious terms from the public square, it would be surprisingly bare.

Religious Contributions to Democracy

Institutional religions have long been familiar with democracy. Some have contributed notably to the development of democratic institutions. In the English context, Presbyterian church order offered the first model for *representative* democracy, through ascending levels of representative bodies. Congregationalists, Methodists, and other sects introduced the lower classes to democratic participation. Puritans John Winthrop and Roger Williams were the fathers of the American principle of "separation of church and state."

Robert Booth Fowler has developed, as one of Tocqueville's insights, the theory that Western religion and political liberalism are actually complementary, supplying each others' deficiencies. Liberalism offers freedom and material welfare, while religion offers restraint and solidarity as protection against the corrosive effects of individualism.[46]

The charge that religious persons are too unworldly to take an interest in politics has faded of late. Recent studies have shown that the more active members of religious bodies are among the more active citizens in the United States.[47] Throughout our history there have been religious viewpoints on public issues, including dueling, gambling, a weekly day of rest, church disestablishment, universal education, educational diversity, prostitution, pornography, public prayer, public drunkenness, slavery, racial discrimination, abortion, same-sex marriage, gender discrimination, prison reform, pacifism, and disarmament. Indeed there may be religious positions on *both* sides of many of these issues. That is no more surprising than that there should be conflicting "philosophical" positions on them.

Religious language is most apt to be heard when the questions are hardest, as in defining the "human" or humane. For who says that all human beings are "equal," and how would one prove it? There are numerous issues in which respect for the human is relevant, in the use of human blood or other body parts, the disposal of fetuses, or the harvesting of living fetal tissue.[48] Should a democracy composed largely of persons professing religious beliefs be forbidden to legislate in these areas because some hold naturalistic philosophies which cannot distinguish human from other life-forms? This is a genuine issue when there are Supreme Court justices who think that a law that says when life begins would be an unconstitutional violation of church/state separation.[49]

If democratic debate is to involve citizens generally, and not just our philosophers, we must be prepared to hear religious terms. Language about wealth, sanity, the humane, human rights, and justice bristles with religious notions of the human good. These concepts are still secure within our democratic society, whatever their status among academic elites. As an example of how things may happen, voters may share an instinctive revulsion, a taboo if you like, against mind-bending drugs. This has kept our "war" on drugs alive without notable protest, without involving much "rational" argumentation. If things change, if drugs become a much more widely accepted fashion, the prohibition may eventually be identified as a religious issue, though it does not seem so now. Actually, it may be a religious issue now, without being recognized as such.

In the end, we may have a hard time saying whether a particular argument was religious or not, being unable to trace it to its source. Elites might not think that our debates are intellectually impressive. But the real test may be how happy the public is with the resolution and whether it commits citizens more firmly to political society. This is the sort of cultural debate that Hollenbach and others think our democracy needs more of, rather than less.[50]

By contrast, courts that were faced with the question of the disposal of aborted fetuses have voided democratically passed laws requiring burial with the dignity accorded human beings, for fear of acknowledging majority sentiments which they identify as religious. Philosophers might hold that no arguments could settle such a matter, because the terms would not have universally agreed meanings. Should a regime whose courts prohibited such a debate on the basis of such a secularist understanding be considered democratic?

Beyond the issue of argumentation, there is the question of whether religious persons should be allowed to vote in accordance with religious tenets. Would that verge on forcing others to be religious? In answer, we assume that religious persons use their vote in the same way nonreligious people use theirs, to produce what they consider to be good for everybody.[51] We shake all these votes down in the ballot box and then impose the will of the more on the less. The accusation that religious people are uniquely guilty of imposing their beliefs on others is therefore odd. In the final analysis, democracy is a system for deciding whose beliefs will guide the state. Beliefs are imposed as rules, not as beliefs.

Everyone has a right to vote one's religious views, since no one in a democracy is forced to justify his vote before we decide whether to count it. Only if the majority forces religious activities on others would this violate the Constitution's establishment prohibition. Even those modern European democracies that still have established churches draw a line at forcing beliefs.[52]

There are problems in factoring faith-related programs into our government's attention to society's intractable problems, many of which now center on the encouragement of personal motivation. John J. DiIulio, Jr., who was the Federal government's first administrator of "faith-based and community initiatives," has discussed how to identify the aspects of religion that need to be isolated for sociological study or political decision in this area. Though not easily summarized, they can all be related to our definition.[53]

Religious Identities and Conversion

In the consideration of what constitutes a permissible debate there is finally the "essentialist" notion that people are either religious or secular. This is not something that our definition of religion can settle. We have argued that religious persons have an amphibious existence, operating in several environments. And even the incommensurability of religious and rationalist viewpoints would leave open the possibility of conversions. People have reported conversions who were far from expecting them, as we will see in chapter 8.

[ichael Polanyi and Thomas Kuhn popularized the term "conversion" in reference to movements within scientific rationality, which may help us see the point more objectively. Polanyi described conversion in the context of scientists having to present their revolutionary findings to each other:

> Proponents of a new system can convince their audience only by first winning their intellectual sympathy for a doctrine they have not yet grasped. Those who listen sympathetically will discover for themselves what they would otherwise never have understood. Such an acceptance is a heuristic process, a self-modifying act, and to this extent a conversion. . . . They think differently, speak a different language, live in a different world, and at least one of the two schools is excluded to this extent for the time being (whether rightly or wrongly) from the community of science. . . . To the extent to which it represents a new way of reasoning, we cannot convince others of it by formal argument, for so long as we argue within their framework, we can never induce them to abandon it. Demonstration must be supplemented, therefore, by forms of persuasion which can induce a conversion.[54]

Remember that this is a description of scientific argumentation, which we take as the model of rationality.

Philosopher Alasdair MacIntyre has insisted that there is not just one thing we can call rationality. In *Whose Justice? Which Rationality?* he describes a number of understandings representing liberal, Aristotelian, Augustinian, Scottish Common Sense versions, and others. He provocatively terms these "traditions" of rationality, using a word that has long indicated mindlessness. They are, he says, different intellectual cultures, any one of which is coherent enough to sustain intellectual debate, but which argue from different bases. "Rationality" thus means consistency or coherence *within* one or another of these traditions. So it is unrealistic to think of one's ideas as uniquely "based on rationality."[55]

MacIntyre does recognize the possibility of conversion from one of these rationalities to another, or even of a competition between them. For though they are incommensurate, they can compete to show that the narrative of one can be incorporated within another, while the reverse is not possible.

> That narrative prevails over its rivals which is able to include its rivals within it, not only to retell their stories as episodes within its story, but to tell the story of the telling of their stories as such episodes.[56]

In short, we need not essentialize secularists or religionists in our discussions of political debate. Greater attention to a toleration of persons and not just ideas should help us to greater understanding in this area.

Democratic Officials

There are other jobs in a democracy than those of debater and voter, and these have different responsibilities regarding religion. Legislators exercise some personal freedom in making laws that answer to the wishes of their constituents or to Rousseau's general will. But they should try to explain their actions in terms that will create agreement. We expect judges to be constrained by the wording of laws they are enforcing. Other officials honor their mandates by representing the state and not their private views. Presidents commonly invoke the symbols of the civil religion, but in such a way as to encourage unity and not division. So freedom decreases as one is more closely identified with the state.

It is understood that legislators will differ from some of their constituents some of the time, reflecting what we hope is their greater knowledge. It is no worse for them to differ from constituents because of their own religious reasons than because of secular ones, if they ran for election in their true colors. Meanwhile, religious citizens would have as great a right to object to being represented by secular figures as secular voters would at being represented by religious figures.[57]

Lobbying for laws, campaigning for candidates, and educational efforts by the parties are also part of the political process. None of these amounts to an exercise of power, so they are governed simply by the rules of free speech. Michael Walzer reminds us of all the other elements of democratic politics that are not deliberative. There is political education, organization, mobilization, demonstration, bargaining, and fund-raising. All of these are necessary, reminding us that politics is a social activity and not just an intellectual one. Without disparaging reason, we must recognize that deliberative democracy includes passion, commitment, solidarity, courage, and competitiveness. Only on juries should deliberation be the only thing.[58]

In short, democracy involves people and not just ideas. Its compromises require virtues such as justice, mercy, and charity. Where does one acquire these virtues within secular liberalism? Government schools are hampered by ideological individualism, by a separation of politics from religion and from moral philosophy generally, and by a dread of being thought preachy. "The family" is often undermined by journalists, psychologists, and bureaucrats who question its authority and its future. Churches are routinely listed among the intervening institutions whose support is needed to prop up the state, but nothing can be done to encourage them in this effort. Quite the opposite, as the message is spread that religion is best kept out of public business.

Some assume that religion is of most use in modern societies when it is most secular. But sociologist Peter Berger has argued that it contributes most when it is most religious. For it is one of the few voices reminding the state of the limits of its justice and the dignity of the individual.[59] We may also think of its occasional involvement in civil, or uncivil, disobedience. Principled disobedience challenges the political civility that is the goal of political philosophers. It may seem paradoxical to see civil disobedience as part of politics, but it can be where it is meant to be constructive. In the past two centuries states have become enormously powerful, capable of exercising nearly total power. When the media are in basic agreement, offering only criticisms of detail, they may unconsciously censor challenges to the state. Only something like religion can motivate people to ignore their own safety in order to protest. Only religion can organize them sufficiently to sustain that protest. This is not "normal" politics, of course, and is likely to be unpopular at the time.

Respect for religion is one of the few limitations that governments might have to respect. Religion has had odd bedfellows in this role. Jefferson used religious appeals to frighten American colonists into rebelling against Britain, which he pictured as crypto-Catholic.[60] Philosopher Karl Popper expressed admiration for certain religious martyrs, for their unpopular contributions to social progress.[61]

Trying to show how our term "religion" relates to a variety of political systems and arguments has created a special responsibility to be faithful to our common understanding of the word rather than to what would be most convenient within our institutions. Our definition of religion implies that tension between religion and politics is their natural condition. Though religion has been known to contribute in a thoroughly political manner, it is reasonable to fear the combination of divine and human power. Some seek formulas of accommodation, in a priestly, mediating manner. Others write polemics, adopting a prophetic or confrontational stance in favor of either religion or secularism. Some have thought that the ideal situation is a preservation of the tension. Still others speculate that, in the United States at least, "religion will increasingly replace electoral politics as the realm where battles for the national soul are fought. . . . Religion is increasingly doing what politics once did: offering an alternative to the values of the free market."[62]

CHAPTER SIX

Science and Reductionism

When the public hears that scientists want to study religion, they may hope to hear conclusive findings on the truth of its ultimate claims, or on its ultimate origins, or a comprehensive report on its functions, so that its future can be predicted. All these are beyond anything an empirical science can achieve. Of course, religion's historical origins are irretrievably lost. And given what the term religion means, the truth claims made for it are beyond testing, and its nonexistence in a population would say nothing of the truth of those claims. For part of its definition is that it transcends ordinary human reality.

What we have instead are studies of the correlations of religious *belief*—with social attitudes, group characteristics, psychological factors, cultural dynamics, brain physiology, evolutionary advantage. These are gathered in hopes of suggesting or confirming hypotheses about religious belief, its origins, or its continuing functions. These could only be entirely conclusive for those who had already decided that religion was a wholly naturalistic phenomenon, to be explained functionally.

Science is popularly (nominally) defined in our culture as that which gives true knowledge. Nature is popularly (nominally) defined as reality. Religion, popularly, means that which lies beyond ordinary knowledge and reality, and its possible demands on us. So there are sure to be efforts to see whether science can reduce religion to true knowledge, in the terms of the natural. In short, we wonder whether religion can be conceptually "reduced" to some more mundane level of reality, and whether that robs it of any distinctive, transcendent character. Exploring that question is the task of this chapter and the next, as we see what kind of challenge they present to our ordinary understanding of religion.

Put another way, what do scientists think they are studying when they want to make scientific studies of "religion." We start with the admitted failure of any real, referential definition of religion to win universal consent among scholars. This reflects the difficulty in isolating the "stuff" of religion, its objective referent. We should expect efforts to continue along that line despite previous disappointments, until our proposal of a nominal definition becomes more widely accepted.

At this point it is important to insist that even a nominal, semantic definition can establish religion's unique character, its reality. If real means irreducible, then even the irreducible *concept* would suggest the reality of religion, for it is concepts that are "reduced," or explained at a deeper level, not *things*. It is not like cases such as a "unicorn." The concept of unicorn can be fully reduced to horse plus horn. By contrast, it is the bonding of spirituality and obligation, not their mere addition, that is essential to religion. This is not to deny that some religious *activities* might be reduced to psychological or sociological terms. Particular religious beliefs and activities may be reduced to the terms or laws of the natural or ordinary, but if this leaves any conceptual remainder, final scientific reduction will have failed. A physicalist reduction of religious experience may show what sustains that experience, without dissolving its meaning as part of us and therefore real to the universe, of which we are a part.

In chapter 2 we recognized the insufficiency of functional definitions, which might prove tempting to scientists. In this chapter we will see how scientists may want to speak of religion substantively. How far can they go in reducing religious activity to the real terms by which they must proceed? When they say they are studying religion, what exactly do they mean?

Can Religion Reduce Science to Its Terms?

First, we might try turning the question around. Can religion make sense of science in its terms? Is science a part of a larger enterprise, the study of a contingent reality—a "creation"—motivated by much the same impulses that inspire theologians? One of the ironic possibilities of our time would involve scientist parents disturbed by their child's addiction to movies that use technology for the production of "religious" or spiritual experiences. When synthetic drugs produce visions which subjects take to be religious, how could one judge them mistaken? Have our modern high-tech hospitals already become the major prayer centers of modern societies? Can we imagine a future in which "science" is valued precisely for being able to produce religious ends? Is the whole point of scientific knowledge and mastery a religious one, directed toward transcendence of some sort? If not, what is the point?

For those raised on the early account of the "warfare of science and religion" the ironies are mounting. Historians and philosophers of science explore the ways that religious concepts and motivation helped to sponsor modern science. Chemist and philosopher Michael Polanyi has explained that in the absence of formulas to generate discoveries, scientists as well as theologians proceed by the principle of *fides quaerens intellectum*, believing in order to understand.[1] Why start a search without a sense of what you will find? William James agreed that the principle of "the right to believe" in advance of the evidence applied to science as well as religion.[2] Philosopher Suzanne Langer found the origins of symbolization and therefore of thought itself within numinous experience.[3] So we must brace ourselves for a tangled account of these relations.

It is notorious these days that scientists have taken to speaking of God, and not only in catchy book titles.[4] In his memoir, Werner Heisenberg recalls a scene in 1927 when four future Nobel Prize-winning physicists (Heisenberg, Pauli, Dirac, and Bohr) sat around a table seriously discussing Einstein's religious views. As Heisenberg was to observe, "What we can say clearly amounts to next to nothing," so that Bohr was right to point out the similarities between scientists' metaphors and those used by religion.[5] Physicist Paul Davies admits that

> among those scientists who are not religious in a conventional sense, many confess to a vague feeling that there is "something" beyond the surface reality of daily experience, some meaning behind existence. Even hard-nosed atheists frequently have what has been called a sense of reverence for nature, a fascination and respect for its depth and beauty and subtlety, that is akin to religious awe. Indeed, scientists are very emotional people in these matters. . . . Through my scientific work I have come to believe more and more strongly that the physical universe is put together with an ingenuity so astonishing that I cannot accept it merely as brute fact.[6]

This chapter will explore the ways that scientists conceive of religion so that they can study it, learn from it, battle with it, or dismiss it. We will see whether any of their views would force us to alter the definition we are refining or subsume religion under another understanding of reality.

Defining Science and Nature

Science is itself a nominal category. That is, cultures differ in the subjects encompassed within it. Whether one includes sociology, psychoanalysis, or linguistics among the sciences is a matter of cultural convention. Some cultures even include history or literary criticism, which would make the question of "science's" relation to religion different. This is not to say that scientific knowledge is socially constructed, but that the larger concept of "science" is. So we will confine ourselves to the relation of particular sciences to religion.

While science is a somewhat uncertain term it cannot simply mean truth, since some of what counted as "science" in past centuries has been superceded or transformed by later claims. One could protest that those earlier attempts were not really science, if they were not true. But then we cannot be sure that what scientists are saying today will prove to be the last word. Since those previous propositions were arrived at by something we can recognize as scientific methods, we can honor them as scientific statements even though they may have been superceded.

Nor is science to be defined as a particular method of investigation. Scientists have used so many methods that it is impossible to find common and essential elements in them all. Imre Lakatos' broader notion of "research program" is an admission of the difficulty of finding a method which defines all scientific study.[7] In a more general way, he points to the elements of formulating and testing of hypotheses, reformulating and retesting, by way of acquiring an account of how things work.

Systematic study will involve different methods, appropriate to the different character of the things being studied. Crucial to any definition is the fact that science is open to replication and verification—or falsification—by others who will take the trouble. The methods used must be explicit, and "scientific proof" amounts to getting the agreement of those who are acknowledged to be in a position to judge.

Crucial to replication is that the things being studied are "real" in the commonsense meaning of always being there when one wants to study them. This suggests a problem when science offers to study religion. Will the putative "object" of religion hold still long enough to be studied under controlled conditions? One could say that the reason science cannot study religion is precisely because it is not real in this sense. But religious thinkers can appeal to philosophers who do not think it meaningful to speak of what is real in general.[8] Concepts are real if they cannot be reduced to other concepts without remainder. Scientific reduction is not of objects or their properties, but of theories and concepts. Science is not "matter" but theories about matter. So reduction is subsuming one theory within a more comprehensive one.

Polanyi's classic study of the "personal" mental processes that go into scientific work begins to break down the differences between it and religion. He starts from the fact that scientists cannot specify their methods exhaustively and that the investigative processes used might be unique to each project. This does not make method merely subjective, for it is still meaningful to speak of research programs. Where things get interesting is when one goes beyond normal science—filling in the details—to "discoveries." For scientific discoveries indicate a problem that involves a logical gap. Such gaps have to be jumped by an experience of "illumination," which often has an element of the mysterious in it. He, and later Thomas Kuhn, used the term "conversion" for this discontinuous process.[9]

Philosopher Karl Popper likewise described the structure of science in terms that makes it seem less than terra firma.

> The empirical basis of objective science has thus nothing "absolute" about it. Science does not rest upon solid bedrock. The bold structure of its theories rises, as it were, above a swamp. It is like a building erected on piles. The piles are driven down from above into the swamp, but not down to any natural or "given" base; and if we stop driving the piles deeper, it is not because we have reached firm ground. We simply stop when we are satisfied that the piles are firm enough to carry the structure, at least for the time being.[10]

Nor does science have within itself a theory explaining its own existence. As William James recognized, the very existence of science is evidence against the determinism that serves as its basic principle. For the scientific enterprise is apparently a freely determined response to the world we find ourselves in.[11] Though science is conscious, goal-directed, and wondering, it pictures the "brute nature" it studies as none of these. So the very existence of science qualifies the image of nature that it promotes.

If science were simply another evolutionary product associated with the hydrocarbon structure we call man, there would be no reason to think of it as "true." If our scientific findings have more or less evolved along with us, we would not call it true. We may say that fingers have evolved, but we cannot say they are true. So science is part of a "human" reality that somehow transcends our official view of nature.

As for nature, we might say that it is something that science cre-ates. It has been said that "nature is what is *not* constructed by the human mind."[12] Nevertheless, we reserve the term for that which we think we understand. Anomalies of experience are studied until they become "nature." Humorist Dave Barry took a stab at a nominal definition in saying that "nature is anything that you would kill if it got inside your house."[13] Nominally, nature is a concept encompass-ing all that we can find a recognized place for within our worldview. The rest is either dismissed from consideration or reserved until we find an explanation which allows us to recognize it as "natural" in that sense.[14] So we might say that nature is the term we use for that which is known to follow the regular laws that we know. If science transcends nature, then we need to be prepared to find that other things do so as well.

Heisenberg observed that the understanding of the most basic elements of nature changed greatly within the scientific mind over the course of the twentieth century:

> The conception of the objective reality of the elementary particles has thus evaporated in a curious way, not into the fog of some new, obscure, or not yet understood reality concept, but into the transparent clarity of a mathematics that represents no longer the behavior of the elementary particles but rather our knowledge of this behavior. The atomic physicist has had to come to terms with the fact that his science is only a link in the endless chain of discussions of man with nature, but that it cannot simply talk of nature "as such." Natural science always presupposes man.[15]

So "nature" is not reality itself, but our present knowledge of real-ity. And that knowledge must often be left in mathematical terms, without hope of visualization.

It is obvious why religion is challenged by science and the con-cept of nature. Our definition made religion the term for a sense of something behind nature, or that remains mysterious within nature, something we are tempted to call "super-natural." There may be theologies that want to soften this distinction, but they have not changed common usage. Thus religion distinguishes itself as that which escapes scientific or naturalistic analysis. If science represents the great human project to understand and master our environment, "religion" may be a sense of the final futility of such a project—and that what we cannot comprehend is the most significant part.

But meanwhile, scientists may seek to bring religious behavior within the circle of the natural. They will look for the physical, psychological, or sociological laws that encompass some aspect of "religion." This is a perfectly natural or understandable effort, extending science so far as possible. When it can be shown that "religious" behavior or awareness shows regular patterns, it may be thought of as "natural." Insofar as that can be shown, scientists become the authorities about religion, as they are about the stars.

Scientists do not need to commit themselves to metaphysical naturalism in order to pursue their studies. But there is a temptation to do so, and to assert that science will eventually encompass or explain everything. This has been called a "materialism of the gaps," in parallel to religious believers' arguments for a "God of the gaps."

Warfare or Standoff?

Since at least 1875, with the publication of John William Draper's *History of the Conflict Between Religion and Science* and Andrew Dickson White's subsequent *A History of the Warfare of Science With Theology in Christendom*, in 1896, there has been a widespread sense that science and religion are in a battle to the death. Our definitions of religion and science suggest that they are not direct rivals, being almost defined by their difference. Yet they might try to conquer and colonize territory held by the other. Psychology might try to account for a religious response, even in pathological terms. Meanwhile, religious apologists might claim that the very notion of "mental health" betrays a religious sense of wholeness that lies unnoticed at the basis of psychology.

Some of these colonizing efforts have recently come into the open. Those who "deprogram" former cult members assert that they are dealing with a medical, not a religious, problem (which may bring them within the funding of Medicare). So even while other forms of behavioral "deviance" are being demedicalized by those who regulate the sciences, religious behaviors may be redefined as pathological. On the other hand, there are religious groups who want a creationist biology taught in public schools as a fully scientific theory. Theologian Langton Gilkey thinks this is a misplaced compliment: "Creation science embodies a common error of our cultural life, that all relevant truth is of the same sort: factual, empirical truth, truth referent to secondary causes—in a word, 'scientific truth.'"[16] Thus, proponents of both religion and secularism are appealing to science as an ideology, not to discover truth but to impose it. Such ideological conflict is not implicit in our definitions of either religion or science.

The same impasse appears in the current arguments over "intelligent design." Some take such discoveries as religious explanations, but as sympathetic a scientist as Paul Davies observes that it actually makes the origin of life "utterly mysterious."[17] Asserting that God created things does not explain them (in terms of other laws) so much as it awakens one to mystery, the realization of the "non-triviality of reality."[18] As Wittgenstein put this point, science is about *how* the world is, while mysticism is the full awareness *that* the world is: "Not *how* the world is, is the mystical, but *that* it is."[19] By our nominal definitions, turning religious concepts into scientific ones makes them cease to be religious, just as finding religious experience to be entirely natural would make it cease to be recognized as religious.

Possibilities of Rapprochement

Despite these possibilities of misunderstanding and conflict, it is striking to see the encouragement that a bare religious awareness, as we have defined it, can give to science. It is a commonplace of the philosophy of science that modern empirical science arose within the context of a monotheistic metaphysics. But Albert Einstein used to suggest something even deeper—that not only the cognitive basis, but the affective or emotional drive behind science must be religious.

> Cosmic religious feeling is the strongest and noblest incitement to scientific research. . . . What a deep conviction of the rationality

of the universe . . . Kepler and Newton must have had to enable them to spend years of solitary labour in disentangling the principles of celestial mechanics! Those whose acquaintance with scientific research is derived chiefly from its practical results easily develop a completely false notion of the mentality of the men who, surrounded by a sceptical world, have shown the way. . . . It is cosmic religious feeling that gives a man strength of this sort. A contemporary has said, not unjustly, that in this materialistic age of ours the serious scientific workers are the only profoundly religious people.[20]

If he was right, not only religious propositions but even the bare religious *awareness* mentioned in our definition may undergird scientific discovery.

Religions are expected to admit some mystery beyond their statements. But the same can be said of some science, most notably at the very basic level of quantum physics. Some scientists have followed Heisenberg in taking his principle of epistemological uncertainty to mean ontological indeterminacy.[21] Thus we are warned that while the statistical expressions of quantum physics work for practical purposes we cannot get beyond them to anything we could visualize. But as physicist John Wheeler admits, "Until we see the quantum principle with this simplicity we can well believe that we do not know the first thing about the universe, about ourselves, and about our place in the universe."[22]

Quantum physics reveals similarities between scientific and religious *awareness*. Physicist and theologian John Polkinghorne observes that the Enlightenment's "clockwork universe could not survive the dissolution of the picturable and predictable into the cloudy and fitful" world of quantum theory. Nor is a recognition of nature's unpredictability only found at the microscale of quantum events. It is also apparent at the macro level of chaotic systems, showing an "openness" at the level of our lifeworld.[23] Thus there is now wonder and mystery on the boundaries of science that suggests a religious awareness if not a religious response.

Cosmology and Humanity

Such mention of cosmology begins our review of the most relevant scientific disciplines, with their different methods and terms, to see how they relate to the concept of religion, as nominally understood. How have scientists imagined religion for their study, or even for their dismissal, and what problems are associated with their efforts?

Physics has always inspired reflections on what is taken to be basic or ultimate. And it is notorious that a number of physicists today echo the creed that Einstein used, in varying forms, to express his sense of "religion."

> The most beautiful thing we can experience is the mysterious. It is the source of all true art *and science*. He to whom this emotion is a stranger, who can no longer pause to wonder and stand rapt in awe, is as good as dead: his eyes are closed. This insight into the mystery of life, coupled though it be with fear, has also given rise to religion. To know that what is *impenetrable to us* really exists, manifesting itself as the highest wisdom and the most radiant beauty which our dull faculties can comprehend only in their most primitive forms—this knowledge, this feeling, is at the center of true religiousness. In this sense, and in this sense only, I belong in the ranks of devoutly religious men.[24]

Karl Popper recalled that "I learned nothing from Einstein directly, as a consequence of our conversations [in the 1950s]. He tended to express things in theological terms, and this was often the only way to argue with him. I found it quite uninteresting."[25]

We have already quoted Paul Davies on the awe that comes over those who are favored with glimpses beyond the boundaries of previous science. We could multiply such testimonies, and the expressions of astonishment and humility remind one of Otto's description of the numinous experience. Their awe has to do with "strangeness" (a common expression), the surprise of counterintuitive aspects, the ingenuity and even wit that seem embedded in things. It hints at personality within something we still call "creation," which makes the experience more than merely aesthetic.

Within cosmology, the obvious problem for religion is humanity's insignificance in relation to the unimaginable size of our universe. After all, worshipers are as much a part of religion as are deities, and it is easy to describe the universe in terms that reduce any human response to perfect insignificance. One could wonder, however, what size has to do with significance. We are led to think that at the Big Bang everything that would become the universe was a mere point, if that is meaningful at such a moment. We also read that humans are something like halfway between the largest and smallest things in the present universe, and that any single person has a higher level of organization and richness of experience than a thousand galaxies.[26] This would give humans something like a front-row seat for the cosmic drama.

Beyond that, as Polkinghorne puts it, "the most remarkable event following the big bang, of which we have knowledge, has been the universe's becoming aware of itself through humanity—the event that . . . has made science possible."[27] When cosmologist Steven Weinberg famously wrote that "the more the universe seems comprehensible, the more it also seems pointless," we must wonder what he meant.[28] For the universe to become *aware of itself* might strike us as quite incredibly interesting. Such awareness is the basis for the whole scientific enterprise. Then, for the beings embodying the universe's awareness to take a hand in their own evolution, first culturally and now through gene-line engineering, is even more astounding. Is the fact that creatures are becoming creators more interesting to theology or to science?

In another place, I have reviewed some of the discussion over the so-called "anthropic coincidences," especially as they bear on rhetorical objections to religion stemming from our physical scale.[29] The so-called "anthropic principle" refers to the astonishingly finely tuned initial conditions of the Big Bang, which apparently made intelligent life of some sort not just possible but even inevitable. They are of interest to both theologians and scientists. Scientists have a harder time discussing them within their terms, and they may express impatience with those whose speculations seem to have no recognized bounds. They are likely to appeal to Stephen Hawking's own speculation that "the Universe does not have any boundaries in space or time. . . . There is thus no problem of boundary [or initial] conditions." But elsewhere, Hawking is more careful to admit that

> this idea that time and space should be finite "without boundary" [sic] is just a *proposal*: it cannot be deduced from some other principle. Like any other scientific theory, it may initially be put forward for aesthetic or metaphysical reasons, but the real test is whether it makes predictions that agree with observation. This, however, is difficult.[30]

So it is not simply the presence of speculation that distinguishes scientists from theologians at this point. Theologians may not offer meanings for such facts, but they are doubtless more willing to use them to keep alive a sense of wonder like that expressed by Wittgenstein. A sense of the limits of our "knowledge" is part of the human condition. Some cosmologists like Freeman Dyson seem to blur the boundary between the scientific and religious sensibilities, when he says that "the more I examine the universe and the details of its architecture, the more evidence I find that the universe in some sense must have known we were coming."[31] The sense of contingency in our universe, the fact that things could have been different, is reintroducing an element of wonder into science as well.

Religious faith as we have defined it may seldom arise from speculation on teleonomy or cosmic design. These are more likely to create simple interest than a religious response. But modern cosmology now allows us to recognize that saying that "we are just part of the universe" is not just a rhetorical flourish meaning that we are not all that special. Rather, it means that a universe that contains us is indeed special. It may still be common to hear that "ethics are made by humans, not found in the world,"[32] as if we were not part of the world. But this is now more likely to come from journalists than scientists.

Neuroscience and Consciousness

As scientists wake up to the fact that human or personal characteristics must be included in an analysis of the universe, they must try to follow naturalistic principles in understanding it. It is their duty to see if science itself can account for the personal. Since cosmology and physics do not appear to have eliminated the notion of "creation," personality, purpose, or ethics, the field of conceptual struggle has moved from the cosmos to inside the brain.

The study of consciousness seems central to the relation of science and religion, since our definition understands religion in terms of consciousness. There are two forms of the study of consciousness, a neurobiological study which searches for its causes, and a philosophical or hermeneutical study which looks for its meaning. Interestingly, that neuroscientific approach has trouble with its reductionistic program. For reductionism must assume that the causes of consciousness are not themselves conscious, being one of those emergent properties that transcends its basis.

Philosopher Thomas Nagel's classic paper on "What is it like to be a bat?" explains that one can reduce mental experiences to more basic terms only if one can exclude the phenomenological features— what they seem like. But consciousness is precisely what things seem like, so that phenomenology is the way to study it. In short, *causal* explanations have problems because whatever is "behind" consciousness might also be present *without* registering in consciousness.[33]

We have found our term "religion" to mean a form of conscious experience (as we will explore more fully in chapter 8). Some of our experience (whatever its causes) seems to suggest a extraordinary power or Power. In Nagel's view, we cannot imagine a physicalist argument that can be used against that understanding.

The study of consciousness may be mankind's greatest intellectual challenge at this point, but there is great uncertainty about how to approach it.[34] There are neurobiological studies of "religious" awareness, which try to establish the uniqueness of the experience. The problem is that they seek physical measures of self-identified "mystical" brain states (of unity, power, rapture, and the like) which may not involve the faith or obligation that make that experience religious. That is, they may establish the measurable reality of the experience, but not its character as religious.[35] So while they might reduce what we call "spirituality" to physicalist terms, our definition of religion has more to it than that. Spiritual awareness is only part of our definition. By itself, this spirituality seems to be an aesthetic category.

Evolutionary Psychology

An older model of science is represented by sociobiology or evolutionary psychology, which was more directly intent on reducing religion to more basic terms. Cosmologists, we noticed, may stumble onto something like religion where they are not looking for it, and do not have to acknowledge it if they do not choose to. But sociobiology offered direct challenges to the integrity of religious concepts. They did not express the same religious awe—when investigating human nature—as physicists may do, who only study the particles we are made of.

Reduction, in the sociobiological context, means contrasting what religious subjects think their religion means with what scientists may show about how it is caused. Social scientists, psychologists, or biologists do that by finding the laws that regularly govern religious expression, or the patterns it takes, which make it part of the "nature" we can understand. Their efforts might show that religion is adequately accounted for by a neurotic compulsion or social need or evolutionary advantage. The tables would be turned if one could show that religion was the cause of activity which subjects *thought* was about something else. Gerhard Lenski's early study, *The Religious Factor*, was such an attempt to show where religion was the independent variable. He found religious affiliation behind political and social attitudes, educational interests and other habits, which subjects barely associated with their formal religion. Religious affiliation discriminated the variables when class and other factors did not.[36] The National Election Studies Biennial Survey group has recently included responses to take account of "religious" factors that may be guiding American electoral behavior.[37] This represents a change from the previous assumption that religion was only a dependent variable.

In perhaps his most challenging book, *On Human Nature* (1979), Edward O. Wilson has popularized the view that we find the functional meanings of religion within the science of species survival. By calling for supreme effort and self-sacrifice against outgroups and other threats, religion has been useful in generating all the nastiness humanity needs to give us a competitive edge. (Interestingly, Darwin had a contrary view of the evolutionary function of religion, thinking that the trait of amazement inspired more flight than fighting.[38]) In expressing his disapproval of religion (especially as an explanatory principle), Wilson seems to be conflicted about religion's evolutionary role. As an evolutionist he ought simply to accept it as a product of the natural process, like he accepts his fingers, but he cannot help thinking that in humans such behavior is shameful. In order to justify that indignation, he begins to treat religion as cultural rather than natural.

Wilson does not explain how culture "hypertrophies" from natural properties to the point that it could transcend its physical basis so as to invite judgment. He clearly thinks that science has broken free of the nature that it studies and transcends evolutionary development. For while the human brain is a product of evolution, constructed "to promote the survival of human genes . . . that direct its assembly," he writes as if it has more disinterested purposes—like science. He cannot bring himself to put religion in the same category; somehow it has gotten on the wrong side of nature and history.

This raises the problem that the evolutionary hypothesis has with rationality. Naturalism must view human thought as the product of evolution, preserving those traits useful for survival. To add that it is "true" seems a gratuitous compliment. Wilson and others argue that religious thinking has been favored by evolution and is now part of our "hard-wiring," helping with the self-maintenance and self-transcendence necessary to survival.[39] They do not claim that this proves religion's truth. But history may make other things assume a greater importance than science, like ecological concerns that seem to be on the other side of the fact/value divide. So even evolutionists should be prepared for changes in our situation that would include a greater scope for religion.

Wilson intimates that the evolutionary struggle has been transferred from the biological to the cultural level, and expresses confidence that science will triumph over religion as superior explanation. (He had previously treated religion as emotional rather than explanatory.) Having speculated about the evolutionary importance of religion, he fails to explain why secularization has now become nature's favorite. He is disdainful of the fact that "knowledge is being enthusiastically harnessed to the service of religion," but does not say why this is bound to fail.[40]

Finally, even in his own project of explaining how all values are contained within survival value, or prudence, Wilson fails to recognize the radical otherness of religion. For he begs the question of why survival is a good thing, which seems to come more directly from religion than from science. For some religions, the idolization of one's species could be viewed as a sin, rather than a virtue.

The Challenge of Personality

Evolutionary psychology and neuroscience have sharpened an awareness that personal qualities may be more irreducible, more ontologically grounded than earlier philosophies recognized. Philosophers and theologians have taken to arguing that agents, those beings that can act, may be said to be more "real" than anything else in the universe. So even before moving on to sciences that take their subject to be human personality, we see that personality has begun to challenge the harder sciences. Philosopher Charles Taylor observes that the appearance of human beings created new realities in the universe. However we appeared, an adequate account of reality now has to include concepts like human, justice, rights, sanity, wealth, and humanities, which cannot be reduced to the terms of a crude naturalism:

> Human science can no longer be couched in the terms of physics. Our value terms purport to give us insight into what it is to live in the universe as a human being, and this is a quite different matter from that which physical science claims to reveal and explain. This reality is, of course, dependent on us, in the sense that a condition

> for its existence is our existence. But once granted that we exist, it is no more a subjective projection than what physics deals with. . . . What is real is what you have to deal with, what won't go away just because it doesn't fit with your prejudices.[41]

In seeming to transcend our standard inventory of natural things, human personality encourages the view that there may be other things that transcend our ordinary world. Our definition of religion witnesses to such powers or beings. And far from finding it conclusively reduced by recent science, we have found openings developing within scientific worldviews.

Finally we must ask how all of this relates to the issue of the *sui generis* character, the independent reality, of religion. The older view of this subject assumed some sort of real definition and therefore a substantial understanding of the objects of religion. The concepts used in describing the "thing" that was religion were those that might be subject to scientific, theoretical reduction. Our nominal definition offers a new understanding of that issue. The unique reality of religion is now seen in our inability to reduce the analytical concept to the categories of any science. The basic sciences touched on in this chapter have not succeeded in their initial challenge. Rather, we seem to have confirmed the incommensurable status of nature and religion that we have long assumed.

CHAPTER SEVEN

Sciences of Human Life

Though sciences like cosmology may be susceptible to an incursion of religious terminology, we may expect the sciences of human life to be more directly involved and more threatening to the concept of religion, even when defined nominally and analytically—as something like faith responding to supernatural power. For it is here that the reduction of the concept of religion and of religious manifestations to naturalistic concepts would seem most likely.

The challenge in this chapter is to find, among the social and psychological sciences, synonyms for what we conventionally call religion. Are there concepts with the same meaning as the one that we have found essential or defining to religion—an active response to the transcendent? If not, the word, the concept, would seem to be irreducible. It could still be true that particular rituals, myths, worldviews, and obsessions might be accounted for (i.e., reduced) within the theories of such sciences. But so long as the concept of religion was not exhaustively contained in any of those, it will have established itself as *sui generis*.

Anthropology

Anthropologists have given the most thought of any scientists to the problems of defining religion. Paradoxically, that is because the less developed societies they study tend not to have words that translate precisely into our term, even though they exhibit a great deal of what looks like religious activity and thinking. The anthropologists' theories about religion contribute to their definitions. These definitions, in turn, are used to identify which rituals and beliefs they consider religious, by a somewhat circular process.[1]

Generally speaking, anthropologists define religion with reference to the "sacred," things to be avoided and things to be accorded ultimate respect. Here we see the two sides of Rudolf Otto's *mysterium tremendum et fascinosum*. Perhaps any object or activity whatever can be taken as sacred. Outsiders would not see it as an intrinsic quality of the object of devotion, but think it resides in the peoples' respect. That respect suggests a response to power, so that this operative definition accords with ours.

In what we call primitive societies, feelings for the sacred are involved with a much wider range of objects and activities than in modern societies. This prompts the common view that religion *means* primitive, and that social development entails the decline of religion. Early anthropologists encouraged this view by using evolutionary theories and making a special search for the origins of religion. Such early theories about origins have been criticized for being entirely speculative. After all, the primitive societies still existing— which serve as laboratories for the study of early human development—may be as far removed from their origins as ours is.

The anthropological definitions are, of course, functional, reflecting the view that religions have some kind of social-cultural importance. Some see the rituals and the explanations that they label religious as early forms of science or technology. The rituals or explanations are mistaken, of course, but anthropologists may give them credit for putting humanity on the path to science. In this "intellectualist" understanding, religion can be reduced to that equivalent science and technology.

Others see religious rituals and ideas as "emotionalist," not concerned with explaining things so much as expressing attitudes in a dramatic form. These could be expressions of awe, of fears or anxieties, of repressed rage or guilt, of confidence, of anything that seems extraordinarily significant. We should note that some anthropologists see the rituals as creating the emotions, rather than the other way around. There is no necessity that this symbolic activity would ever disappear from culture. But it makes religion only a heightening of emotion.

Still other anthropologists, like Geertz, see religion as distinctive and self-contained within its own context. What they are getting at is that symbolization itself—that which made human thought possible and enabled humanity to transcend nature—was probably born in ritual, which we ordinarily think of as religious. Myth and rite "fix and organize abstract conceptual relationships in terms of concrete images and thus make speculative thought possible." In other words, religion relates humans to the universe in the widest sense, not just scientifically and technologically, and not just emotionally, but also morally and existentially. It *links* meaning and motivation, and celebrates our relation to the environment.[2]

This "structuralist" view tends to see religion as nonreferential. Or one could say that religion refers to its own reality and not to the features of the social or natural world that it uses symbolically. Religion is taken to be the scheme of ultimate classification, not a part of technology or emotional experience. Some criticize this understanding as antiscientific, since it seems to take the rituals or ideas drawn from social relations to a "religious" level treated as more basic. And indeed, one can find anthropologists speaking of the *religious* basis of symbol and language, of logic, of society, and of "man" as a concept.[3] Thus, critics call the approach "fideist."[4] For it leaves religion so basic as to be inexplicable, and outside the area of theory and function.

Thus, within anthropology there may be a standoff in the matter of theoretical reduction. This is also seen in a disagreement over whether magic is part of religion or something else altogether. The usual definition of magic, again, proves to be nominal, distinguishing

it as more purely instrumental than religion. There is some speculative consensus that magic derived from religion rather than the
other way around (following Durkheim rather than Weber on this
issue). That is, magic is commonly seen as a profanation of communal religious rituals, for private and often antisocial ends.[5]

Magic would not qualify as religious by our definition if it were
purely instrumental, making no ultimate demands on the practitio-
ner. Of course there is plenty of "inauthentic" religion around. But
such religion is understood as deceptive, whereas magic is not pretending to be something different.

It might be that these different anthropological theories fit different cases. That would mean, however, that "intellectualist" or
"emotionalist" reductions of particular rites would not prove the
case universally. And it seems unlikely that these essentially hermeneutic considerations will ever be definitively resolved.

Sociology

Sociology, of course, favors functionalist views of religion, in its
search for a social theory of religion. This may assume what needs
to be proved, and we have already dealt with the deficiencies of
functional approaches in defining religion (in chapter 2). Generally
speaking, sociologists see religion as providing the symbols and rituals of social cohesion. Religion might be considered irreducible if
that function could not be accomplished in another way. But many
would see nonreligious ideologies as functional equivalents in this
bonding role.

If these ideological surrogates are called "religions" there will be
the hint of quotes around the term, but it would not be far from
the mark. Any society must appeal to transcendent values in calling
for the sacrifice of personal interests, or life itself, for the common
good. We discussed one such ideology in the "civil religion" we noted
in chapter 5. To abandon any notion of transcendent justice, and
reduce authority to simple power, might be seriously dysfunctional.
So if the transcendent is considered religious by definition, sociologists run the risk of arguing the impossibility of secularization.

There has been long discussion of this issue and the current mood is to speak of religious change rather than religious decline.[6]

Economics

Recently there have been attempts to reduce religion to the terms of economics, according to rational choice models of behavior. This functionalist or instrumentalist approach is an alternative to seeing religion as essentially irrational or ignorant. Sociologist Rodney Stark and his associates recognized the difficulties of "secularization theory," which had predicted a universal religious decline. And they noticed that religion fared better in a "free market" than in a monopolistic cultural situation. Rational choice theory was invoked to explain how religion could flourish in a world governed by economic rationality. The "compensators" that they thought religion offers could not exactly be called rewards since they tend to be invisible to others. They were intangible substitutes for real rewards, but proved to satisfy the steady customers.[7]

The criticisms we have made of functional definitions pertain here. Rational choice models could well describe the place of religion in many lives, but it does not define religion. Are all intangible rewards religious? Are all religious rewards intangible? Beyond that, the theory has the same philosophical difficulties as other forms of utilitarianism. How do we identify something as a reward except by its being chosen? What one person sees as a cost (a prayer meeting, for example) another might see as a benefit. With utilitarianism, "pleasure" proved to be so personal that the theory lacked predictive value. In any event, insofar as religion compels rather than calculates, this rationality would only be *using* religion. In its purest form religion seems to involve a *loss* of self, so that rational choice religion would describe an inauthentic type.

Some economists have actually turned the tables, to speak of "Economic Rationality as a Religious System." In an article with that title Neil Smelser observed that rational choice theory itself bristles with assumptions about an idealized human nature and environment, about values and violations. Like religion, he says, economics has to do not with goods per se, but with gratifications more generally, including religious ones as conventionally defined.[8] Like the concept of sanity, a definition of economic well-being (wealth) seems ultimately to relate to *religious* ideas of what is optimal for humans.

Religion and Social Science Professionals

It may be relevant to mention what is known of the attitude of social scientists toward religion. After surveying the scholarship on this subject, sociologist Robert Wuthnow holds that the expected inverse relation between science and religion is markedly more evident among social scientists than physical scientists. In a survey in 1974, only 37 percent of those in the "hard sciences" described themselves as nonreligious, compared to 49 percent of those in the "softer" social sciences. Physicists and chemists were also less likely to be nonreligious than scholars in the humanities (46%).

Wuthnow hypothesizes that part of the more antireligious stance of the latter groups may derive from institutional insecurity. Social scientists may think they are not taken as seriously as those in the natural sciences and must maintain intellectual boundaries between themselves and the public, which they identify as religious.[9] Under these circumstances "science" easily becomes an ideology, used to justify their elite status. It is natural for a scientific ideology to define itself in opposition to religion, and the cruder the definition of religion the better it serves the purpose of justification.

From all reports, scientists would not be wrong in thinking of the American public as religious. We may be suspicious of attitude questionnaires, but even when studies concentrate on the reports of paranormal *experiences* the figures seem almost "medieval." By a Gallup survey of 1991, a sixth of a national sample said they had been in touch with someone who had died, a tenth had seen a ghost, a tenth had been in the presence of the Devil, and three-fourths had experienced at least one of several paranormal experiences. Only seven percent denied believing in any of the listed possibilities. The likeliest to report such experiences were from privileged groups— middle aged and younger, college graduates, with higher incomes, who did not think of themselves as conventionally religious.[10] A national survey of 1973 had reported similar results, with almost a fifth of the population reporting frequent paranormal experience. It noted that these "mystics" were disproportionately older, wealthier, better educated, and male.[11]

All this raises the question of how social scientists can supplement self-report or official statistics as the measure of religiosity. Even "unobtrusive measures," such as charitable giving, religious book and music sales, shrine attendance, or political support of religious issues, may also be problematic. Religion as we are defining it may be too elusive to register a clear presence for the scientists' tools of measurement. Scientists may need to get inside the person to be more confident of encountering whatever religion might be.

Psychology

Psychology seems to offer the most possibilities of reducing religious awareness to an aspect of nature. It intersects with religion in the three areas of experimental psychology, psychoanalysis, and parapsychology. Experimentalists want to see how a subject's religion is related to (and perhaps caused by) other factors. Psychoanalysts want to get behind their subjects' religious expressions to find any unacknowledged meaning. Parapsychologists would like to catch their subjects at the point of a paranormal (religious?) experience to see what is going on. The experimentalists and parapsychologists are engaged in normal science, inviting verification. Psychoanalysis is more commonly a hermeneutic approach.

These three offer different problems with respect to our definition. Experimentalists have been forced to think whether religion is a single variable. They have been led to formulate different religious types or dimensions. One of the most successful typologies, in terms of its discriminations and correlations, contrasts intrinsic with extrinsic (instrumental) religion. This has been broadened to include a third, "quest" type.[12] Such distinctions, like William James' healthy/sick-minded religion, suggest value judgments having to do with authenticity, which are awkward in science. This would be a problem for a real definition but not for a nominal one. In chapter 2 we discussed how inauthentic religion or religious pretense could also be given meaning within our terms.

Parapsychologists' main problem is convincing others of their scientific credentials. They rely on correlational studies and the uncertainties of self-report and questionnaires, since it is difficult to schedule such experiences as one would a laboratory experiment. For our purposes, their problem is in showing that these events deserve the term religious. Of course, "paranormal" does suggest the supernatural, which generates much of the popular interest in the field as well as the scholarly resistance.

While experimental psychologists accept quite conventional definitions of the religious, parapsychology's special subject is "wondrous events" that defy "ordinary" explanation. Those include extra-sensory perception, out-of-body and near-death experiences, apparitions and poltergeists (noisy spirits), spiritual possession, pain and heat immunity, psychokinesis, and miraculous healing. By our definition, these seem religious in suggesting supernatural activity. It is not so clear that they create a response of faith or otherwise "make a difference." Indeed, several studies have indicated that "religious skeptics" were more likely than "religious believers" to accept paranormal claims. Different studies have revealed positive, negative, and null correlation with self-reported religiosity in their subjects. Only a quarter of one investigator's informants reported that such anomolous experiences affected any religious faith they had. Nevertheless, the general assumption is that, historically, religion has been built on such experiences.[13]

The objective reality of such incidents is argued on the basis of group experience, as well as cross-cultural and historical studies.[14] Studies so far have not discovered differences according to age, race, education, income, marital status, or religious preference that would suggest obvious explanations. The other question is whether the paranormal is to be classed with the pathological. Some studies note that such experiences may be deliberately cultivated by "healthy, high-functioning individuals." For there seems to be a "normal dissociative capacity" unrelated to trauma.[15] Later in this chapter we will need to consider the concepts of mental health and disease in relation to ideas of religion and of nature.

Since reports of the miraculous or paranormal seem to challenge current views of the natural and naturalism, studies are made with extreme attention to controls. Controlled experiments have involved LSD, wilderness experience, contemplative prayer, epileptic seizures, hypnosis, and stimulating the temporal lobes with electromagnetic charges. The point is to correlate these experiments to measures of "well-being," alcohol recovery, childbirth, religious rituals, personality types, and national variations. Findings are sometimes recognized as contradictory. As one literature review wryly concludes, "future investigations will generate belief and skepticism rather than consistent results."[16]

The resistance that scientists often show toward parapsychology seems to stem from the fear that it could provide a beachhead for religion within science.[17] Actually, the reverse is true. The hope of parapsychologists is to reduce such phenomena to the kind of laws and theories that other sciences can boast. Religious apologists would have more to fear from their investigations, except that they can always question the religious identification of the phenomena, especially if they adopted our definition.

Psychoanalysis

Like parapsychology, psychoanalysis exists on the uncertain, shifting boundaries of science. Psychoanalysts interact with patients rather than with experimental subjects, in a search for insight and helpful interpretation. They have less hope of refining laws; it is enough if their insights can be validated by their patients. Typically, they take religious expressions to be the disguise of something deeper, and perhaps a danger signal. Sigmund Freud early came to the view that collective "religion is a universal obsessional neurosis," and that "neurosis is an individual religion."[18] His analysis of such obsessions, involving the ambivalence of "Oedipal conflict," made sense of both sides of Otto's numinous, the attraction and the terror—the *mysterium tremendum et fascinosum*. (We use Freud, not as the whole story of psychoanalysis, but as the most representative figure.)

There are various objections to defining "religious" as obsessional. Some hold that obsessional neurosis describes magic rather than religion. Others object to finding the causes of a cultural institution like religion within individual psychology. Some go the other direction, deriving individual pathologies from a sick culture. But then the question becomes whether general behaviors can be considered pathological if they are functional within the culture.

The issue of defining religion within this context turns on whether Freud distinguished religious pathologies from other, more "healthy" manifestations of religion. That would suggest that he was differentiating on the basis of some other, implicit definition. In *Totem and Taboo* (1913) Freud remarked that "taboo is not a neurosis but a social institution. We are therefore faced with the task of explaining what difference there is in principle between a neurosis and a cultural creation such as taboo." He never did, but at that point he had recognized a difference between primitive religious phenomena and similar manifestations as they appear in modern patients. What would need explaining in the case of a modern patient would not in a primitive believer, or not on the level of individual psychology. Durkheim, for example, had claimed that children learn rituals *before* emotionalizing them.[19]

If one cannot reduce collective religion to individual projections then one cannot simply *define* religion as neurosis. Cultures cannot be termed neurotic, if it is only in the context of particular cultures that neurosis has meaning.[20] The social functions served by religion (while not defining religion) boost it into the category of the rational rather than the obsessional. Some of Freud's disciples, like Erik Erikson, have drawn back from medicalizing religion, even finding some forms to be therapeutic.

More promising as an approach to defining religion was Freud's paper on "The Uncanny" (1919), which appeared two years after Otto's *Das Heilige*. Freud associated this phenomenon with aesthetics rather than religion, but the uncanny does seem close to what we have described as religious awareness. Freud defines it as something familiar but repressed, and therefore attractive but also troubling. It is therefore close to Otto's view. Freud's explanation (involving Oedipal conflicts) is not open to falsification and might be considered only speculative on that account. His discussion of his own experiences of the uncanny may indicate that he did not think of it as pathological.[21]

There have been attempts within psychoanalysis to define an experience which is irreduceably transcendent or mystical. The most prominent of these was Abraham Maslow's concept of "peak-experiences." Maslow casually separates religious and nonreligious peak experiences, without saying how to distinguish them.[22] Thus, like R. C. Zaehner in chapter 2, he sees mysticism as a broader subject than religion.

Religion as Pathology, or Health as Religious?

The terms pathological and therapeutic raise an important question about religion within science, contrasting concepts of health and sanity with disease. Stigmatizing religion as pathology might be considered the ultimate dismissal in our medicalized culture. But the concept of disease is itself in question, lacking scientific credentials.

Health and disease are meant to distinguish the natural from the aberrant or nonnatural, but a moment's reflection shows that they do not. Diseases are every bit as much a part of "nature" as their hosts. That is, they function according to the laws of their being. Philosophers of science suggest that the concept of disease has no ontological significance. It is a normative term, like "weed," and it is culturally relative.

Philosophers are now calling disease a "convenient fiction" that requires a nominal definition rather than an "essentialist" or substantive one.[23] Some wryly conclude that "disease" only refers to something that a physician can cure better than someone else.[24] This points up the political nature of the issue, like the medicalization of cult activities and normalization of homosexuality, referred to earlier. If our medical culture decides that there is no "proper" sexuality, then sexual pathology become problematic.

Obviously we cannot do without the concepts of health and disease. One way to save them is to see them as religious perspectives. Defining disease need not be dismissed as an exercise of power. It reflects notions of wholeness, of what human life is, optimally. So when physicians and psychologists speak of pathology or therapy, they are using concepts derived from something like a religious worldview. We can give them credit for wanting people healed, and not just simply returned to the work force. They believe human life is a good thing in itself. A philosophical statement of that sentiment might need to use religious terms.

Here we have an important case of the "reduction" of a scientific concept to the more basic level of religion, which makes better sense. It seems unthinkable that we would simply give it up notions of health or sanity for lack of a rigorously naturalistic explanation. If one accepts the language of healthy versus neurotic, some religious behavior should probably be considered neurotic while some should not.

Psychologist R. D. Laing was famous for raising the question of whether even the pathological elements in religion discredit it. This was part of his famous attack on the reigning notions of mental health. Laing thought psychotics might be especially open to religious experience, without calling that experience into question. Schizophrenics, he says, have more experience of "how insubstantial the pageant of external reality can be," and of the "sublime and grotesque presences that can replace it, or exist alongside it." As for the rest of us, "When the ultimate basis of our world is in question, we run to different holes in the ground."

The ego, Laing observes, is our instrument for living in the world, and when it is broken up we are exposed to other worlds. One of those other worlds is our mind! In his view "mind" is what the ego is unconscious of. After we encounter this other world, therapists encourage us to "lose" our minds again and climb back to the safety—the alienation—of the ego. Laing is claiming that our conscious minds privilege a different reality from that which we discover underneath it. Society was healthier, he implies, when there was access to both worlds.[25]

In a spirit opposite to that of Freud, he observes that the "transcendental experiences that seem to me to be the original well-spring of all religions" are experienced by psychotics and sane people alike. So he did not want them medicalized, since these people are mad, not sick. He needed to be convinced that we should privilege the reality of the rational ego.

Others have tried to show that while schizophrenics may be mystics, mystics are not necessarily schizophrenic. As one report concludes, "The disruption of thought seen in the acute psychoses is not a component of the accounts of acute mystical experience reviewed here."[26] Indeed, Edward Podvall explains how schizophrenics may use mystical experience in attempts to overcome their situation. Some can produce their mental states at will and are depressed by a cure, which they view as "spiritual defeat." "No one wishes to be 'cured' of psychosis," he asserts, though they might want relief from certain symptoms. He does not think that psychotic states are the best way of coping with their problems, but he recognizes their "addiction" to these altered states. Nietzsche was one who expressed this joy in his madness.[27]

Several recent studies have tried to distinguish mysticism from psychosis.[28] But they are like the discussions of religious consciousness within neuroscience that we mentioned. That is, they failed to show that the mystical brain states are religious, in the sense of involving commitment.

Theology as Science

The ostensible science of religion, of course, is theology, which we will reserve for the next chapter. It is not included among the sciences by the nominal English definition of science. But Western theologians have had much to say about how we should understand our sense of the supernatural. This has a bearing on historical discussions of an understanding of religion and "natural science."

From the beginning, Christian theologians took the view that supernatural or paranormal experience cannot automatically be associated with religion. St. Augustine pointed out that whether a "marvel" amounts to a "miracle" is a matter of interpretation and not of evidence—an issue for hermeneutics rather than epistemology. All sorts of events happen that we cannot explain; some seem pointless. If we are convinced that others have a religious significance—are "miracles"—the important response is not belief but faith. That is, simple acknowledgment or belief is not the religious response; rather religion calls for some kind of commitment. So Augustine defined the religious as we are doing, by including a response.

In his widely influential treatment, Augustine taught that neither marvels nor miracles were "against nature, but only against what we know of nature." He viewed nature as "regular" but not absolute. It sometimes missed the mark, as when a child is born with six fingers.[29] What made certain anomalies miracles was not their cause but their significance or moral use. Actually, he liked to think of the world itself as a miracle ("the miracle of miracles") in the sense of being divinely significant. Unfortunately, he recognized, many persons need cheap tricks to remind them of the miracle of being. Wise men did not, nature itself being a "sign" for them. While Augustine pictured miracles as *above* rather than contrary to nature, he insisted that they were not more divine than the natural course of things.[30]

It was in twelfth century Europe that these concepts of *natura*, *mirabilis*, *miraculosus*, and *magicus* began to harden. Magic was usually stigmatized as diabolic. The marvelous, always more at home in polytheism, was increasingly dismissed as superstition and found a cultural home in knightly romances or tales of earthly paradise, sometimes as a form of subtle resistance to the Church.[31] Those churchmen that turned to the study of "nature" did so not to distinguish themselves from the Church but from the people, whom William of Auvergne said "turn too quickly to God's power, calling things miracles, when it is merely the case that they do not know how to go about investigating the cause."[32] Thus our current academic culture began to emerge.

By the thirteenth century, the idea of miracle as an *explanation* rather than a revelation became common, within an increasing interest in explanation. Miracles came to be treated as if they revealed primarily God's power, rather than purposes.[33] So the stage was set for science, more interested in mechanics than in meaning.

Coexistence

These last two chapters have sought to clarify the relation between the various sciences and religion, understood analytically. We need not think of this as showing a difference between religious people and scientific people but between two activities of our minds. We do not deny the obvious possibilities of sociology and psychology to reduce many instances of religious behavior to other levels of analysis. Our task was rather to see whether the concept of religion could escape that effort. We found that scientists admit to differentiating religious from nonreligious instances within their investigations. Even Freud distinguished religious obsessions from other obsessions, thereby acknowledging that he had failed to define "religion" as such.

The question of the "reality" of the religious is ultimately beyond the reach of science. Things are taken as real when they are necessary to one's thinking. Even within science, each level of organization—each science—has its own criteria. Philosophers think things are real *to each other* at particular levels of being, and avoid speaking of what is real per se.[34]

This lends support to the position, most recently promoted by Stephen Jay Gould, that we observe a truce between the non-overlapping disciplines of science and religion. He may not be right that they have "non-overlapping subject matter." But he is right to point out that they do not describe two sides of society but two sides of ourselves.[35] As theologian Reinhold Niebuhr put it, humanity is part of nature and also transcends nature, and religion is born of that experience.[36]

William James observed that mystical experiences "establish a presumption" in their favor for those that have them, but might not do so for others. On the other hand, he thought the "scientific attitude" had an element of superficiality: "So long as we deal with the cosmic and the general, we deal only with the symbols of reality, but *as soon as we deal with private and personal phenomena as such, we deal with realities in the completest sense of the term.*" Religion operated on that more existential or personal level, and will therefore "necessarily play an eternal part in human history."[37] Subsequent studies have shown that mystical encounters tend to be remembered longer and more vividly than ordinary experiences, even though they offer something more like perspective than knowledge.[38]

Wittgenstein, who was familiar with the languages of science and religion, noticed their difference. Religion's oddity is in its "terror"—which we could interpret as the power which elicits a religious response.

> That is partly why you don't get in religious controversies, the form of controversy where one person is *sure* of the thing, and the other says: "Well, possibly." ... One would be reluctant to say: "These people rigorously hold the opinion (or view) that there is a Last Judgement." "Opinion" sounds queer. It is for this reason that different words are used: "dogma," "faith." We don't talk about hypothesis, or about high probability. Nor about knowing. In a religious discourse we use such expressions as: "I believe that so and so will happen," and use them differently to the way in which we use them in science. ... [For scientific] indubitability wouldn't be enough to make me change my whole life.[39]

As Wittgenstein saw, since the power one senses in religious encounter is an absolute power the response is likely to be absolute as well.

Religious believers are often accused, even by theologians, of looking for religion in the gaps of a scientific worldview. Clinging to a god of the gaps is taken as the mark of an exhausted faith. However, even if religion were primarily explanation, science may be so unfinished that the charge would not stick. We cannot know whether science is almost "complete" or *mostly* gaps. Scientists are only puzzled by the question of whether they are nearly finished, whatever that would mean.[40] And even when we have that long awaited Theory of Everything, uniting the basic forces of physics, it will explain very little at the highest levels of our lifeworld.

It should not be surprising that religion tends to find its hints of ultimacy not at the center but at the edges of the world or of consciousness. While science is our way of *defining* things as natural, religious awareness is prompted by glimpses beyond the ordinary. Religion is simply more at home in the "gaps." Tillich thought it was when we are threatened by nonbeing—at the extreme limits of evil, or of knowledge, or physical endurance—that we will be thinking religiously, if we can think at all at such times.[41]

CHAPTER EIGHT

Religion and Theologies at Odds

Theology is the discipline, or even the science, that offers to make sense of religion. While other religious scholars may take a cultural studies approach—interpreting religions within the context of particular cultures—theologians accept the integrity of a religion, to explore its own structure. So it is time that we asked what theologians think they are dealing with when they speak of religion in a general sense. Having seen reasons to think that our word religion is most at home in a Western context, informed mainly by Jewish and Christian traditions, we will focus in the area of the "Abrahamic" faiths. Other spiritual traditions, more at home in other societies and cultures, would naturally have rather different terms and require a different analysis.

If a nominal and analytic definition of "religious" is not vacuous, what issues relative to it appear in the context of theology, which studies religion from within? Paradoxically, we will find that our understanding of the term seems to fit most naturally with the famous *rejection* of the concept of "religion" that was associated with the theologies of Karl Barth and Dietrich Bonhoeffer in the mid-twentieth century. By contrast, our definition's most obvious problems are with the ostensibly neutral fields of natural theology, natural religion and the "religious *a priori.*" Surveying these possibilities will indicate how our common usage of the term religion can challenge even the friendliest of intellectual systems, theology itself.

The most notable recent effort to sort out the different meanings of religion within Western theologies is George Lindbeck's *The Nature of Doctrine: Religion and Theology in a Postliberal Age* (1984). He had noticed, as a member of ecumenical commissions, that ostensibly Christian theologians were not always speaking the same language when they tried to formulate statements of agreement. It made him doubt that religion, or theology, was best understood as doctrines, or as particular experiences either. In line with recent developments in linguistic philosophy, Lindbeck thought that religions might more fruitfully be considered "cultural-linguistic" traditions. Theologies are like Wittgenstein's different "forms of life." Lindbeck even used Wittgenstein's concept of "language-game," as the expression of these different forms of life.

Lindbeck did not mean any playfulness by this phrase but only sought to contrast his linguistic understanding of religion with the more familiar "cognitive" and "experiential-expressive" theories, as he called them. He noted that the liberal theologies which have dominated the last century in the West have viewed religion either as doctrinal systems or as an understanding of human experience of a certain sort. His postliberal approach rests on the linguistic, philosophical, and anthropological evidence for the idea that we cannot even *experience* something unless we are already culturally programmed to interpret it.[1] That evidence persuaded him that some kind of linguistic and mental structure must precede not only the *expression* of an experience but must precede even *noticing* the experience. Lindbeck argued that religious experience is no different in this regard; one must have a religion before one can have a religious experience. (Similarities can be seen with the view we met in the last chapter, when anthropologists embraced a structuralist understanding of primitive religions.)

To Lindbeck, the cultural-linguistic model seemed not just one way of conceiving religion, but the most satisfactory way. Briefly, he presented the rival cognitive theory as the idea that the essence of a religion lies in propositions (doctrines) and their truth claims. By contrast, according to the experiential-expressive view the essence of religion lies in unique experiences, personal feelings, or existential orientations.[2] As he noted, the cognitive understanding has been fading among theologians for some time, leaving the expressive approach dominant. But nontheological students of religion have been moving toward a more linguistic and cultural understanding, and Lindbeck urged theologians to follow suit.

Actually, there may be a flaw in Lindbeck's initial point—that religious experience depends upon already having a religious vocabulary and awareness. A "phenomenological" school (e.g., Rudolf Otto, Gerardus VanderLeeuw, Mircea Eliade) starts from the position that the experience of the "numinous" depends on a prior *non*religious awareness, rather than a religious one. That is, a sense of the "holy" or "sacred" is striking precisely because of the contrast with one's general expectation of ordinariness. The holy is initially recognized as completely alien and uncanny. If this is true, then a "numinous" experience may well precede any religious concepts or expectations. That experience creates the need for a religious language, which must first use metaphors from more ordinary experience. So something like *sounds* may come first—or at least weird noises—and a religious *language* then develops, with words and syntax to guide expression and thought.[3] Doctrines and whole theologies develop with this language.

This is a critical point so we will restate it. Lindbeck makes the familiar argument that there is no such thing as uninterpreted experience. So anything that counts as "an experience" must be more than an immediate intuition. Wayne Proudfoot likewise insists that an "epistemic element" is an essential feature of all religious experience, and this element amounts to an idea of the explanation behind the experience.[4] They do not differentiate between two moments in experience: (1) awareness of something truly anomalous, outside normal experience, which gets one's attention, and (2) the identification of that awareness or experience as religious. Our definition of religion suggests that an essential feature of religion is (1) its uniqueness within experience—in that it baffles any normal or natural interpretation. But somehow that moment seems bonded to (2) a sense of responsibility to forces of another kind, for which we often use the word supernatural. If the relation is more intuitive than logical, then the beginning of religion would seem to be prior to the language—the interpretive system—that Lindbeck has in mind.

The bonding of these distinct elements of Louis Dupré's analysis, considered above (chapter 3), says that religious experience is exceptional in that its "object" seems to provide its own meaning, rather than receiving a meaning from the human subject. This, he thought, was religion's defining characteristic, and we will offer examples later.

If this is so, then it seems that religion can begin with (1) that initial awareness of the anomalous within ordinary reality. We are capable of religious intuitions even in the absence of cultural suggestion. The sense of the anomolous implies the logical and chronological priority of the ordinary, which we might call the secular. It also implies that the ordinary is not *recognized* as such until we have experienced the other reality, of the religious. So we recognize the religious and the secular in one revelatory instant.

Religious and secular discourses may use much the same words, but in different "games." Given the priority of secular experience, religion will tend to rely on metaphorical usages.[5] These are heightened by contrast with everyday usage.[6] To say that religious language is metaphorical need not mean that it is unsatisfactory. We may feel that we recognize this new territory though we have never visited it before, as happens with poetry.

In time, languages develop that are specific to religious experience. This is the work of communities rather than of individuals or philosophers. Wittgenstein used the concept of language-game to emphasize that there is no metalanguage, mediating all discourses. Lindbeck uses it to suggest that there will not be one language of religion, felt as satisfactory by all traditions. As philosopher George Santayana put it, "the attempt to speak without speaking any particular language is not more hopeless than the attempt to have a religion that shall be no religion in particular. . . . Every living and healthy religion has a marked idiosyncracy. Its power consists in its special and surprising message."[7]

As religious languages develop there come to be other ways to produce a sense of the holy than direct intuition. It might be induced by rituals or narratives or religious education. Lindbeck and Proudfoot were obviously thinking of these cultural methods of generating religious or mystical experience when they insisted that explanation is prior to experience. They were not thinking of stumbling into the sacred by accident. But it makes a difference if anybody at all is surprised by a direct experience, for this seems to validate religion for others. Max Weber thought that most people in all ages were religiously tone-deaf, and depended on the few virtuosi who were religiously gifted.[8]

Of course, none of this proves anything about the *object* of this religious sense; theories of "religion" are not theories of God. Theories of religion refer more to the human subject than to a divine object. And having a "basic religious sense" need not be thought of as especially meritorious, or the same as having a proper relation to God, in the view of some particular religion.

Uninterpreted Experiences

The idea of uninterpreted experience is widely denied. And for an experience to count as "knowledge" there must be an interpretation at hand. We might say that we were speaking only of uninterpreted *awareness*. We have argued that spirituality is an awareness, akin to or part of an aesthetic awareness. When it remains without consequence, we might not call it religious. When it points beyond itself, as the aesthetic does not, our culture calls it religious. And it may do this for persons who had no religious preoccupations. It might even take a while for persons to make the connection of this religious consciousness and the cultural meanings of "religion."

One sees this in our first example of such uninterpreted experience. It describes an event which was not seen as religious until much later, and which had no antecedent in religious "suggestion."

I remember that it was a cool, clean, fresh, calm, blue, radiant day, and I stood by the shore, my feet not in the waves. And now—as then—I find it difficult to explain what did happen. I expect that the easiest thing is to say that suddenly SOMETHING WAS. My whole soul was cleft clean by it, as a silk veil slit by a shining sword. And I *knew*. I do not know now what I knew. I remember, I didn't know even then. That is, I didn't know with any "faculty." It was not in my mind or heart or blood stream. But whatever it was I knew, it was something that made ENORMOUS SENSE. And it was final. And yet that word could not be used, for it meant *end*, and there was no end to *this* finality. Then joy abounded in all of me. Or rather, I abounded in joy. I seemed to have no nature, and yet my whole nature was adrift in this immense joy, as a speck of dust is seen to dance in a great golden shaft of sunlight.

I don't know how long this experience lasted. It was, I should think closer to a second than to an hour—though it might have been either. The memory of it possessed me for several months afterward. At first I marveled at it. Then I reveled in it. Then it began to obsess me and I tried to put it in some category of previous experience. . . . Gradually I forgot it. The memory of it never returned to me until one day several years after my conversion, during the first minute of the liturgy of the Mass, where the server says: "Ad Deum qui laetificat juventutem meum . . . (Unto God who giveth joy to my youth)."[9]

Thus she could finally see the experience in the ecclesiastical and moral context to which it had contributed.

Examples like this reveal not the effects of religious education but something so unexpected that language falters. William James, in his classic survey of religious experience, recounts several such experiences and is in no hurry to explain them. He approved Jonathan Edwards' caution about theologizing these religious experiences, and he quotes him as opposing rigid expectations concerning religious conversions:

A rule received and established by common consent has a very great, though to many persons an insensible influence in forming their notions of the process of their own experience. I know very well how they proceed as to this matter, for I have had frequent opportunities of observing their conduct. Very often their experience at first appears like a confused chaos, but then those parts are selected which bear the nearest resemblance to such particular steps as are insisted on, and those are dwelt upon in their thoughts, and spoken of from time to time, till they grow more and more conspicuous in their view, and other parts which are neglected grow more and more obscure. Thus what they experienced is insensibly strained, so as to bring it to an exact conformity to the scheme already established in their minds. And it becomes natural also for ministers, who have to deal with those who insist upon distinctness and clearness of method, to do so too.[10]

This, then, is a description of how a cultural-linguistic religion incorporates religious experience, rather than how it prompts it.

So Edwards was not surprised by the fact that most later accounts of religious awakening or conversion mention the person's prior introduction to religious concepts, by way of background. Whether that is due to the meaning the subject later found for the experience, or was foremost in their mind at the time, is usually not clear. In our own time, as religion becomes less salient in culture, religious experiences may increasingly be puzzling at first, coming unsought and without cultural preparation.

There are recent examples of those who made no connection between their experience and a religious vocabulary they had long rejected. The religious experience actually had to work against an inherited religious vocabulary.

I was going up Headington Hill on the top of a bus. Without words and (I think) almost without images, a fact about myself was somehow presented to me. I became aware that I was holding something at bay, or shutting something out. Or, if you like, that I was wearing some stiff clothing, like corsets, or even a suit of armour, as if I were a lobster. I felt myself being, there and then, given a free choice. I could open the door or keep it shut; I could unbuckle the armour or keep it on. Neither choice was presented as a duty; no threat or promise was attached to either, though I knew that to open the door or to take off the corslet meant the incalculable. The choice appeared to be momentous but it was also strangely unemotional. I was moved by no desires or fears.

In the following days professor and author C. S. Lewis began to see his adversary in this struggle as God, someone to whom he had long given little thought:

> People who are naturally religious find difficulty in understanding the horror of such a revelation. Amiable agnostics will talk cheerfully about "man's search for God." To me, as I then was, they might as well have talked about the mouse's search for the cat. . . . You must picture me alone in that room in Magdalen [College], night after night, feeling, whenever my mind lifted even for a second from my work, the steady, unrelenting approach to Him whom I so earnestly desired not to meet. That which I greatly feared had at last come upon me. In the Trinity Term of 1929 I gave in, and admitted that God was God, and knelt and prayed: perhaps, that night, the most dejected and reluctant convert in all England. . . . It must be understood that the conversion . . . was only to Theism, pure and simple, not to Christianity. I knew nothing yet about the Incarnation. The God to whom I surrendered was sheerly non-human.[11]

Clearly, the experience suggested the kind of moral or existential response that made it more than simply a new perspective on reality.

Author Joy Davidman was similarly unprepared to meet God, having been raised in a secular Jewish household and having found her spiritual home in the Communist Party. There was a crisis when her first husband, a fellow writer and Communist, abandoned her during his own nervous breakdown. (Though Davidman later married C. S. Lewis, the following account was published a year before she met Lewis and several years before he published the account given above.)

> For the first time in my life I felt helpless; for the first time my pride was forced to admit that I was not, after all, "the master of my fate" and "the captain of my soul." . . . How can one describe the direct perception of God? It is infinite, unique; there are no

words, there are no comparisons. Can one scoop up the sea in a teacup? Those who have known God will understand me; the others, I find, can neither listen nor understand. There was a Person with me in the room, directly present to my consciousness—a Person so real that all my previous life was by comparison mere shadow play. And I myself was more alive than I had ever been; it was like waking from sleep. So intense a life cannot be endured for long by flesh and blood; we must ordinarily take our life watered down, diluted as it were, by time and space and matter. My perception of God lasted perhaps half a minute.

In that time, however, many things happened. I forgave some of my enemies. I understood that God had always been there, and that, since childhood, I had been pouring half my energy into the task of keeping him out. I saw myself as I really was, with dismay and repentance; and, seeing, I changed. I have been turning into a different person since that half minute, everyone tells me.

When it was over I found myself on my knees, praying. I think I must have been the world's most astonished atheist. . . . My awareness of God was no comforting illusion, conjured up to reassure me about my husband's safety. I was just as worried afterward as before. No; it was terror and ecstacy, repentance and rebirth.[12]

Joy Davidman's husband at the time, William Gresham, confirmed her story, quoted above.

Joy had been raised by dogmatically atheist parents, and was more inflexible in her materialism than I—until in a moment of panic, out of fear for me, she let her defenses drop and became suddenly aware of the presence of God. This was the turning point in both our lives. She was completely astonished, but she had to believe it; she had no choice. The sudden awareness gave her no comfort in her anxiety about me—it simply threw her life into a new perspective; it made her see that her attitudes had been wrong, running against the current, all her life. I knew something of mystical experience, through accounts I had read, and I received the news with a great surge of hope. Together, accepting God, we started tentatively, and at first unwillingly, to remake our spiritual lives.[13]

We find it natural to search such stories for suggestions of a psychological interpretation. Some of those who have had the experiences can remember having used the same explanations themselves, before their own encounters overcame such resistance. So we have a standoff on this point.

Some people find an inherited religious vocabulary to stand in the way of their initial experiences of religious awakening. Journalist Hugh Redwood's life-changing experience of "Reality" came during a religious service, but seemingly without reference to it. He had been sent to cover a talk by a Salvation Army speaker:

> It seemed to him [to Redwood himself] that something was being said to him, not so much through the words of the preacher, but between the lines of what she was saying. When he went out into the damp Bristol streets there was a raw wind blowing, but he felt no chill. He felt instead a glow of excitement, a sense of adventure. He walked in the grip of wonder. And this was because he knew that at last he had met Reality. He gave it no other name as yet, it was not yet entirely his, but here was something brought within his ken as truth and substance which never before had been very much more than theory. . . . He pictured himself as some minor body in space which has suddenly felt the pull of an unseen world. . . . Except that it was something phenomenal, he had no words to describe it.[14]

Playing along with the current religious "language-game" is not a necessary accompaniment of the experience.

One can even find clergy who are not entirely prepared for such religious experiences, and may find them an embarrassment. William James quoted one such:

> I remember the night, and almost the very spot on the hilltop, where my soul opened out, as it were, into the Infinite, and there was a rushing together of the two worlds, the inner and the outer. . . . It is impossible fully to describe the experience. . . . I could not any more have doubted that He was there than that I was. Indeed, I felt myself to be, if possible, the less real of the two. . . . There was, as I recall it, no sudden change of thought or of belief,

except that my early crude conception had, as it were, burst into flower. . . . I am aware that it may justly be called mystical. I am not enough acquainted with philosophy to defend it from that or any other charge. I feel that in writing of it I have overlaid it with words rather than put it clearly to your thought.[15]

His theological vocabulary continued to fail him when he tried to describe his discovery of the religious.

One might well object that few of those who count themselves religious are original mystics, or have had this numinous experience in its immediate, original force. Many religious people hear about the experiences of others and only then recognize something like it in their own lives. But our examples reverse the order Lindbeck sets out, putting religious experience before religious language in the experience of some. Indeed, something of the sort seems necessary in order to account for the historical origins of religions. Lindbeck could insist that numinous experience was not really religious until one had words to conceptualize it *as* religious. But that argument stumbles over the fact that he has not yet defined religion.

To try to say what was going on in these minds, we note that they are reversing the order of thought that Descartes described. His assumption was of himself as primary reality, of his mind as the touchstone of truth. This is reversed in those like Rudolf Otto, whose sense was of his own reality in the face of a greater.[16] So many of the props for Descartes' modern view have been removed, in the discovery of the unconscious, subatomic indeterminacy, a sociology of knowledge, the counterintuitive aspects of relativity, and the contingent nature of the universe. Perhaps our culture is thus prepared for something of a revival of the uninterpreted religious response.

Sociologist Peter Berger mentions recent writers who have described moments when ordinary reality—"the world taken for granted"—gives way and "something terrifyingly *other* shines through." The Austrian author Robert Musil, and perhaps Marcel Proust, are noted for this. In cases of violence, disorientation, sexual frenzy, mathematical or musical ecstacy, and other cases seemingly absurd or trivial, our assumed security is shown to be artificial and fragile. We sense a reality behind the facade of our lifeworld. "Even if the other condition remains a rare experience in the life of an individual, the memory will remain and ensure that normal living will never again be completely spontaneous."[17]

A Theologian Tries a Definition

Lindbeck is hesitant to offer his own definition of religion. He speaks rather of the "identifying mark of religion," the "class name" for the cultural system he is describing, as against competing "notions of what religion is." Whatever the source of his reluctance, he finally comes out with it: religions are "idioms for dealing with whatever is most important—with ultimate questions of life and death, right and wrong, chaos and order, meaning and meaninglessness."[18] It is a definition.

It may be a functional definition, depending on how "most important" is understood. Important to some other end? "Ultimate" questions in the plural? Like all functional definitions, it is incomplete (see chapter 2). When Paul Tillich announced his similar definition (religion is ultimate concern) he soon wanted to criticize those who put things in the position of ultimacy which were not (or should not be) truly ultimate. They were therefore idolatrous—worshiping business success or their nation, for example.[19] At this point one must either decide that idolatry is a religion, or specify the proper *object* of this concern—in a normative definition. Tillich was a theologian, and eventually specified that ultimate concern should be for ultimate-Being-itself. As Michael Eldridge notes, for Tillich "the one term, 'ultimate,' characterizes [both] the concern of the religious person and the object of that concern."[20] Indeed, Tillich expressed the mystical view that ultimate concern is the concern of the Ultimate for the ultimate. Therefore our "knowledge of God is the knowledge God has of himself."[21] The point here is that functional definitions are only preliminary to more "substantive" ones, which Lindbeck does not provide.

Lindbeck's definition includes religion among society's cultural idioms. He must still distinguish the religious ones from the nonreligious ones and "most important" may be too slippery. Whatever he chooses for the substance of the definition will probably be in the area of doctrine or experience—which he had earlier tried to ignore.[22] Were Lindbeck to choose between them, it appears that he would put the substance of religion in the area of doctrines and truth claims, where theology operates. He often refers to "truth," but almost never to what I take to be the more basic analytical aspect of religion, which is power. A discussion of religion which does not mention power will seem empty to those who think of religion more as a thing of the "spirit" than of the mind.

As Lindbeck notes, there are persons and communities that have only a latent religion, having learnt the language or form but not having the spirit of the thing within them.[23] Where our culture recognizes differences in religious authenticity, those who only learn the *language* of religion would be considered potentially religious. Only after responding to a *message* in the language would we speak of them as religious. So the cultural-linguistic or "language-game" theory of religion implies a more complex model of which it is only a part. To take account of origins one must include experience. To offer the substance of religious discourse, we get into the cognitive area. For it is not just ultimate "questions" that religion deals with, but ultimate experiences and ultimate commitments. These were, indeed, the terms of our definition.

All of this is beside Lindbeck's most important point, however, which is that particular religions must be granted their intratextual integrity. Confessional theologies will not acknowledge that there is a larger philosophy of religion, a metareligion, which makes sense of them. Truth claims are at the level of particular theologies and not in some higher-order discourse. As philosopher D. Z. Phillips points out, we know that these religious discourses have some sort of coherence because people speaking these languages understand each other, make jokes in them, and recognize nonsense in the statements they hear.[24] Those from very different national cultures may find a bond with coreligionists in other cultures through a shared religious idiom. On the other hand, even the Christian elites that Lindbeck saw talking past each other seemed to have trouble with their different dialects.

Philosophies of Religion

The other intellectual disciplines that deal with religion may not acknowledge that religious language-games have this autonomy. Those who want to deal in philosophical theology, natural religion or natural theology, may be promoting a master-game. They are often refining terms that transcend cultural difference and will therefore want a referential definition of religion.

Philosophical theology involves analyzing concepts, like God or creation, which are advanced products of religious thought. The terms cease to be metaphorical and become elements within a philosophical structure, anchoring ideas more than demanding a response. We need not question the results of this philosophical enterprise in order to point out that it is not meant as a religious activity. That is, the philosophers are not using the religious terms within a religious discourse or religious life. Beyond that, it may be self-defeating, in accepting an alien foundationalism, the "reason" which is part of a different discourse.[25]

The situation with "natural religion" is somewhat different. It seeks to derive religion from the sphere of the "natural" as we have defined it—the regular and the expected. It searches for a natural human religiousness—a reverence for life, perhaps. In common usage, however, religion is our word for that which brackets or qualifies those regularities, making natural religion close to a con-tradiction. A product of Enlightenment Deism, natural religion has difficulty avoiding a philosophical naturalism.[26]

"Natural theology" is the opposite, showing the place of nature within theology. That is, natural theology seeks to show how religious doctrines encompass universally acknowledged experience.[27] Its goal is to encourage agreement, not generate faith. Its actual effect will confirm the faith of those who already believe on other grounds. For it offers reasons for not rejecting what one knows intuitively. This may have ironic consequences, such as the fact that nineteenth-century natural theology helped popularize the very science it was wrestling with.[28] Natural theology was meant to provide a bridge for philosophers to cross, but of course bridges work in both directions.

Theologies, like other sciences, may seek to compel acceptance rather than to awaken faith. Our definition of religion would lead us to side with David Hume in thinking that general standards of proof work against *arguments* derived from religious experience. But that is only a statement about proof. Faith is for more important matters.

Personalism and Religion

There are philosophical perspectives such as personalism that preserve more of the element of anomalous experience that we associate with religion than these philosophies of religion do. Never a major tradition in philosophy, personalism takes personal being as the model of all being, all reality. Those things in the universe were considered most real that could act—that is, personal agents. The value terms associated with personality represent fundamental realities, as real as anything in the universe. They are the place to start some investigations, and are not epiphenomenal, as they are often treated.

As we mentioned in chapter 6, personalist philosophies ask: What does the fact that humans are part of nature say about *nature*? Science asks the opposite question: What does the fact that we are part of nature say about *us*? We expect an answer to the latter question to reduce us to physicalist terms. But against those who assume that being means matter, personalists think being means value. So "person" is a basic, fundamental philosophical category.

Personalism finds resonance in theological terminology. For example, in the words of Erazim Kohák, "being is value born of the intersection of time and eternity," and "a person is a being through whom eternity enters time."[29] Eternity is the word Kohák uses for transcendent value. Because humans are "witnesses of creation" they are eternal, in the sense of escaping time. We can see reality as creation rather than accident, and accordingly recognize categories of personal being like beauty, truth, goodness, justice, love, and holiness.[30]

Kohák borrows from phenomenologist Edmund Husserl, speaking of a "radical bracketing" of experience, like one feels in a forest clearing. Thus one can sense a "presence" in a surrounding nature, such as we met in our earlier examples of spiritual awareness. Darkness, solitude, moral judgment, pain, and death are also good at helping us see beyond the blinders of objective reality. Kohák does not mean that these epiphanies show us a psyche within "nature" or personal traits in everything. It is more like viewing things with respect, sensing a moral relationship even with the inanimate. It may go beyond the aestheticism of Kant's "sublime," which locates the numinous within nature.[31]

This may be as close as philosophy comes to what we have been calling the religious awareness and response. Religion, we have been saying, asks us to bracket our accustomed reality. Kohák's notion of "respect" approaches what we have called the religious response, as some Asian spiritualities do. He notes that some "anthropologists use the evidence of worship as the distinguishing mark of a human rather than simply higher primate presence."[32]

Modernity included the effort to depersonalize things, not excluding ourselves. The positivistic project of eliminating the first-person perspective, to find the objective "view from nowhere in particular," has come close to dominance in Western secular cultures.[33] In relation to human personality it is counterintuitive, and personalists may not propose arguments against it. Rather, they can adopt a "second naïvete." As Kohák observes, "arguments are reasons for *not disbelieving* what we believe because we have seen"—his way of saying that knowledge rests on faith.[34]

Taking personal being as basic to any universe that includes humans, taking life as a gift, acknowledging a moral relationship to creation, may qualify as religious in ordinary English. The structure of our definition directs our attention to more than we are used to seeing and recognizes a personal relation to our reality. So personalism might be considered a form of natural religion. Whether it should be called a philosophy would be depend on another nominal definition.

Jewish and Christian theologians have adopted and even pioneered personalist insights. One thinks of Martin Buber, Franz Rosenzweig, John Macmurray, John Zizioulas, and various Christian existentialists.[35] Others like Martin Heidegger have become nonreligious in the process.

A Religious a Priori

Closer to traditional philosophy is the effort to find a religious a priori, like the cognitive principles of Kant's philosophy. Some proponents of religion have held that finding religion among the a priori elements in human thinking would demonstrate its reality and universality. It became a project of theologian Anders Nygren to show that religion was thus "valid," by being more than subjective. His claim was that religion was not discovered *by* experience but was seen to be necessary *to* all experience. He did this by arguing that claims to absolute validity, which are common within philosophy, science, and ethics, are religious by definition, being related to the eternal. One might refuse to acknowledge this religious element, but only by a flaw in thinking like the refusal to acknowledge Kant's categorical imperative. Nygren allowed that the content of this category is for scholars of comparative religion to fill in, using theological categories.[36]

At about the same time, Rudolf Otto was announcing his a priori category of the numinous, which he described as less cognitive than emotional.[37] Tillich agreed that Otto's analysis was phenomenological rather than psychological. For Otto's sense of the holy was not simply an aspect of human thought, but of the ground of our being.[38] In short, Otto considered religion a fundamental aspect of human consciousness, something deeper than cognition.

Otto came to this position not, like Nygren, from philosophy but from history and the study of religions. He was inspired by the mystical tradition to investigate the *sensus numinis*. Beyond the often absurd superstitions of religions he detected an ineradicable sense of mystery and awe. He considered this—"the holy"—to be the defining characteristic of religion. In the West it had been theologized and moralized into little more than "the good." So Otto tried to recapture an original sense of the *mysterium tremendum et fascinans*. Both daunting and fascinating, there is an essential tension between repulsion and attraction, between dread and love[39]—or, in our terms, between power and response.

Claiming this as an a priori element meant that Otto saw it not as offering ideas so much as a "receptivity and a principle of judgement and acknowledgment" of a unique category of experience. As an a priori element it does not evolve from experience but receives experience. The holy or numinous or religious is experience that everyone is capable of having. But it is not an innate cognition, such as is claimed for natural religion, which Otto said "does not exist."[40]

Otto did not want it thought that he was only describing the mind of savages. He claimed the numinous is best studied in "souls of the highest individual development, and of uniquely gifted people."[41] Many things "call forth the feeling of the numinous" most immediately, such as second sight, clairvoyance, foreboding, healing powers, visions, ecstacy, alienation, and thought transference. But this nonrational core of religion attracts rational elements also, related to purpose, personality, morality, necessity, and the like.

In this way, Otto thought the numinous feeling or state of mind can rightly be thought of as a source of theological knowledge.[42] Otto supposed that religious symbolization began in ritual and liturgy rather than in concepts, but he assumed that as primitive dread became worship and then doctrine it became truer as it grew further from its source.[43] Thus he went against the common tendency to think of pristine religion as its primitive forms. The question remains whether any religious a priori subverts a transcendent understanding, by making religion something of a natural endowment.

Sociologist Peter Berger has attested to Otto's importance after a century of arguing over his insights, calling his "the most useful definition of the phenomenon that lies at the core of religious experience."[44] And he points to the two-stage recognition process we mentioned earlier in this chapter. Religion involves not only the numinous experience, but it also requires a religious identification of this radical "otherness." Berger notes that this can be a problem to believers on "the morning after." "Faith at this point means *faith in my own experience*. The second level is attained by deciding that the transcendent reality I have perceived is not only *there* but is there *for me*."[45] Responding to this reality in faith completes our definition of religion.

Philosopher Paul Ricoeur found an analogy to the experience of the wholly other and one's response to it in the experience of speech.

Nietzsche and Freud, he points out, could account for religious fear but not for religious joy, thinking that there must be a concealed contradiction involved. Borrowing from Heidegger, Ricoeur views faith as a response to a message, more like "hearkening" than like philosophical consideration. Words do not impose something on us so much as they call forth a response from our own desire. The "word" of numinous experience, though daunting, evokes a sense of personal significance felt unexpectedly within ordinary reality.[46] The structure of our definition seems almost a commonplace in Jacques Derrida's remark that "in the authentic sense of the word, religion comes into being the moment that the experience of responsibility extracts itself from that form of secrecy called demonic mystery."[47]

Completing Our Survey

The nominal definition of religion we have offered here envisions a validating experience of the transcendent, whether it was the cause or perhaps the result of an individual's concept of religion. So we should note the variety of experiences that have been considered in this respect. Caroline Franks Davis' taxonomy of six types of religious experience is becoming a standard view.[48] She reports conventional views, beginning with (1) interpretive experiences, which have no unusual features except that we associate them with religious beliefs, as when unwelcome events are assumed to be divine judgments. Next are (2) "quasi-sensory" experiences, which find anomalies within normal perceptions. They are interpreted as religious either because they involve familiar religious symbols or because they are so unusual as to seem miraculous. Paranormal experiences fit here, and are seen as religious or not, depending on the subject.

A third category are (3) revelations, by which Franks Davis means expanded insights or perspectives. They may not deliver a message so much as enlarge the mind. They do not appear to be part of a reasoning process but come unbidden. We are most likely to consider them religious if they are induced by religious exercises or reading, when familiar words or concepts take on a new reality. (4) Regenerative experiences have less to do with knowledge than with feelings, confirming one in joy, strength, peace, or hope. They are religious when associated with religious activities or teachings. Franks Davis also describes Otto's (5) numinous experience, and ends with (6) mystical experience, which is notable for a sense of freedom from limits of time, space, and ego. Mystical states involve apprehensions of ultimate reality and union with it.

Only the first of Davis' types suggests an important role for cultural-linguistic preparation in identifying the experience. One can imagine some hesitation in regard to the others, as subjects begin to recognize them as religious. Peter Berger adds to this list by showing how several apparently ordinary experiences could well serve as "signals of transcendence." The sense of basic order in experience (important to the birth of science), the "redemptive" experiences of play and of humor, the pull of hope, and the conviction of evil as damnable, may not strike us as religious because they are so familiar. But Berger argues that they make most sense in a religious or theological framework.[49] They would simply be puzzles within a naturalistic evolutionary psychology.

Schleiermacher and Barth: Religion or Theology?

Finally, we can ask how a Christian theology, that which is most closely related to the meaning of "religion" for English speakers, could be derived from these ineffable experiences. For this has been a matter of some controversy.

Friedrich Schleiermacher's *On Religion: Speeches to its Cultured Despisers* (1799) is famous for having raised the question of the place of experience in theology, and for rejecting an overintellectualized religion. He reacted against the Enlightenment's treatment of religion as dogma or explanation, and argued that true religion began in feelings or awareness. He rejected the view that theology was a deduction from an objective nature, as the Deists' natural religion had supposed, asserting instead that theology was an understanding of humans' basic feeling of dependence.

Schleiermacher's relation to theology was ambiguous. He thought that a feeling of absolute dependence implied the things at the heart of Christian religion, like humility, faith, hope, and charity. But he was not surprised to find that such essential features of religion were absent from the theology of his day. It showed him that religion should not end in dogmatic theology but go beyond it. Its goal is not explanations or truths, but motivation. Theology, for him, was useful in confirming religious intuitions.[50]

In Tillich's view, Schleiermacher's "feeling of absolute dependence" avoided naturalistic reduction.

> [It] referred not to a psychological function but to the awareness of that which transcends intellect and will . . . a dependence which has a moral character, which includes freedom and excludes a pantheistic and deterministic interpretation of the experience of the unconditional. . . . It was a misunderstanding of Schleiermacher's definition of religion and a symptom of religious weakness when successors of Schleiermacher located religion in the realm of feeling as one psychological function among others.[51]

Thus, Schleiermacher avoided the notions of natural religion current in his day, as well as the naturalism of our own.[52]

But did his religion end the same way it began, without a theology? Herbert Richardson observes that Schleiermacher's "feeling" did not refer to a particular thing, nor was it simply an experience. Rather, it was a gestalt revealing a situation in its totality. Such a whole is not defined by its parts and is therefore not perceived by our senses. It is perceived cognitively, in entire revelation.[53] Does this end in mysticism or suggest that one still has theological work to do?

Schleiermacher's project had a powerful influence on theology over the following century, but Karl Barth thought it was wholly inimical. Barth's very influential reaction took the form of a strenuous rejection of the very idea of "religion." Because of the power of Barth's ideas in the mid-twentieth century, his was recognized not simply as a sectarian theological response, but as a major philosophical event.

Schleiermacher's attempt "to show you from what capacity of humanity religion proceeds" may have inspired Otto's search for the religious a priori. But Barth, at exactly the same time, objected to such a diversion of Christian theology. He and Dietrich Bonhoeffer made an issue of rejecting anything that suggested a natural religious capacity or a natural theology. Their opposition extended to a theological rejection of the concept of religion itself, if it must be grounded in feeling.

Ironically, Barth's theological treatment of faith is one of the best formulations of our definition of religion. This is not to argue that it is the best theology, or the best Christian theology, on offer. It only indicates still another confirmation of our approach by one of the seminal minds of recent times. For Barth was not rejecting religion so much as the cultural understanding of it current in his day.

Barth thought that the theological liberalism dominant in his time was based on the idea of religion as a universal human trait, a trait that generated various forms such as Christianity. Barth, by contrast, took seriously Otto's notion of a "wholly other" to which religion witnessed. He was afraid that theologians had gotten into the habit of thinking of religion as human efforts to understand God. Understanding and considering were a long way from awe and terror. To consider theology might be a way of keeping one's distance from God, which was behind Barth's famous charge that "religion is unbelief."[54]

Barth and Bonhoeffer thought that liberalism actually proved the truth of philosopher Ludwig Feuerbach's atheistic view that religion was humanity's projection of its own image onto the heavens.[55] But that was religion; faith was the opposite. True faith came through revelation of something utterly different, as unlooked for and unsettling as Otto's *mysterium tremendum*. Such an experience does not confirm us, but reveals our estrangement and inadequacy. As Feuerbach said, the religion that resulted from human perspectives was an idolizing of humanity, tainted by self-congratulation. Barth agreed. With Luther, he held that "religion" was the attempt to establish one's own righteousness in defiance of a divine judgment already declared. So the rejection of religion was a necessary step toward recovering a transcendent faith.[56]

This resonated in the West after World War I, when liberal concepts of human nature were under attack. This was also a time when scholars had begun to reject the notion of penetrating texts to find what was behind them. Barth can be seen as the first narrative theologian, who sought guidance not in experience (Schleiermacher) or reason (Kant) but in Christian revelation, in the light of faith.[57]

Christian faith, for Barth, was philosophically radical. He saw it not as finding meaning but as confronting meaninglessness. With contemporary existentialists, he held that a condition of meaninglessness was the ground of a truly human life, as opposed to a comforting but alienating culture. As Karen Carr interpreted Barth, "The confrontation with nihilism has the power to transform individuals because it throws into question the world in which they are unreflectively immersed." (Echoes of our definition are striking.) So humanity can be seen as both the need for certainty and its absence. Alienation or estrangement might be necessary to religious awakening.

For Barth, accepting "a religion" is a betrayal of faith. It means the acceptance of a culture that alienates one from the human condition. The difference between human and divine is absolute, not bridged by religious culture. Faith is therefore neither a natural endowment nor embodied in cultural truths, but is more like hope, tension, or paradox. Just as our definition seems to do, this avoids understanding religion as theodicy, presuming on providence, or guaranteeing health, salvation, or superiority. Rather, true faith was self-emptying and self-giving. God is revealed only when we despair of our natural knowledge and effort.

Barth wrote many weighty volumes, but he said they were to keep questions open more than to give answers. He agreed with Nietzsche that Christianity had self-destructed as a philosophy. That is, it had set a standard of truth that its metaphysics could not meet. But turning the tables on Nietzsche, Carr maintains that Barth thought nihilism was actually the triumph of the purest Christian faith and morals, and not a mark of its decline.[58]

Barth fought off his friend Emil Brunner's writings on natural theology. He objected that Christian revelation did not emerge from some "capacity for revelation" or "receptivity for [certain] words." Insofar as there is a natural theology, he says, even its elements depend on the revelation in Scripture.[59] In this Barth may have gone too far. James Barr points out that the Scripture that Barth insists on taking whole and undiluted itself uses concepts of natural religion to explain itself.[60]

Dietrich Bonhoeffer joined in the effort to free divine revelation from "religion." He understood the latter as the appropriation of God for the service of humanity. And he puzzled readers by references to "religionless Christianity."[61] Executed by Hitler, Bonhoeffer did not have the leisure to develop these ideas at length. But he seems to have meant that he wanted Christianity to be understood as righteousness in the midst of a secular world rather than as individual salvation from that world. God was not an answer to our questions, or a guarantor of privilege. Rather, faith was participation in God's suffering in the world. Bonhoeffer professed to welcome the disappearance of Europe's religious culture. If it left a void, that is what faith feels like. He was not distressed that silence and responsible action were replacing religious chatter and pietism.[62]

Barth heralded the disappearance of Christendom in something of the same spirit as Nietzsche did. He did not want to pass through nihilism to faith, but to take nihilism as part of Christian faith. This was not a human possibility, he said, but a gift found wrapped in the narrative of biblical revelation. Barth worried that he was creating a theology, and his many volumes of *Church Dogmatics* might be taken for such. But by responding to answers with questions he tried to challenge readers rather than confirm them. For, in his understanding, faith is not a thing to think about but a way of thinking, or living.[63]

Barth and Bonhoeffer's treatment of revelation and faith has much in common with the definition of religion presented here. They do not think of religious "revelation" as providing information of the usual sort, but see it as a call to repentance in the sphere of the intellect.[64] Our definition of religion makes it our word for the appropriate response to that which is beyond everything. For Barth, faith is hearing a word which places one under judgment. It is ironic that the theological approach which seems most congenial to our bare definition would be something like Barth's.[65]

None of this is meant to show that our analysis confirms a dialectical theology. Rather, it may be taken as one theological confirmation of our analysis of common terms.

A coda will bring us up to date. Postmodernism answered Barth's theology by denying that nihilism is a challenge. Whereas Nietzsche thought nihilism was a stage to get through, and Barth thought it was an invitation to faith, philosopher Richard Rorty thinks it might simply be accepted. Such a "banalization" of nihilism (Karen Carr's phrase) would justify the liberal status quo, or any other for that matter, having no truth with which to challenge it. While Barth rejected knowledge for truth, Rorty rejects truth for knowledge. The latter understands power to have replaced argument.[66] Rorty's a-theology would truly represent the absence of religion, for it is human rather than transcendent power that is seen as ultimate.

While Barth looked to the Church as the community of truth, Rorty likewise looks to community as final arbiter: "Truth is nothing more than a particular community's understanding of what is good in the way of belief."[67] Still, the irreducible term "religion" presents a challenge to the view that rationality is the defining characteristic of the human. Descartes and Kant thought that humanity fulfilled its nature by being the guarantor of knowledge. But we may be more remarkable simply for being conscious of our situation. As we have said, following Wittgenstein, the mystical arises not from knowing what the universe is, but in knowing *that* it is. Our distinctiveness is in hearkening to something we can identify as a word, perhaps from beyond.

If religion does not draw us beyond all we know, it is not what we mean by religion. And there is no likelihood of our outgrowing such an awareness. For as Milton Munitz points out,

> the ineliminable presence of conceptual bounds in the use of any cosmological model, however successful a particular model may be, provokes attempts to overcome the horizons of understanding enforced by those conceptual bounds. At any state of inquiry, the known universe points beyond itself.[68]

Addendum
Artistic Expression of Religion

Artists as well as theologians help to elaborate our religious experience. This can either take the form of developing religious traditions or of very personal expressions. When Robert Wuthnow tried to study "creative spirituality" he found that those who refused to think of themselves as "religious" got little help from the artistic traditions developed among religions. But it is hard to make a highly personal vision resonate among the public. If "spirituality" is determined to be original and authentic, it may be foregoing any cultural impact.

The ineffability of religious awareness is a notable challenge for artists. Michael Polanyi spoke of music being an instance of "important discourse about nothing."[69] He did not mean nothing exactly, but nothing that we can argue about. There is an example of the ineffable, perhaps, in William Faulkner's *The Sound and the Fury*, which recounts a sermon and its effect on a black congregation. The preacher made no real sense, but

> the voice consumed him, until he was nothing and they were nothing and there was not even a voice but instead their hearts were speaking to one another in chanting measures beyond the need for words, so that when he came to rest against the reading desk, his monkey face lifted and his whole attitude that of a serene, tortured crucifix that transcended its shabbiness and insignificance and made it of no moment, a long moaning expulsion of breath rose from them, and a woman's single soprano: "Yes, Jesus!"

Afterwards, a deeply moved member of the congregation explained "He seed de power and de glory. . . . I seed de beginnin, en now I sees de endin."[70]

Artists like Wordsworth are reluctant to see transcendent glory "fade into the light of common day," or as we might say, to see it put into ordinary language. The 1985 movie *Agnes of God* was a test of its audience along these lines. It portrayed a nun who gave birth in her convent, though apparently entirely innocent of sex. Whether she was a classic case of multiple personality is not important, nor is our current fascination with issues of child abuse, lust, or hypocrisy. Rather, the focus remains on the uncanny radiance of Agnes' character, which opens into a place where the worldly characters hesitate. The movie leaves one suspended over possibilities. Our tendency toward moral judgment seems to be standing in the way of something possibly more interesting.

Even God's absence can be a religious theme in art, rather than—as one would assume—a secular theme. Critics complain that divine intervention within literature is too clumsy to be effective. Divine silence can be treated as secularization. But it might be a frustrated author's struggle with her response. Faith may be expressed in creedal statements, to be sure, but it might also be the assurance that there is more in our situation than others see. If knowledge is what no one can deny, faith engages with what one can always doubt, like love, purpose, or redemption. It is intriguing in a way that knowledge is not.

It is tempting to give up on religion when one's childish expectations were disappointed, or when the words first used of God are no longer convincing. Others react differently, searching for terms to hint at the inexpressible or finding new meaning for old words. And if we ever make contact with beings on other planets, we can expect that they will also have had glimpses beyond the boundaries in the way we associate with religion.[71] Otherwise we will hesitate to say we have met with intelligent life.

CHAPTER NINE

What We Mean by Secular

Having a sense of what religion means in a number of connections, it might now seem easy to define secular by way of contrast. But secular and its derivatives have given scholars and policy-makers no end of trouble recently. Not a few have declared that "secularization" is meaningless, ambiguous, incoherent, or self-contradictory. Actually, the problem is that there are different rules with regard to its use, depending on different aspects of the subject. It is true that one cannot use "secular" simply as referring to the opposite of religious. Nor can secularization refer simply to a general decline of religion. But that does not mean that the term cannot be used consistently, when the different aspects of the subject are kept in mind. In fact, all the various meanings of the term are recognized in common, though not always in academic, usage. Scholars confuse the issue with arbitrary definitions.

First, we may suggest where some of the confusion entered. For forty years, scholars have recognized that secularization is not a unitary process.[1] But those who tried to sort out the differences have thought of them *either* in terms of different processes—like decline, differentiation, disengagement, or rationalization[2]—or in terms of different forms of analysis—like structural, cultural, organizational, or individual.[3] So it has not been clear that the different processes are specific to the different analyses. That is, these are not *alternative* processes toward the secular or alternative ways of looking at the change. So we must try to relate the processes and the areas affected, to show the different senses of "secularization."

In reviewing these different meanings, we can elaborate recognized sociological usage. But we can also show that they correspond to common usage of very long standing, as evidenced in the *Oxford English Dictionary* (hereafter, the OED). So we are using the same technique of nominal definition as before, in differentiating the ways the terms are used.

(1) When discussing social structures—or "societies" with regard to their structures or symbol systems—secularization is used to mean *differentiation*. Here, secularization means the separation of religious activities, groups, or ideas from others present in the society. This may seem a rather technical use of the term, since it is primarily scholars who view things structurally. But actually, the general public also uses the term in this sense. Since the thirteenth century, English usage (according to the OED) has included such phrases as secular rulers, secular judges, secular lords, and secular historians, to mean those who have no connection with the "church." It does not mean that these rulers, judges, et al., are personally nonreligious, which would be a confusion of this sense with (4) below. It only means they lack an official connection to religion or religious institutions, due to such differentiation.

When the general public uses the term society, it usually does not mean a structure, but rather the *population* contained within the social structure. That creates an ambiguity that we will discuss below in (5). Nevertheless, the public understands that there are autonomous activities and institutions, differentiated from religion in the sense of being free from religious direction or association, and in that sense "secular." Confusion arises when we forget that most of these activities once did have a connection to religious organizations. There were processes of differentiation that cut them loose. Even the creation of religious institutions (e.g., churches) could be considered an instance of secularization, in which specifically religious institutions separated from some original "primitive cultural fusion." That is a use that will never be common outside of anthropology.

Please note that we are not saying that differentiation *leads to* secularization. It *is* secularization. For we are not speaking here of a *theory* of what causes religious decline, or secularization, but only speaking descriptively. We can assume, however, that this differentiation will entail some loss of religion's power or authority, since the religious institution becomes one of many institutions, sharing authority with the others as a result of this differentiation.

(2) When discussing *institutions*, we use secularization to mean the *transformation* of an institution that had once been considered religious in character into something not thought of as religious. This is also the sense in which we speak of the secularization of things and of words which were once associated with religion but have lost that connection. It is easy to think of examples of such things, like the European university, or "perjury," or nationalized church property. Again, this is a usage of long standing. The OED lists an English example from 1570, Henry VIII's secularization of monastic lands. The clergy that lost their jobs in the church at that time were also said to have been "secularized," which again, did not mean that they lost their religious faith.

(3) When discussing *activities*, secularization is taken to mean the *transfer* of activities from institutions of a religious nature to others without that character. The list of such activities is longer than one may think. For nothing is intrinsically secular; anything whatsoever can be considered as part of one's religion, including cooking, dancing, agriculture, military technology, and measuring time.[4] The transfer of artistic patronage from the church to private individuals would be an instance of secularization, and it might in turn encourage a change of artistic themes from religious to secular ones. One would refer to the early modern transfer of welfare services from the church to the state as the secularization of that function.

(4) When discussing *mentalities*, we take secularization to mean a significant shift of attention from ultimate concerns to proximate ones. The secularization of mentality can, of course, take a more decided turn against religion, in active doubt or open disbelief.

Again, this is a usage of long standing. According to the OED the use of secular to describe a mentality was recognized in English as early as 1395 to describe worldly minded clergy, and around 1425 in a reference to "secular affections."

The term "secularism" must be differentiated from these processes of secularization. "Secularism" was coined around 1852 to describe an ideology organized to oppose religious loyalties, in an effort to complete or enforce secularization.

(5) As mentioned above, the secularization of a society is not the same thing as the secularization of a population. For social scientists at least, "society" means a structure (or even a process) rather than the persons contained within that structure. So we can quite properly speak of a secular society which contains an entirely religious population. That would mean that the rules under which such a society operates are recognized as having a different character from the religious beliefs held by the population. On the other hand, where a whole population is characterized by a neglect of religious habits or convictions, one might speak of the secularization of that population—a generalization of (4) above.

Most of our present confusion on the subject of secularization is due to this ambiguity in the term society—whether we mean the role structure or those filling the roles. If we were to ask scholars to change their practice with regard to any of this terminology, it should be to become more consistent as to whether they were speaking of a "society" or a population.

(6) Finally, the term secular can only be used unambiguously in contrast to religion in a generic sense. Ordinarily it is used in contrast to specific religions, like Christianity. The reason that this inevitably creates confusion is that it is impossible to define Christianity to everyone's satisfaction. We differ over normative understandings of that term. For example, what some would lament as the decline of a Christian culture others might welcome as the purification of Christian spirituality. The decline of popular respect for the clergy, or faith in vows, might be assessed quite differently, depending on one's views of Christianity. The term religion may be tricky to define

generically, but it is obviously impossible to satisfy everyone on the inescapably normative definitions of particular religions.

Those who intend to discuss de-Christianization[5] should say so, and should specify the aspects of Christianity they are referring to (church attendance, for example). They may find that religion in the population was increasing at the same time that secularization in the social institutions was also increasing!

Testing the Definitions

We might test these meanings of secularization on the most puzzling, almost oxymoronic use of the term, which speaks of "the secularization of the Church."[6] This could mean one of several things. It could mean that a religious organization had become something *other* than that, as the YMCA has done. That would be secularization by transformation—(2) above. Or it could mean that a church was becoming something *broader* than a religious organization, by engrossing what had been "secular" activities. For we should remember that there are no intrinsically secular activities or objects. If the church succeeded in *sacralizing* some previously secular activities in public opinion this should not count as secularization at all, but rather the opposite. On the other hand, if the church were broadened so greatly that it ceased to be regarded as religious, it would again count as a case of transformation (2). And finally, the "secularization of the Church" could mean the secularization of that church's members in sense (5), meaning a loss of interest in religious experience or concepts or activities.[7]

These rules are easy to forget. Some insist on thinking of secularization as a general decline of religion. Then, if they want to deny the reality of such secularization, they may shift from one sense of the term to another, more hopeful meaning. But there is no need for secularization to proceed in all these dimensions simultaneously for it to be a meaningful concept. As we have said, it is sometimes possible to show secularization and the intensification of religion going on simultaneously. Confining religion to a narrower channel can give more force to its flow. The idea of a general decline of religion is a dubious concept, given the variety of forms that religion can take.

It is also common to object that since religious belief survived the social processes we have just described, one cannot speak of secularization. To those critics, secularization has the *telos* of eliminating religion. Again, this misses the sense—common to sociology and also to ordinary use—of secularization simply as the separation of religion from particular aspects of life—(1) above. In historical societies, the secular and the religious have always coexisted, so that the degrees of secularization are relative and not absolute.

Students of the recent past often assume that to speak of secularization means to speak of "secularism." Presumably, for them secularization has to be conscious, intentional, philosophical, and perhaps even political, to deserve the name. But the secularization of Western culture did not begin as a challenge at the intellectual level.[8] Many of the secularizing processes were actually promoted by religious groups (most notably extreme Protestants) who wanted to define religion more narrowly, excluding "superstitions" that had once been central to religious practice.

Finally, many scholars assume that to speak of secularization means to embrace "the secularization hypothesis" or "secularization theory." That thesis made secularization a linear and inevitable process within modern economic and social development. It has been attacked from many sides as an unfalsifiable hypothesis.[9] But one does not need to accept a hypothesis in order to talk of secularization in a descriptive sense. Some of those attacking the *thesis* imply that this will close off any further discussion of the processes of secularization.

Actually, the collapse of secularization theory should be a stimulus to greater descriptive study of secularization. It will enable us to see that different societies or cultures have had very different experiences of secularization.[10] So long as scholars thought that these processes always followed the same course, there was little interest in those differences.

Not only that, but the disappearance of the secularization thesis would allow us to recognize what a huge topic secularization is.

There are innumerable books on the growth of the modern European state, on industrialization, on the development of capitalism, and on the growth of modern science and rationalism. Secularization, in all its aspects, is as big as any of these topics. But it can only be seen from the other side of the medieval/modern divide, as we learn more about the extent of the religious culture that was displaced. Far from being a "Whiggish" approach to history, the study of secularization will force historians to recover a time we can barely conceive. One need not argue that earlier ages were uniformly devout in order to see that religious meanings permeated every aspect of their complex cultures. Recovering a time when all aspects of life carried religious meanings will take substantial efforts of historical imagination. We may not be arguing that people were more "religious" then, but that the culture was.

Still, we must end with another ritual reminder that we should not assume that "secularization" is an inevitable process—a developmental arrow. Religion is more likely to change its form than to decline, and we may not be looking in the right place for it. One could most reasonably expect the religious and the secular to coexist indefinitely, since humanity seems to have an amphibious existence in both.

Secular Judgments

Secular viewpoints may assume an ability to transcend religious ones in the sense of understanding and judging them. We have already dealt with the possibility of scientific reductions of religious experience. There may be hermeneutical ones as well, which object that particular religions are not worthy of the name. First, some assume that if a particular religion is simply unacceptable, it should not be considered a religion at all. Another name must be found for it, like cult, superstition, or fanaticism, implying that religion per se is above criticism. Second, one may object to religion in a general, moral sense, where a criticism of any particular religion becomes a criticism of all religion. Defining religion generically and analytically, as we have done, might seem to encourage this.

But it will probably not be the analytical concept so much as the substance of particular religions that will be at issue. We can, of course, refuse to accept that religious awareness connects to anything beyond itself. That is simple unbelief, not judgment. Such unbelief may take an effort, given the intuitive sense of the term that we have remarked upon.

When we begin to make our judgments of particular religions explicit, we will discover something about ourselves. We find that, ultimately, we can only judge one religion on the basis of another religion. Judgments in this area take us down to bedrock. Bedrock turns out to be, not self-validating rational truths, but our personal faiths or even our rejection of any commitment. What we gain from an honest exercise of judgment is the discovery of just what we do believe.

The only truly general thing one can say about religion is analytic and semantic—that it is our word for an awareness of something staggering, for which we lack the words at first but which seems to demand our response. We cannot say anything further without considering particular traditions. These are the forms in which it can be said to be helpful, destructive, reasonable, hateful, or illuminating.

Particular religions can be judged according to moral standards, or logical, psychological, utilitarian, or pragmatic ones. How well does it explain, or motivate, or restrain? What has it produced in the way of art, ethics, political culture, theology, philosophy, and science? How does it measure "success," and how much has it achieved? But again, the criteria used will represent alternative ultimate concerns, the very marks of a particular faith.

Religions may have similar elements, but scholars find them finally incommensurable. As Mark Heim argued (chapter 3) religions have different goals, different salvations. As George Lindbeck indicated (chapter 8) they have their own languages, their own discourses. It is difficult enough to judge them by their own standards and authoritative texts. Journalists want to refute terrorists on the basis of quotes from the Koran, but Islamic theologians may not be persuaded. The worldwide reality of Islam embraces Germans, Nigerians, Persians, Filipinos, Uzbeks, Canadians, Pakistanis, and Malays, as well as Arabs and Turks. Christianity has an even more complex history and a wider racial and cultural reach. Judgments must be complex, and will reveal one's own commitments.

Letting A Religion Judge Us: When Religion Frames the Secular

So in the course of judging religions we become aware that our fundamental standards are themselves coming into question. Ethical judgment on history can never be rendered from within history but only from beyond it, where religion seems to dwell. The transcendence of ultimate standards suggests that the question is not so much whether we are religious, but the character of our final appeal.

Our current belief in secular education is not seen as a belief, but as self-evident or at least necessary. We are urged to teach religious diversity by shifting the basis to "intelligence." In her advocacy of this program, Nel Noddings holds that the Supreme Court, in *Wisconsin v. Yoder*, was wrong in allowing the Amish to build on their own basis.[11] But what we call intelligent beliefs are those whose basis we have forgotten. Some, like tolerance, may have religious roots, but this was so long ago that they now lie buried among the sacred foundations of secularism. Education must proceed from some prior settlement, since a debate of first-order principles might never end. Cultural differences may grow so great that they justify separate schools, all of which may try to be fair to others.

Secularity is our word for an absence—the absence of religion—but secularism seems to denote a whole ideology. As such, it too might be subject to scientific reduction or hermeneutical deconstruction. In such an effort, it might be religion that would be framing the secular. We may be used to thinking of the secular as rationality itself, and yet the pure state may have been very rare in history. If it meant that one had no intellectual or personal commitments at all, nothing like a faith, it would indicate the lack of a personal core, nothing offering consistency in choice. If one argued that this was a pathological condition, we would be reminded of our discussion of whether considerations of health, sickness, and sanity are themselves religious at basis (chapter 7).

Finally, the thing that makes a nominal definition of religion hardest to accept is that it makes no claim to universality of meaning or of judgment. We want our scholarship or science to speak a universal language of reality. If religion can only be given a culture-specific definition, it will seem to have failed the reality test. But this is the reality that United Nations translators already live with, who must deal with documents on religious liberty and who find themselves interchanging the English terms religion, thought, conscience, and belief.[12]

So we have not settled whether Confucianism, Satanism, secular humanism, Buddhism, witchcraft, or civil religion are religions or not. Those who are more intimately involved with them are the ones to decide the matter on the basis of our definition, if they see a point in doing so. They may decide that other terms are more appropriate, like worldview, ideology, ethos or spirituality, which would also be defined nominally.

Notes

Chapter 1

1   Paul C. Vitz, *Religion and Traditional Values in Public School Textbooks: An Empirical Study* (Washington: Department of Education, Government Printing Office, July 15, 1985).

2   "Defining a Religion," *Gainesville Sun* (June 16, 2001), D8.

3   Wade Clark Roof, *Spiritual Marketplace: Baby Boomers and the Remaking of American Religion* (Princeton: Princeton University Press, 1999), 35, 44, 81. See also Robert C. Fuller, *Spiritual, But Not Religious* (New York: Oxford University Press, 2001), 5.

4   Roof, *Spiritual Marketplace*, 34.

5   Robert Wuthnow, *Creative Spirituality* (Berkeley: University of California Press, 2001), 7.

6   Brian J. Zinnbauer, Kenneth I. Pargament, et al., "Religion and Spirituality: Unfuzzying the Fuzzy," *Journal for the Scientific Study of Religion* 36 (1997): 549–64. See also Penny Long Marler and C. Kirk Hadaway, "'Being Religious' or 'Being Spiritual' in America: A Zero-Sum Proposition?" *Journal for the Scientific Study of Religion* 41 (2002): 289–300, and Wade Clark Roof, *A Generation of Seekers* (San Francisco: Harper, 1993), 76.

7   Peter Van Ness, *Spirituality, Diversion and Decadence* (Albany: State University of New York Press, 1992), 13.

8   Steve Bruce, "Secularization and the Impotence of Individualized Religion," in *Hedgehog Review* 8 (2006): 43.

9   Stephen L. Carter, *God's Name in Vain: The Wrongs and Rights of Religion in Politics* (New York: Basic Books, 2000), 19.

10   Richard Rorty, "Religion as Conversation Stopper," *Common Knowledge* 3 (1994): 2.

11   Quoted in Richard John Neuhaus, "When Tolerance is Trump," *First Things* (February 2001), 65.

12   Marsha Mercer, quoting Senator Joseph Lieberman, *Gainesville Sun* (March 6, 2001), 13A.

13   "How China Beat Down Falun Gong," *Time* (July 2, 2001), 32–35.

14   C. John Sommerville, *The News Revolution in England: Cultural Dynamics of Daily Information* (New York: Oxford University Press, 1996), 10, 135–45; and, in a more popular vein, C. John Sommerville, *How the News Makes Us Dumb; The Death of Wisdom in an Information Society* (Downers Grove, Ill.: InterVarsity, 1999), 45–54, 131–39.

15   Carter, *God's Name in Vain*, 70. This is despite the fact that left-voting black churches are notorious for ignoring the stipulated restrictions.

16   The quotes appear in "Bill Clinton and the American Character," *First Things* (June/July 1999), 72.

17   Thomas Nagel, *The Last Word* (New York: Oxford University Press, 1997), 130.

18   See the various essays in Jan G. Platvoet and Arie L. Molendijk, eds., *The Pragmatics of Defining Religion: Contexts, Concepts and Contests* (Leiden: Brill, 1999).

19   There are other terms for this nominal definition by linguistic difference. Wittgenstein called it "definition in use." "Definition," in *Cambridge Dictionary of Philosophy*, ed. Robert Audi, 2nd ed. (Cambridge: Cambridge University Press, 1999), 214. Logicians have termed it nominal definition by synthesis (i.e., by relating words to their surroundings, rather than by analysis, finding their constituent elements). See Richard Robinson, *Definition* (Oxford: Clarendon, 1950), 98.

20   S. N. Balagangadhara, *"The Heathen in His Blindness": Asia, the West and the Dynamic of Religion* (Leiden: Brill, 1994), 29.

21   David A. Pailin, *Attitudes to Other Religions; Comparative Religion in Seventeenth- and Eighteenth-Century England* (Manchester: Manchester University Press, 1984), 34, 53, 137–40, 160, 236–39, 245–51.

22   Pailin, *Attitudes*, 59.

23 Philip C. Almond, *The British Discovery of Buddhism* (Cambridge: Cambridge University Press, 1988), 10–13, emphasis in original.

24 Almond, *British Discovery*, 14, 138–40. See also Thomas A. Tweed, *The American Encounter with Buddhism, 1844–1912* (Bloomington: Indiana University Press, 1992); and Gustaaf Houtman, "How a Foreigner Invented 'Buddhendom'," *Journal of the Anthropological Society of Oxford* 21 (1990): 113–28.

25 Heinrich von Stietencron, "Hinduism: On the Proper Use of a Deceptive Term," in *Hinduism Reconsidered*, ed. Günther-Dietz Sontheimer and Hermann Kulke (New Delhi: Manohar, 1997), 33, 40, 46. See also "Articles and Response on 'Who Speaks for Hinduism?'" *Journal of the American Academy of Religion* 68 (2000): 705–835. I am indebted to conversations with Vasudha Narayanan and Gene Thursby in this area. See the more general discussion in Richard King, *Orientalism and Religion* (London: Routledge, 1999).

26 Marc Galanter, *Law and Society in Modern India* (Oxford: Oxford University Press, 1989), 237–58. See also Robert D. Baird, *Religion and Law in Independent India* (Delhi: Monohar, 1993), 41–58.

27 Lionel M. Jensen, *Manufacturing "Confucianism": Chinese and Western Imaginings in the Making of a Tradition* (Durham, N.C.: Duke University Press, 1995).

28 Wilfred Cantwell Smith, *The Meaning and End of Religion* (New York: Macmillan, 1962), 69.

29 Balagangadhara, *"The Heathen in His Blindness,"* 18.

30 W. C. Smith, *Meaning and End of Religion*, 70–73.

31 Jonathan Z. Smith, "Religion, Religions, Religious," in *Critical Terms for Religious Studies*, ed. Mark C. Taylor (Chicago: University of Chicago Press, 1998), 276.

32 Werner Cohn, "On the Problem of Religion in Non-Western Culture," *International Yearbook for the Sociology of Religion* 5 (1969): 7–19; Timothy Fitzgerald, *The Ideology of Religious Studies* (New York: Oxford University Press, 2000), 9.

33 Edward W. Said, *Orientalism* (New York: Pantheon, 1978), 272.

34 Bellah, "Religious Evolution," 20–50.

35 Murray L. Wax, "Religion as Universal: Tribulations of an Anthropological Enterprise," *Zygon* 19 (1984): 5–20.

36 J. Z. Smith, "Religion, Religions, Religious," 281.

37 W. C. Smith, *Meaning and End of Religion*, 50, 195.

38 Richard King, *Orientalism and Religion* (London: Routledge, 1999), 40.

39   E.g., John Hick, *An Interpretation of Religion: Human Responses to the Transcendent* (New Haven: Yale University Press, 1989), 3; William P. Alston, "Religion," in *Encyclopedia of Philosophy*, ed. Paul Edwards (New York: Macmillan, 1967), 7:140–45; Ninian Smart, "Religion: The Study and Classification of," *The New Encyclopedia Britannica*, 15th ed., 26:509; Peter B. Clarke and Peter Byrne, *Religion Defined and Explained* (New York: St. Martin's, 1993), 7, 12, 16; Benson Saler, *Conceptualizing Religion* (Leiden: Brill, 1993), 159; Thomas A. Idinopulos and Brian C. Wilson, eds., *What is Religion? Origins, Definitions, and Explanations* (Leiden: Brill, 1998), 158–60.

40   Alston, "Religion," 7:140–45.

41   Anthony F. C. Wallace, *Religion: An Anthropological View* (New York: Random House, 1966), 52.

42   Mark C. Taylor, "Introduction," in *Critical Terms for Religious Studies*, 6; emphasis in original.

43   W. C. Smith, *Meaning and End of Religion*, 20, 195.

44   Cf. Rodney L. Taylor, *The Religious Dimensions of Confucianism* (Albany: State University of New York Press, 1990).

45   Ludwig Wittgenstein, *Philosophical Investigations*, trans. G. E. M. Anscombe (New York: Macmillan, 1953), section 43.

46   Norman Malcolm, *Wittgenstein: A Religious Point of View?* (London: Routledge, 1993), 74.

47   E.g., Hilary Putnam, *Renewing Philosophy* (Cambridge, Mass.: Harvard University Press, 1992), 167.

48   George A. Lindbeck, *The Nature of Doctrine: Religion and Theology in a Postliberal Age* (Philadelphia: Westminster, 1984), 33. And yet there are problems with his approach too, as detailed in chapter 5. See also D. Z. Phillips, *Wittgenstein and Religion* (New York: St. Martin's, 1993), 56–78; Ray Monk, *Wittgenstein* (New York: Free Press, 1990), 302–8, 338.

Chapter 2

1   Paul W. Pryser, *Between Belief and Unbelief* (New York: Harper & Row, 1974), 55.

2   Bernard Spilka, Ralph W. Hood, Richard L. Gorsuch, *The Psychology of Religion: An Empirical Approach* (Englewood, N.J.: Prentice-Hall, 1985), 4.

3   Winston L. King, *Introduction to Religion* (New York: Harper & Brothers, 1968), 5.

4   Smart, *New Encyclopedia Britannica*, 26:509.

5   Saler, *Conceptualizing Religion*, 27–69, 159.

6   Paul J. Griffiths, "On the Future of the Study of Religion," *Journal of the American Academy of Religion* 74 (2006): 66–74.

7   To complicate things, Paul Ricoeur argues that understanding and explanation (or as the Germans first distinguished them, *verstehen and erklären*) must complement each other. One cannot assume one understands the subjectivity without some preliminary use of analysis or comparison of the phenomena, or that objectivity captures the entire human reality without disciplined efforts at understanding. See Steven D. Kepnes, "Bridging the Gap Between Understanding and Explanation Approaches to the Study of Religion," *Journal for the Scientific Study of Religion* 25 (1986): 504–12.

8   E.g., J. L. Austin, *Philosophical Papers*, 3rd ed. (Oxford: Oxford University Press, 1979), 58; William C. Wimsatt, "Reductionism, Levels of Organization, and the Mind-Body Problem," in *Consciousness and the Brain*, ed. Gordon G. Globus, Grover Maxwell, and Irwin Savodnick (New York: Plenum, 1976), 242, 248.

9   See Alfred Schutz, "On Multiple Realities," *Collected Papers* (Hague: Nijhoff, 1962–1966), 1:209–59; and Thomas Nagel, *Mortal Questions* (Cambridge: Cambridge University Press, 1979), 211.

10   Incidentally, it is concepts that are reduced, not entities. Hans H. Penner, *Impasse and Resolution: A Critique of the Study of Religion* (New York: Peter Lang, 1989), 23. And lest it be thought that my argument would justify the reality of unicorns, I admit that one can reduce that concept to horse + horn. A closer equivalent to "religion" would be the irreducibility of the term "organism" or "life." Any attempted reduction would leave out the essential feature of the concept.

11   Hick, *Interpretation of Religion*, 3–6.

12   William James, *The Varieties of Religious Experience* (London: Longmans, Green, 1908), 27.

13   E.g., Wilfred Cantwell Smith wonders what to make of the fact that scientists have a prior faith in science: *Faith and Belief* (Princeton: Princeton University Press, 1979), 16.

14   John R. Searle, *Speech Acts; An Essay in the Philosophy of Language* (Cambridge: Cambridge University Press, 1969), 12.

15   Danièle Hervieu-Léger, *Religion as a Chain of Memory*, trans. Simon Lee (New Brunswick, N.J.: Rutgers University Press, 2000).

16   W. C. Smith, in *Meaning and End of Religion*, flirted with the possibility of a nominal definition (of religious, as an adjective, on 16, 20, 49, 195) but settled on real definitions—of faith and tradition. Nicholas Lash (*The Beginning and End of "Religion"* [Cambridge: Cambridge University Press, 1996], 22) recognized the difference between real and nominal definitions, but took no position on the matter.

17   Melford E. Spiro, "Religion: Problems of Definition and Explanation," in *Anthropological Approaches to the Study of Religion*, ed. Michael Banton (London: Tavistock, 1966), 86–91; Clifford Geertz, *The Interpretation of Cultures* (New York: Basic, 1973), 119–22.

18   Geertz uses a number of terms to suggest the distinctive character of the religious as opposed to the nonreligious aspects of his phenomena: all pervading vitality, unconditioned end, transcendent truths, fundamental nature of reality, ultimate, and the "really real" (Geertz, *Interpretation*, 98, 108, 112).

19   Geertz, *Interpretation*, 90.

20   Thomas Luckmann is the most notable of those who hold that American churches have been secularized from within, because they cannot detect a theological pulse. *The Invisible Religion: The Problem of Religion in Modern Society* (New York: Macmillan, 1967), 35.

21   E.g., Victor W. Turner, *The Ritual Process: Structure and Anti-Structure* (Chicago: Aldine, 1969), 4, where Turner alludes to "the extreme importance of religious beliefs and practices, for both the maintenance and radical transformation of human social and psychical structures."

22   Frits Staal, "The Meaninglessness of Ritual," *Numen* 26 (1979): 2–22.

23   Paul Tillich, *Dynamics of Faith* (New York: Harper, 1957), 11. Michael Eldridge has shown that Tillich actually held that only an ultimate concern for the Ultimate qualified as religious, making this a normative definition. "The Wonderful Ambiguity of Paul Tillich's Concept of 'Ultimate Concern'," *Ultimate Reality and Meaning Monographs* 1 (Toronto: Regis College Press, 1994): 234–41.

24   Of course, in investigating the intuition of essences, phenomenology is the study of religious people and not of the religious "object." Eric J. Sharpe, *Comparative Religion: A History*, 2nd ed. (LaSalle, Ill.: Open Court, 1986), 220–36.

25   Rudolf Otto, *The Idea of the Holy* (Harmondsworth: Penguin, 1959), 34–39; Gerardus Van Der Leeuw, *Religion in Essence and Manifestation* (New York: Harper, 1963), 1:23; Mircea Eliade, *The Sacred and the*

Profane: The Nature of Religion (New York: Harcourt, Brace & World, 1959), 8–13.

26   Hans G. Kippenberg, "Rivalry among Scholars of Religions: The Crisis of Historicism and the Formation of Paradigms in the History of Religion," *Historical Reflections/Reflexions Historiques*, 20 (1994): 386.

27   See Brian Morris, *Anthropological Studies of Religion* (Cambridge: Cambridge University Press, 1987), 100, 103f., 118, 167; and similar indications in Philip C. Almond, *Rudolf Otto: An Introduction to His Philosophical Theology* (Chapel Hill: University of North Carolina Press), 62; Carl Gustav Jung, *Psychology and Religion* (New Haven: Yale University Press, 1938), 5; Bryan R. Wilson, *The Noble Savages* (Berkeley: University of California Press, 1975), vii; Streng, *Understanding Religious Man*, 5, 73; Robert G. Hamerton-Kelly, *Sacred Violence* (Minneapolis: Fortress, 1992), 28; Wallace, *Religion: An Anthropological View*, 5. Even Paul Tillich ventured a definition of religious experience in terms of power, or the "power of being." While "being" is the ultimate term in his analysis, he spoke evocatively of God as "the power of being" which overcomes the "non-being" which is human finitude. Faith and love are affirmations inspired by this sense of the power of being. The religious experience is "the feeling of being in the hand of a power which cannot be conquered by any other power . . . which is the infinite resistance against non-being and the eternal victory over it" (*Love, Power and Justice* [New York: Oxford University Press, 1954], 35–53, 110). Robert Wuthnow also understands Geertz's definition as involving power. *Rediscovering the Sacred* (Grand Rapids: Eerdmans, 1992), 58.

28   Max Weber, *The Sociology of Religion* (Boston: Beacon, 1993), 25. See also Morris, *Anthropological Studies of Religion*, 69, 85.

29   Alister Hardy, *The Spiritual Nature of Man* (Oxford: Clarendon, 1979), 134. I owe this reference to Professor Diogenes Allen.

30   Griffiths, "On the Future of the Study of Religion," 68.

31   Charles Taylor, *A Secular Age* (Cambridge, Mass.: Harvard University Press, 2007), 510.

32   Talal Asad, *Genealogies of Religion: Discipline and Reasons of Power in Christianity and Islam* (Baltimore: The Johns Hopkins University Press, 1993), 29, 42.

33   Hardy, *Spiritual Nature of Man*, 133.

34   Luckmann, *Invisible Religion*, 109–16; Robert Bellah, *Beyond Belief: Essays on Religion in a Post-Traditional World* (New York: Harper & Row, 1970), 11.

35   Spiro takes up this issue in "Religion: Problems of Definition and Explanation," 85–96. See also Jensen, *Manufacturing "Confucianism."*

36   Martin Southwold, "Buddhism and the Definition of Religion," *Man* (now *Journal of the Royal Anthropological Institute*) 13 (1978): 364–66.

37   Helen Hardacre, *Shintō and the State, 1868–1988* (Princeton: Princeton University Press, 1989), 9, 18, 39, 63, 66, 77.

38   Frederick J. Streng, *Understanding Religious Man* (Belmont, Calif.: Dickenson, 1969), 65.

39   *Marsh v. Chambers*, 463 U.S. 783 (1983), at 810, quoting A. Sabatier.

40   Brian J. Zinnbauer, Kenneth I. Pargament, et al., "Religion and Spirituality: Unfuzzying the Fuzzy," *Journal for the Scientific Study of Religion* 36 (1997): 549–64; Penny Long Marler and C. Kirk Hardaway, "'Being Religious' or 'Being Spiritual' in America: A Zero-Sum Proposition?" *Journal for the Scientific Study of Religion* 41 (2002): 289–300.

41   Michael Paffard, *Inglorious Wordsworths* (London: Hodder & Stoughton, 1973), 213.

42   Earle J. Coleman, *Creativity and Spirituality* (Albany: State University of New York Press, 1998), 188, 195.

43   Cf. William Lad Sessions, *The Concept of Faith: A Philosophical Investigation* (Ithaca: Cornell University Press, 1994).

44   Richard King, *Orientalism and Religion* (London: Routledge, 1999), 7–15.

45   Evelyn Underhill, *Mysticism*, 12th ed. (London: E. P. Dutton, 1930), 24, 71.

46   R. C. Zaehner, *Mysticism: Sacred and Profane* (London: Oxford University Press, 1961), xiii, 101–5, 200.

47   E.g., J. Milton Yinger, *Religion in the Struggle for Power* (Durham, N.C.: Duke University Press, 1946), 6.

48   David Hume, *The Natural History of Religion*, in *Hume on Religion*, ed. Richard Wollheim (New York: World, 1963), 40, 47, 54, 56.

49   Thomas Aquinas, *Summa Theologiae* (London: Eyre & Spottiswoode, 1964), 39:11–15; J. Milton Yinger, *The Scientific Study of Religion* (New York: Macmillan, 1970), 10.

50   Clifford Geertz, *Islam Observed: Religious Development in Morocco and Indonesia* (New Haven: Yale University Press, 1968), 98.

51 Peter L Berger, *The Heretical Imperative* (Garden City, N.Y.: Doubleday, 1979), 36.

52 Paffard, *Inglorious Wordsworths*, 165, 213.

53 Paul Ricoeur, "Philosophy and Religious Language," *Journal of Religion* 54 (1974): 84.

54 Peter L. Berger, *A Far Glory: The Quest for Faith in an Age of Credulity* (New York: Doubleday, 1992), 133–39.

55 John Skorupski, *Symbol and Theory: A Philosophical Study of Theories of Religion in Social Anthropology* (Cambridge: Cambridge University Press, 1976), 14; and Peter Winch, "Meaning and Religious Language," in *Reason and Religion*, ed. Stuart Brown (Ithaca: Cornell University Press, 1977), 193.

56 Gordon Allport and J. Michael Ross, "Personal Religious Orientation and Prejudice," *Journal of Personality and Social Psychology* 5 (1967): 432–43.

57 Berger, *A Far Glory*, 133.

Chapter 3

1 *Abington School District v. Schempp*, 374 U.S. 203 (1963), at 224.

2 Tanya Storch, "Quietly Sitting under a Tree . . ." *CLASnotes* (University of Florida) 13 (1999): 1, 10.

3 E.g., Margaret Wertheim, *Pythagoras' Trousers: God, Physics, and the Gender Wars* (New York: Norton, 1997).

4 Alastair MacIntyre, "Is Understanding Religion Compatible with Believing?" in *Rationality*, ed. Bryan R. Wilson (Oxford: Basil Blackwell, 1977), 74.

5 Michael Polanyi, *Personal Knowledge: Towards a Post-Critical Philosophy* (London: Routledge, 1962), 123–27.

6 Polanyi, *Personal Knowledge*, 151, 159.

7 Steven Shapin, *A Social History of Truth; Civility and Science in Seventeenth-Century England* (Chicago: University of Chicago Press, 1994).

8 *Gainesville Sun* (June 9, 2005), from a report in *Nature*.

9 Classically in Carl L. Becker, *The Heavenly City of the Eighteenth-Century Philosophers* (New Haven: Yale University Press, 1932).

10 Huston Smith, "Western Philosophy as a Great Religion," in *Transcendence and the Sacred*, ed. Alan M. Olson and Leroy S. Rouner (Notre Dame: University of Notre Dame Press, 1981), 21–23. See

214 || NOTES TO PP. 59–63

also John Milbank, *Theology and Social Theory: Beyond Secular Reason* (Oxford: Basil Blackwell, 1990).

11   Warren A. Nord, *Religion and American Education* (Chapel Hill: University of North Carolina Press, 1995), 298.

12   Nel Noddings, *Educating for Intelligent Belief or Unbelief* (New York: Teachers College Press, 1993); Polanyi, *Personal Knowledge*, 266.

13   See also Leszek Kolakowski, *Religion, If There Is No God* . . . (New York: Oxford University Press, 1982), 54; and Nord, *Religion and American Education*, 186.

14   *Abington School District v. Schempp*, at 225.

15   Amy Gutmann, *Democratic Education* (Princeton: Princeton University Press, 1987), 108.

16   Mark Tushnet, *Red, White, and Blue: A Critical Analysis of Constitutional Law* (Cambridge, Mass.: Harvard University Press, 1988), 261.

17   Elmer John Thiessen, *Teaching for Commitment* (Montreal: McGill-Queen's University Press, 1993), 25, 233.

18   Thiessen, *Teaching for Commitment*, 130, 141–43.

19   Wilfred Cantwell Smith, "Methodology and the Study of Religion: Some Misgivings," in *Methodological Issues in Religious Studies*, ed. Robert D. Baird (Chico, Calif.: New Horizons, 1975), 9–11.

20   Edward W. Said, *Orientalism* (New York: Pantheon, 1978), 272.

21   Michel Foucault, *The Order of Things: An Archaeology of the Human Sciences* (New York: Pantheon, 1970), 377.

22   "The Santa Barbara Colloquy: Religion within the Limits of Reason Alone," *Soundings* 71 (1988): 267, 228.

23   "The Santa Barbara Colloquy," 200–204, 215–19, 274–77.

24   "The Santa Barbara Colloquy," 249; and Eric Sharpe, *Comparative Religion: A History*, 2nd. ed. (LaSalle, Ill.: Open Court, 1986), 220–36. See also George Alfred James, *Interpreting Religion* (Washington, D.C.: Catholic University of America Press, 1995), for a fuller history of phenomenological approaches.

25   Louis Dupré, "Phenomenology of Religion: Limits and Possibilities," *American Catholic Philosophical Quarterly* 66 (1992): 175–88.

26   Robert A. Segal, "In Defense of Reductionism," *Journal of the American Academy of Religion* 51 (1983): 97–124.

27   George Marsden, *The Outrageous Idea of Christian Scholarship* (New York: Oxford University Press, 1997), 80.

28   Nord, *Religion and American Education*, 267–69.

29   Bruno Bettleheim, *The Uses of Enchantment* (New York: Random House, 1977).

30   See Thiessen, *Teaching for Commitment*, 93.

31   William K. Kilpatrick, *Why Johnny Can't Tell Right From Wrong* (New York: Simon & Schuster, 1992), 228–33; Nel Noddings, "Character Education and Community," in *The Construction of Children's Character*, ed. Alex Molnar (Chicago: National Society for the Study of Education, 1997), 1–13. She cites Alastair MacIntyre, Michael Oakeshott, Robert Nisbet, and Robert Bellah.

32   Robert Coles, *The Spiritual Life of Children* (Boston: Houghton, Mifflin, 1990), 108, 121.

33   Robert Coles, "Youngsters Have Lots To Say About God," *Time* (January 21, 1991), 16–18.

34   Jonathan Z. Smith, *Imagining Religion: From Babylon to Jonestown* (Chicago: University of Chicago Press, 1982): 102–20.

35   S. Mark Heim, *Salvations: Truth and Difference in Religion* (Maryknoll, N.Y.: Orbis, 1995), 219.

36   J. A. DiNoia, *The Diversity of Religions* (Washington, D.C.: Catholic University of America Press, 1992), 34.

37   Neil Postman, *The End of Education: Redefining the Value of Schools* (New York: Alfred A. Knopf, 1995), 154; George M. Marsden, *The Soul of the American University: From Protestant Establishment to Established Unbelief* (New York: Oxford University Press, 1994), 432.

38   Winnifred Fallers Sullivan, *Paying the Words Extra: Religious Discourse in the Supreme Court of the United States* (Cambridge, Mass.: Harvard University Press, 1994), 82 n. 2.

39   Nord, *Religion and American Education*, 161–68, 249–59.

40   *McCullom v. Board of Education*, 333 U.S. 203 (1948), at 227.

41   *Abington School District v. Schempp*, at 288.

42   *Lee v. Weisman*, 505 U.S. 577 (1992), at 593.

43   *Board of Education v. Mergens*, 496 U.S. 226 (1990), at 269.

44   *Lemon v. Kurtzman*, 403 U.S. 602 (1971), at 622.

45   Joe Maxwell, "The Textbook Reformation," *Christianity Today* (September 16, 1991), 47–50.

46   Stephen L. Carter, *God's Name in Vain: The Wrongs and Rights of Religion in Politics* (New York: Basic, 2000), 179; Charles Leslie Glenn Jr., *The Myth of the Common School* (Amherst: University of Massachusetts Press, 1988), 264.

47 Stephen Bates, *Battleground: One Mother's Crusade, The Religious Right, and the Struggle for Control of our Classrooms* (New York: Poseidon, 1993), 298.

48 Charles L. Glenn, "War in the Classroom," *First Things* (January 1994), 39–42.

49 Jeremy A. Rabkin, "Let Us Pray," *American Spectator* 28 (1995): 46.

50 Stephen L. Carter, *The Culture of Disbelief* (New York: Basic, 1993), 174.

51 *Board of Education v. Mergens*, at 269.

52 *Wisconsin v. Yoder*, at 218, 211.

53 Justice Douglas, dissenting in *Wisconsin v. Yoder*, at 249, referred to the decision in *U.S. v. Seeger*, 380 U.S. 163 (1965), as recognizing certain philosophies as religious, which he thought was a recognition of a more "exalted view of religion" than traditional religions merited.

54 Nord, *Religion and American Education*, 169–71.

55 *Time* (October 27, 1986), 94. The definitions of humanism in Paul Kurtz, ed., *The Humanist Alternative: Some Definitions of Humanism* (Buffalo, N.Y.: Prometheus, 1973) agree in denying anything outside humanity that would provide guidance or goals for humanity. There is a strong ethical emphasis, of responsibility for the human race. And there is always some form of denial of religion as ordinarily understood.

56 John Dewey, *A Common Faith* (New Haven: Yale University Press, 1934), 1–6, 16.

57 Christopher Dawson, *The Crisis of Western Education* (New York: Sheed & Ward, 1961), 104.

58 Cf. James Davison Hunter, "'America's Fourth Faith': A Sociological Perspective on Secular Humanism," *This World* 19 (1987): 101–10.

59 Nord, *Religion and American Education*, 179, 372.

60 George M. Marsden, "Liberating Academic Freedom," *First Things* (December 1998), 11.

61 Nel Noddings, in *Curriculum, Religion, and Public Education*, ed. James T. Sears and James C. Carper (New York: Columbia University Teachers College Press, 1997), 121.

62 *Lemon v. Kurtzman*, at 615–17.

63 Nord, *Religion and American Education*, 251–54.

64 Marsden, *Outrageous*, 80.

65 Silvano Arieti, *Creativity; The Magic Synthesis* (New York: Basic, 1976), 249.

66 Paul Radin, *Primitive Man as Philosopher* (New York: Appleton, 1927), 323, 375.

67 Dawson, *Crisis of Western Education*, 63, 102–6.

68 Pierre Hadot, *Philosophy as a Way of Life* (Oxford: Basil Blackwell, 1995), 24, 17, 280, 267–74.

69 See my discussion of this subject in *The Decline of the Secular University* (New York: Oxford University Press, 2006).

Chapter 4

1 E.g., Steven D. Smith, *Foreordained Failure: The Quest for a Constitutional Principle of Religious Freedom* (New York: Oxford University Press, 1995); Sharon L. Worthing, "'Religion' and 'Religious Institutions' Under the First Amendment," *Pepperdine Law Review* 7 (1980): 313, 351; Stanley Ingber, "Religion or Ideology: A Needed Clarification of the Religion Clauses," *Stanford Law Review* 41 (1989): 241.

2 Perry, *Religion in Politics*, 29; Steven G. Gey, "Why is Religion Special? Reconsidering the Accommodation of Religion Under the Religion Clauses of the First Amendment," *University of Pittsburgh Law Review* 52 (1990): 75–187; Scott C. Idleman, "The Sacred, the Profane, and the Instrumental: Valuing Religion in the Culture of Disbelief," *University of Pennsylvania Law Review* 142 (1994): 1313–81; Christopher L. Eisgruber and Lawrence G. Sager, "Congressional Power and Religious Liberty after *City of Boerne v. Flores*," *1997 The Supreme Court Review* (Chicago: University of Chicago Press, 1998), 111–16, 123.

3 *Torcaso v. Watkins*, 367 U.S. 488 (1961), at 495 n. 11.

4 Ronald Dworkin, *Life's Dominion* (London: HarperCollins, 1993), 160–68.

5 Phillip E. Johnson, "Concepts and Compromise in First Amendment Religious Doctrine," *California Law Review* 72 (1984): 821.

6 Kent Greenawalt, "Religion as a Concept in Constitutional Law," *California Law Review* 72 (1984): 763; George C. Freeman III, "The Misguided Search for the Constitutional Definition of 'Religion,'" *Georgetown Law Journal* 71 (1983): 1519–65.

7 Winnifred Fallers Sullivan, "Judging Religion," *Marquette Law Review* 81 (1998): 441–60.

8 *U.S. v. Seeger*, 380 U.S. 163, at 180–83.

9   See C. John Sommerville, *The Secularization of Early Modern England: From Religious Culture to Religious Faith* (New York: Oxford University Press, 1992).

10   Sanford Kessler, "Locke's Influence on Jefferson's 'Bill for Establishing Religious Freedom,'" *Journal of Church and State* 25 (1983): 231–52.

11   Laurence H. Tribe, *American Constitutional Law* (Mineola, N.Y.: Foundation, 1978), 818 n. 19. My emphasis.

12   Explicitly in *Cantwell v. Connecticut*, 310 U.S. 296 (1940).

13   Thomas J. Curry, *The First Freedoms: Church and State in America to the Passage of the First Amendment* (New York: Oxford University Press, 1986), 200, 207.

14   Laura Underkuffler-Freund, "The Separation of the Religious and the Secular: A Foundational Challenge to First Amendment Theory," *William and Mary Law Review* 36 (1995): 891–929, 958, 963.

15   Richard Rorty, "Religion as Conversation Stopper," *Common Knowledge* 3 (1994): 2.

16   Bette Novitt Evans, *Interpreting the Free Exercise of Religion* (Chapel Hill: University of North Carolina Press, 1998), 218.

17   Johan D. van der Vyver, *Religious Human Rights in Global Perspective: Legal Perspective* (The Hague: Martinus Nijhoff, 1996), xviii–xxxix.

18   P. N. Bhagwati, "Religion and Secularism Under the Indian Constitution," in *Religion and Law in Independent India*, ed. Robert D. Baird (Delhi: Manohar, 1993), 12–20; J. Duncan M. Derrett, *Religion, Law and the State in India* (New York: Free Press, 1968).

19   *Davis v. Beason*, 133 U.S. 333, at 341.

20   E.g., William G. Hollingsworth, "Constitutional Religious Protection: Antiquated Oddity or Vital Reality," *Ohio State Law Journal* 34 (1973): 78; Anita Bowser, "Delimiting Religion in the Constitution: A Classification Problem," *Valparaiso University Law Review* 11 (1977): 166; "Note: Toward a Constitutional Definition of Religion," *Harvard Law Review* 91 (1978): 1056, 1072; Jesse Choper, "Defining 'Religion' in the First Amendment," *University of Illinois Law Review* (1982): 594–601.

21   For other doubts of the utility of functional definitions, see Peter Berger, "Some Second Thoughts on Substantive versus Functional Definitions of Religion," *Journal for the Scientific Study of Religion* 13 (1974): 125–33.

22   For these as subsequent quotes, see *U.S. v. Seeger*, 380 U.S. 163, at 172–88.

23 Choper, "Defining 'Religion' in the First Amendment," 597–604.

24 Quoted in Robert T. Miller and Ronald B. Flowers, eds., *Toward Benevolent Neutrality: Church, State, and the Supreme Court*, 6th ed. (Waco, Tex.: Baylor University Press, 1977), 569.

25 Michael J. Sandel, "Freedom of Conscience or Freedom of Choice?" in *Articles of Faith, Articles of Peace*, ed. James Davison Hunter and Os Guinness (Washington, D.C.: Brookings Institution, 1990), 75.

26 Arlin M. Adams and Charles J. Emmerich, *A Nation Dedicated to Religious Liberty* (Philadelphia: University of Pennsylvania Press, 1990), 64.

27 *U.S. v. Seeger*, 380 U.S. 163, at 188–93.

28 *U.S. v. Macintosh*, 283 U.S. 605, at 633.

29 Gey, "Why is Religion Special?" 167.

30 *Welsh v. U.S.*, 398 U.S. 333, at 342.

31 *Wisconsin v. Yoder*, 406 U.S. 205, at 216.

32 Jesse Choper, *Securing Religious Liberty: Principles for Judicial Interpretation of the Religious Clauses* (Chicago: University of Chicago Press, 1995), 71; D. G. Leitch, "The Myth of Religious Neutrality by Separation in Education," *Virginia Law Review* 71 (1985): 161; Ben Clements, "Defining 'Religion' in the First Amendment: A Functional Approach," *Cornell Law Review* 74 (1989): 541.

33 See Thomas Robbins and Dick Anthony, "Deprogramming, Brainwashing and the Medicalization of Deviant Religious Groups," *Social Problems* 29 (1982): 283–97.

34 The phrase made famous by Michael J. Sandel, *Liberalism and the Limits of Justice* (Cambridge: Cambridge University Press, 1998).

35 Evans, *Free Exercise of Religion*, 19–21, 43, 54. She cites Choper, Gey, Clements, and Sandel as agreeing on this point.

36 *Reynolds v. U.S.*, 98 U.S. 145, at 166.

37 Dworkin, *Life's Dominion*, 162–66, citing *Gillette v. U.S.*, 401 U.S. 437. H. Jefferson Powell has pointed out to me that Christian just war doctrine would allow such selective objections.

38 Charles M. Whelan, "'Church' in the Internal Revenue Code: The Definitional Problem," *Fordham Law Review*, 45 (1977), 885–926.

39 Evans, *Free Exercise of Religion*, 177–79, 190, 197.

40 Mark Tushnet, *Red, White, and Blue: A Critical Analysis of Constitutional Law* (Cambridge, Mass.: Harvard University Press, 1988), 270–73.

41 Frederick Mark Gedicks and Roger Hendrix, *Choosing the Dream: The Future of Religion in American Public Life* (New York: Greenwood, 1991),

68–71; Craig Anthony Arnold, "Religious Freedom as a Civil Rights Struggle," *Nexus: A Journal of Opinion* 2 (1997): 154.

42   *Everson v. Board of Education*, 330 U.S. 1, at 8.

43   Douglas Laycock, "Continuity and Change in the Threat to Religious Liberty: The Reformation Era and the Late Twentieth Century," *Minnesota Law Review* 80 (1996): 1087–89.

44   *Lemon v. Kurtzman*, 403 U.S. 602, at 622.

45   As described in Frederick Mark Gedicks, *The Rhetoric of Church and State: A Critical Analysis of Religion Clause Jurisprudence* (Durham, N.C.: Duke University Press, 1995), 12.

46   Gey, "Why is Religion Special?" 154.

47   Adams and Emmerich, *Nation Dedicated to Religious Liberty*, 37; Stephen L. Carter, *God's Name in Vain* (New York: Basic, 2000), 77–81.

48   Steven D. Smith, "Separation and the 'Secular': Reconstructing the Disestablishment Decision," *Texas Law Review* 67 (1989): 955–1031.

49   *Sherbert v. Verner*, 374 U.S. 398, at 403.

50   *Employment Division v. Smith*, 494 U.S. 872 at 883, referring to Lyng.

51   Catherine Cookson, *Regulating Religion: The Courts and the Free Exercise Clause* (New York: Oxford University Press, 2001), 122.

52   Evans, *Free Exercise of Religion,* 206.

53   *Employment Division v. Smith*, at 878.

54   Evans, *Free Exercise of Religion,* 201.

55   *Employment Division v. Smith*, at 888.

56   *Employment Division v. Smith*, at 877.

57   See *U.S. v. Kauten*, 133 F. 2d 703 (1943); *Berman v. U.S.*, 156 F 2d 377 (1946); *U.S. v. Macintosh*, 283 U.S. 605 (1931). These are all quoted in *Welsh v. U.S.*, at 348.

58   Choper, "Defining 'Religion' in the First Amendment," 591.

Chapter 5

1   Gey, "Why is Religion Special?" 173. For other examples, see Kathleen M. Sullivan, "Religion and Liberal Democracy," *University of Chicago Law Review* 59 (1992): 222; Mary Segers and Ted G. Jelen, *A Wall of Separation?: Debating the Public Role of Religion* (Lanham, Md.: Rowman & Littlefield, 1998); Isaac Kramnick and R. Laurence Moore, *The Godless Constitution: The Case Against Religious Correctness* (New York: W. W. Norton, 1996).

2   Sommerville, *Secularization of Early Modern England.*

3   Harry Harootunian, "Memory, Mourning, and National Morality: Yasukuni Shrine and the Reunion of State and Religion in Postwar Japan," in *Nation and Religion: Perspectives on Europe and Asia*, ed. Peter vanderVeer and Hartmut Lehmann (Princeton: Princeton University Press, 1999), 144–60.

4   Hardacre, *Shintō and the State*, 134.

5   Douglas Johnston and Cynthia Sampson, eds., *Religion, The Missing Dimension of Statecraft* (New York: Oxford University Press, 1994), 13; Douglas Johnston, ed., *Faith-Based Diplomacy: Trumping Realpolitick* (New York: Oxford University Press, 2003).

6   See Langton Gilkey, *Reaping the Whirlwind: A Christian Interpretation of History* (New York: Seabury, 1976), 39–69.

7   Mark Juergensmeyer, *The New Cold War? Religious Nationalism Confronts the Secular State* (Berkeley: University of California Press, 1993), 1–20, 22, 156, 191–94. See Rene Girard, *Violence and the Sacred* (Baltimore: The Johns Hopkins University Press, 1977), for the theory behind this analysis.

8   Quoting Todd M. Johnston and David B. Barrett, in Thomas F. Farr, "The Diplomacy of Religious Freedom," *First Things* (May 2006), 18.

9   Matthew C. Moen and Lowell S. Gustafson, eds., *The Religious Challenge to the State* (Philadelphia: Temple University Press, 1992).

10   Farr, "Diplomacy of Religious Freedom," 18.

11   In Johnston, *Religion, The Missing Dimension of Statecraft*, 8–19.

12   E.g., John R. Mott (1946), Friends Service Committee (1947), Albert Schweitzer (1952), Father Dominique Pere (1958), Albert Luthuli (1960), Dag Hammarskjold (1961), M. L. King Jr. (1964), Mother Teresa (1979), Adolfo Perez Esquivel (1980), Lech Walesa (1983), Desmond Tutu (1984), the Dalai Lama (1989), and Bishop Carlos F. X. Belo (1996).

13   Johnston, *Religion, The Missing Dimension of Statecraft*, 1–36.

14   Johnston, *Religion, The Missing Dimension of Statecraft*, 258–333.

15   Ashutosh Varshney, "Contested Meanings: India's National Identity, Hindu Nationalism, and the Politics of Anxiety," *Daedalus* 122 (1993): 227–61.

16   Samuel P. Huntington, *The Clash of Civilizations and the Remaking of World Order* (New York: Simon & Schuster, 1996), 54, 96–113.

17   Clifford Geertz, "Ideology as a Cultural System," in *Ideology and Discontent*, ed. David E. Apter (New York: Free Press, 1964), 63.

18 Robert N. Bellah, *Beyond Belief: Essays on Religion in a Post-Traditional World* (New York: Harper & Row, 1970), 179.

19 Russell E. Richey and Donald G. Jones, eds., *American Civil Religion* (New York: Harper & Row, 1974), 152.

20 Steven Lukes, "Political Ritual and Social Integration," *Sociology* 9 (1975): 289–308; Robert E. Goodin, "Rites of Rulers," *British Journal of Sociology* 29 (1978): 281–99.

21 Robert Bellah and Phillip E. Hammond, *Varieties of Civil Religion* (San Francisco: Harper & Row, 1980), 17; Sydney E. Ahlstrom, *A Religious History of the American People* (Garden City: Doubleday, 1975), 2:450.

22 Sanford Levinson, *Constitutional Faith* (Princeton: Princeton University Press, 1988), 54–56, 91, 165.

23 Jean-Jacques Rousseau, *On the Social Contract*, ed. Roger Masters (New York: St. Martin's Press, 1978), book 4, viii.

24 Norman Cohn, *The Pursuit of the Millennium*, 2nd ed. (New York: Harper & Row, 1961), 290–305.

25 Harold Berman, *Law and Revolution: The Formation of the Western Legal Tradition* (Cambridge, Mass.: Harvard University Press, 1983).

26 Darren Kew, "Why Nigeria Matters," *First Things* (November 2007), 17–19.

27 Quoted by Michael Sandel, "Freedom of Conscience or Freedom of Choice?" in Hunter, ed., *Articles of Faith*, 88.

28 Quoted by Miller and Flowers, *Toward Benevolent Neutrality*, 569.

29 *Wallace v. Jaffree*, 472 U.S. 38, at 53 (Justice Stevens).

30 James Madison, "Memorial and Remonstrance Against Religious Assessments," in *The Complete Madison*, ed. Saul K. Padover (New York: Harper & Brothers, 1953), 301 (his emphasis), quoting Article 16 of the *Virginia Declaration of Rights* (1776).

31 Paul J. Weithman, ed., *Religion and Contemporary Liberalism* (Notre Dame: University of Notre Dame Press, 1997), 67.

32 Richard John Neuhaus, *The Naked Public Square: Religion and Democracy in America* (Grand Rapids: Eerdmans, 1984), 250; Sandel, "Freedom of Conscience," 87.

33 Gey, "Why is Religion Special?" 75–187.

34 Ronald E. Thiemann, *Religion in Public Life: A Dilemma for Democracy* (Washington, D.C.: Georgetown University Press, 1996), 20, 72–74.

35 Adams and Emmerich, *A Nation Dedicated to Religious Liberty*, 85.

36 John Rawls, *A Theory of Justice* (Cambridge, Mass.: Harvard University Press, 1971), 208–18.

37 *Board of Education v. Allen*, 392 U.S. 236, at 254.

38 Gedicks and Hendrix, *Choosing the Dream*, 141.

39 Stephen Macedo, ed., *Deliberative Politics* (New York: Oxford University, 1999); and Ashley Woodiwiss, "Democracy Agonistes," *Books and Culture* (March/April 2001), 22–25.

40 Theimann, *Religion in Public Life*, 74.

41 Paul K. Griffiths and Jean Bethke Elstain, "Proselytizing for Tolerance," *First Things* (November 2002), 30–36.

42 Jeremy A. Rabkin, "Let Us Pray," *American Spectator* 28 (1995): 46.

43 David Hollenbach, "Contexts of the Political Role of Religion: Civil Society and Culture," *San Diego Law Review* 30 (1993): 894.

44 Rorty, "Religion as Conversation Stopper," 4.

45 Christopher Lasch, *The Revolt of the Elites and the Betrayal of Democracy* (New York: W. W. Norton, 1995), 16, 243.

46 Robert Booth Fowler, *Unconventional Partners: Religion and Liberal Culture in the United States* (Grand Rapids: Eerdmans, 1989), 4, 157–60.

47 Michael Walzer, "Michael Sandel's America," in *Debating Democracy's Discontent*, ed. Anita Allen and Milton Ragan (New York: Oxford University Press, 1998), 180; David C. Leege and Lyman A. Kellstedt, eds., *Rediscovering the Religious Factor in American Politics* (London: M. E. Sharpe, 1993), 129.

48 Michael J. Perry, *Love and Power: The Proper Role of Religion and Morality in American Politics* (New York: Oxford University Press, 1991), 41; Robert J. White, "Fetal Brain Transplantation: Questionable Human Experiment," *America* 167 (November 28, 1992): 421.

49 Stephen L. Carter, *The Dissent of the Governed* (Cambridge, Mass.: Harvard University Press, 1998), 92; Clarke E. Cochran, *Religion in Public and Private Life* (New York: Routledge, 1990), 98.

50 Perry, *Religion in Politics*, 47–49.

51 Raimundo Panikkar, "Religion or Politics: The Western Dilemma," in *Religion and Politics in the Modern World*, ed. Peter H. Merkl and Ninian Smart (New York: New York University Press, 1983), 44–60.

52 Perry, *Religion in Politics*, 16.

53 John J. DiIulio Jr., *Godly Republic: A Centrist Blueprint for America's Faith-Based Future* (Berkeley: University of California Press, 2007), chap. 5.

54   Polanyi, *Personal Knowledge*, 151; Thomas S. Kuhn, *The Structure of Scientific Revolutions* (Chicago: University of Chicago Press, 1964), 147, 157.

55   Alasdair MacIntyre, *Whose Justice? Which Rationality?* (Notre Dame: University of Notre Dame Press, 1988), 335, 1–9, 370–88.

56   Alasdair MacIntyre, *Three Rival Versions of Moral Enquiry* (Notre Dame: University of Notre Dame Press, 1990), 81.

57   MacIntyre, *Three Rival Versions*, 50; Kent Greenawalt, *Religious Convictions and Political Choice* (New York: Oxford University Press, 1988), 52, 156; Weithman, *Religion and Contemporary Liberalism*, 86.

58   Michael Walzer, "Deliberation, and What Else," in Macedo, *Deliberative Politics*, 58–69.

59   In Hunter and Guinness, *Articles of Faith*, 117.

60   Garry Wills, *Under God: Religion and American Politics* (New York: Simon & Schuster, 1990), 359–62.

61   K. R. Popper, *The Open Society and Its Enemies*, 2nd ed. (London: Routledge & Kegan Paul, 1952), 2:23, 273.

62   "Will Politicians Matter?" *Time* (February 21, 2000), 68–71.

Chapter 6

1   Michael Polanyi, *Science, Faith and Society* (London: Oxford University Press, 1946), 1–31; Polanyi, *Personal Knowledge*.

2   Putnam, *Renewing Philosophy*, 192.

3   Suzanne K. Langer, *Philosophy in a New Key* (New York: New American Library, 1962), 100–102, 133–48.

4   John Horgan, *The End of Science* (New York: Helix, 1996), 14, 24, 37, 58, 252, 257; cf. 76, 119.

5   Werner Heisenberg, *Physics and Beyond* (New York: Harper & Row, 1971), 82–92, 209–13.

6   Paul Davies, *The Mind of God: The Scientific Basis for a Rational World* (New York: Simon & Schuster, 1992), 15.

7   See Nancey Murphy, *Theology in the Age of Scientific Reasoning* (Ithaca: Cornell University Press, 1990), 59, 121.

8   Schutz 1:209–59, and Nagel, *Mortal Questions*, 211.

9   Polanyi, *Personal Knowledge*, 123–32, 151.

10   Karl Popper, *The Logic of Scientific Discovery* (London: Hutchinson, 1968), 111. See discussion in Derek Stanesby, *Science, Reason and Religion* (London: Croom Helm, 1985), 51, 67.

11   Hans Joas, *The Genesis of Values* (Chicago: University of Chicago Press, 2000), 38.

12   Holmes Rolston, quoted in Anna L. Peterson, *Being Human: Ethics, Environment, and Our Place in the World* (Berkeley: University of California Press, 2001), 71. His emphasis.

13   *Gainesville Sun* (June 17, 2001), D1.

14   Walter Burkert, *Creation of the Sacred: Tracks of Biology in Early Religions* (Cambridge, Mass.: Harvard University Press, 1996), ix.

15   Werner Heisenberg, "The Representation of Nature in Contemporary Physics," *Daedalus* (Summer 1958): 100.

16   Langton Gilkey, *Creationism on Trial* (Charlottesville: University of Virginia Press, 1998), 171.

17   Paul Davies, *The Fifth Miracle: The Search for the Origin and Meaning of Life* (New York: Simon & Schuster, 1999), 31.

18   Willem B. Drees, *Religion, Science and Naturalism* (Cambridge: Cambridge University Press, 1996), 114.

19   Ludwig Wittgenstein, *Tractatus Logico-Philosophicus* (New York: Routledge, 1990), 187. His emphasis.

20   Albert Einstein, *The World As I See It* (London: John Lane, The Bodley Head, 1941), 27.

21   John Polkinghorne, *Faith, Science and Understanding* (New Haven: Yale University Press, 2000), 144.

22   John Wheeler, quoted in *Between Quantum and Cosmos*, eds. Wojciech Hubert Zurek, et al. (Princeton: Princeton University Press, 1988), 10.

23   Polkinghorne, *Faith, Science and Understanding*, 166; John Polkinghorne, "The Quantum World," in *Physics, Philosophy and Theology: A Common Quest for Understanding* (Vatican City: Vatican Observatory, 1988), 333–35.

24   Henry G. Leach, ed., *Living Philosophies* (New York: Simon & Schuster, 1931), 6. My emphasis.

25   Adam Gopnik, "The Porcupine," *New Yorker* (April 1, 2002), 92.

26   Ian G. Barbour, *Religion in an Age of Science* (London: SCM, 1990), 147.

27   Polkinghorne, *Faith, Science and Understanding*, 188.

28   Steven Weinberg, *The First Three Minutes* (New York: Basic, 1977), 149. Weinberg later allowed that "people can grant significance to life by loving each other, investigating the universe, and doing other worthwhile things." Gregg Easterbrook, "Science and God: A Warming Trend," *Science* (August 15, 1997), 893. But he did not justify the terms "grant," "significance," or "worthwhile."

29 C. John Sommerville, *The Decline of the Secular University* (New York: Oxford University Press, 2006), 80.

30 Quoted in Karl W. Giberson, "The Guy in the Wheelchair," *Books and Culture* (September/October 2007), 21. His emphasis.

31 Quoted in Ian G. Barbour, *Religion in an Age of Science* (London: SCM, 1990), 136.

32 *The New Yorker* (December 10, 2001), 84.

33 Nagel, *Mortal Questions*, 167.

34 See John R. Searle, *The Mystery of Consciousness* (New York: New York Review Books, 1997).

35 Drees, *Religion, Science and Naturalism*, 180, 194.

36 Robert A. Segal, "In Defense of Reductionism," *Journal of the American Academy of Religion*, 51 (1983), 97–124, misses this point. Gerhard Lenski, *The Religious Factor* (Garden City, N.Y.: Doubleday, 1961).

37 David C. Legger and Lyman A. Kellstedt, *Rediscovering the Religious Factor in American Politics* (London: M. E. Sharpe, 1993), 27, 129, 132.

38 John Onians, *Sight and Insight* (London: Phaidon, 1994), 13–15.

39 E.g., Eugene G. D'Aquili and Andrew B. Newberg, "The Neuropsychological Basis of Religions, or Why God Won't Go Away," *Zygon* 33 (1998): 187–201.

40 Edward O. Wilson, *On Human Nature* (New York: Bantam, 1979), 3–6, 170–72, 177, 184, 191, 200.

41 Charles Taylor, *Sources of the Self: The Making of the Modern Identity* (Cambridge, Mass.: Harvard University Press, 1989), 59.

Chapter 7

1 See Brian Morris, *Anthropological Studies of Religion* (Cambridge: Cambridge University Press, 1987), 69, 115, 142, 167, 177, 216, 313–15.

2 Clifford Geertz, "Religion: Anthropological Study," in *International Encyclopedia of the Social Sciences*, ed. David Sills (New York: Macmillan, 1968), 13:406. See also Morris, *Anthropological Studies of Religion*, 297–305.

3 Rene Girard, *Violence and the Sacred* (Baltimore: The Johns Hopkins University Press, 1977), 306; Morris, *Anthropological Studies of Religion*, 246.

4   Robin Horton, "Tradition and Modernity Revisited," in *Rationality and Relativism*, ed. Martin Hollis and Steven Lukes (Cambridge: MIT Press, 1982), 208.

5   Daniel Lawrence O'Keefe, *Stolen Lightning: The Social Theory of Magic* (New York: Continuum, 1982), 7, 14–16, 464. I owe this reference to Richard Fenn.

6   See Peter L. Berger, ed., *The Desacralization of the World: Resurgent Religion and World Politics* (Washington, D.C.: Ethics and Public Policy Center, 1999).

7   Rodney Stark and William Sims Bainbridge, *A Theory of Religion* (New York: Peter Lang, 1987); cf. Steve Bruce, "Religion and Rational Choice: A Critique of Economic Explanations of Religious Behavior," *Sociology of Religion* 54 (1993): 193–205; and Laurence R. Iannacone, "Voodoo Economics?" *Journal for the Scientific Study of Religion* 34 (1995): 76–88.

8   Neil Smelser, "Economic Rationality as a Religious System," in *Rethinking Materialism*, ed. Robert Wuthnow (Grand Rapids: Eerdmans, 1995), 73–92.

9   Robert Wuthnow, "Science and the Sacred," in *The Sacred in a Secular Age: Toward Revision in the Scientific Study of Religion*, ed. Phillip E. Hammond (Berkeley: University of California Press, 1985), 187–203.

10   George H. Gallup Jr. and Frank Newport, "Belief in Paranormal Phenomena Among Adult Americans," *Skeptical Inquirer* 15 (1991): 137–46. The phenomena associated with New Age religions hardly turned up in Gallup's survey, with two percent reporting participation.

11   William C. McCready and Andrew Greeley, *The Ultimate Values of the American Population* (Beverly Hills, Calif.: Sage, 1976), 132–37.

12   C. Daniel Batson and W. Larry Ventis, *The Religious Experience: A Social-Psychological Perspective* (New York: Oxford University Press, 1982).

13   James McClenon, *Wondrous Events: Foundations of Religious Belief* (Philadelphia: University of Pennsylvania Press, 1994), 14, 21, 56.

14   McClenon, *Wondrous Events*, xiv. Carol Zaleski, *Otherworldly Journeys: Accounts of Near-Death Experience in Medieval and Modern Times* (New York: Oxford University Press, 1987), 189, refers to both persistence and change over time. There has even been talk of studies of "religious" behavior in animals, which falter on points of interpretation and definition. Ronald K. Siegel, "Religious Behaviour in Animals and Man: Drug-Induced Effects," *Journal of Drug Issues* 7 (1977): 219–36.

15   Colin A. Ross and Shaun Joshi, "Paranormal Experiences in the General Population," *Journal of Nervous and Mental Disease* 180 (1992): 357–61.

16   David Lukoff and Francis G. Lu, "Transpersonal Psychology Research Review Topic: Mystical Experience," *Journal of Transpersonal Psychology* 20 (1988): 161–84, 206.

17   E.g., Paul Kurtz, "Two Sources of Unreason in Democratic Society, the Paranormal and Religion," in *Flight From Science and Reason*, 493–504.

18   Sigmund Freud, "Obsessive Actions and Religious Practices," in *The Standard Edition of the Complete Psychological Works of Sigmund Freud*, trans. James Strachey (London: Hogarth, 1959), 9:126.

19   Quoted in D. Z. Phillips, *Religion Without Explanation* (Oxford: Basil Blackwell, 1976), 75, 60–64, 51.

20   Erik H. Erikson, *Childhood and Society*, 2nd ed. (New York: Norton, 1963), 182–86.

21   Sigmund Freud, "The Uncanny," in *Collected Papers*, trans. Joan Riviere (New York: Basic Books, 1959), 4:368–407.

22   Abraham H. Maslow, *Religions, Values, and Peak-Experiences* (New York: Viking, 1970), 27; Jack Tyrus Hanford, "A Synoptic Approach: Resolving Problems in Empirical and Phenomenological Approaches to the Psychology of Religion," *Journal for the Scientific Study of Religion* 14 (1975): 225.

23   J. G. Scadding, "Diagnosis: The Clinician and the Computer," *Lancet* 2 (1969): 877–82, and the resulting debate on his paper. I owe this reference to Roger Blashfield.

24   Robert A. Woodruff Jr., Donald W. Goodwin, and Samuel B. Guze, *Psychiatric Diagnosis* (New York: Oxford University Press, 1974); Robert E. Kendal, *Issues in Psychiatric Classification: Science, Practice and Social Policy* (New York: Human Sciences Press, 1986); Lawrie Reznek, *The Nature of Disease* (New York: Routledge & Kegan Paul, 1987).

25   R. D. Laing, "Transcendental Experience in Relation to Religion and Psychosis," in *Exploring Madness*, ed. James Fadiman and Donald Kewman (Monterey, Calif.: Brooks/Cole, 1973), 97–105.

26   Peter Buckley, "Mystical Experience and Schizophrenia," *Schizophrenia Bulletin* 7 (1981): 520.

27 Edward Mitchell Podvall, "Psychosis and the Mystic Path," *Psychoanalytic Review* 66 (1979–1980): 571–90.

28 E.g., Kenneth Stifler, Joanne Greer, William Sneck, and Robert Dovenmuehle, "An Empirical Investigation of the Discriminability of Reported Mystical Experiences Among Religious Contemplatives, Psychotic Inpatients, and Normal Adults," *Journal for the Scientific Study of Religion* 32 (1993): 366–72; and David Lukoff, "Transpersonal Perspectives on Manic Psychosis: Creative, Visionary and Mystic States," *Journal of Transpersonal Psychology* 20 (1988): 111–36. William James avoided this dichotomy, by acknowledging both healthy-minded and sick-minded religion: *The Varieties of Religious Experience; A Study in Human Nature* (London: Longmans, Green, 1908).

29 See Lorraine Daston and Katherine Park, *Wonders and the Order of Nature, 1150–1750* (New York: Zone, 1998), 120.

30 Benedicta Ward, *Miracles and the Medieval Mind: Theory, Record and Event, 1000–1215* (Philadelphia: University of Pennsylvania Press, 1982), 2–4.

31 Jacques LeGoff, *The Medieval Imagination* (Chicago: University of Chicago Press, 1988), 28–32.

32 Carolyn Walker Bynum, "Wonder," *American Historical Review* 102 (1997): 9, paraphrasing William of Auvergne (in 1235).

33 Ward, *Miracles and the Medieval Mind*, 19, 24, 31, 205.

34 Austin, *Philosophical Papers*, 58; William C. Wimsatt, "Reductionism, Levels of Organization, and the Mind-Body Problem," in *Consciousness and the Brain*, ed. Gordon G. Globus, Grover Maxwell, and Irwin Savodnik (New York: Plenum, 1976), 242–48.

35 Gould, *Rocks of Ages*, 22, 65, 69.

36 Cited in J. Milton Yinger, *The Scientific Study of Religion* (New York: Macmillan, 1970), 1.

37 James, *Varieties*, 424, 498, 502. Emphasis in original.

38 D'Aquili, "Neuropsychological Basis of Religions," 187–201

39 Ludwig Wittgenstein, *Lectures and Conversations* (Berkeley: University of California Press, 1967), 56.

40 E.g., Richard Schlegel, *Completeness in Science* (New York: Appleton-Century-Crofts, 1967).

41 Paul Tillich, *The Courage to Be* (New Haven: Yale University Press, 1952), 40.

Chapter 8

1   George A. Lindbeck, *The Nature of Doctrine: Religion and Theology in a Postliberal Age* (Philadephia: Westminster, 1984), 37. He cites the works of Wittgenstein, Noam Chomsky, and Clifford Geertz, especially.

2   Lindbeck, *The Nature of Doctrine*, 16.

3   I am using "numinous" less as a noun than an adjective; it characterizes a certain moment within experience.

4   Wayne Proudfoot, *Religious Experience* (Berkeley: University of California Press, 1985), 187.

5   Kai Nielsen, "Wittgensteinian Fideism," *Philosophy* 42 (1967): 201.

6   D. Z. Phillips, *Faith and Philosophical Enquiry* (New York: Schocken, 1971), 97, 107. Ian T. Ramsey, in *Religious Language* (New York: Macmillan, 1957), 51, calls it "logically odd," even involving "significant tautologies. "

7   George Santayana, *The Life of Reason* (New York: Charles Scribner's Sons, 1953), 180.

8   Mircea Eliade and David Tracy, eds., *What is Religion? An Inquiry for Christian Theology* (New York: Seabury, 1980), 26.

9   Clare Boothe Luce, quoted in *Famous Conversions*, Hugh T. Kerr and John M. Mulder, eds. (Grand Rapids: Eerdmans, 1994), 249. Text in all capitals and italics is in the original.

10 William James, *The Varieties of Religious Experience* (London: Longmans, Green, 1908), 200 n. 1.

11 C. S. Lewis, *Surprised By Joy* (London: Fontana, 1959), 179–82.

12 David Wesley Soper, ed., *These Found the Way* (Philadelphia: Westminster, 1951), 23.

13 Soper, *These Found the Way*, 75.

14 Paraphrased by A. E. Gould, in *Changed Men of Our Time* (Derby: Peter Smith, 1964), 68, from Hugh Redwood, *God in the Shadows* (New York: Fleming H. Revell, 1932), 32.

15 Quoted in James, *Varieties of Religious Experience*, 66.

16 Merold Westphal, *God, Guilt, and Death: An Existential Phenomenology of Religion* (Bloomington: Indiana University Press, 1984), 27.

17 Berger, *A Far Glory*, 128–30. Emphasis in original.

18 Lindbeck, *Nature of Doctrine*, 40.

19 Tillich, *Dynamics of Faith*, 11.

20 Michael Eldridge, "The Wonderful Ambiguity of Paul Tillich's Concept of 'Ultimate Concern,'" *American Philosophers' Ideas of Ultimate Reality*

and Meaning, ed. A. J. Reck, et al. (Toronto: Regis College Press, 1994), 234–41.

21 Tillich, *Dynamics of Faith*, 11.

22 William P. Alston, *Perceiving God: Epistemology of Religious Experience* (Ithaca: Cornell University Press, 1991), 16, makes a similar point.

23 Lindbeck, *Nature of Doctrine*, 62.

24 Phillips, *Faith and Philosophical Enquiry*, 93.

25 Mark I. Wallace, *The Second Naiveté: Barth, Ricoeur and the New Yale Theology* (Macon, Ga.: Mercer University Press, 1990), 95.

26 Peter Byrne, *Natural Religion and the Nature of Religion: The Legacy of Deism* (London: Routledge, 1989), 185–96.

27 James Barr, *Biblical Faith and Natural Theology* (Oxford: Clarendon, 1993), 3.

28 Barr, *Biblical Faith*, 148; John Brooke and Geoffrey Cantor, *Reconstructing Nature* (Edinburgh: T&T Clark, 1998), 152, 202.

29 Erazim Kohák, *The Embers and the Stars; A Philosophical Inquiry into the Moral Sense of Nature* (Chicago: University of Chicago Press, 1984), 196, 122.

30 Kohák, *The Embers and the Stars*, 84, 197.

31 Kohák, *The Embers and the Stars*, 209, 184, 46, 200, 128.

32 Kohák, *The Embers and the Stars*, 190, 185.

33 William Wimsatt, "Reductionism, Levels of Organization, and the Mind-Body Problem," in *Consciousness and the Brain*, ed. Gordon G. Globus, Grover Maxwell, and Irwin Savodnik (New York: Plenum, 1976), 262.

34 Kohák, *Embers and the Stars*, 210, 186, 66, 130, 175.

35 See Alan J. Torrance, "What Is a Person?" in *From Cells to Souls—and Beyond; Changing Portraits of Human Nature*, ed. Malcolm Jeeves (Grand Rapids: Eerdmans, 2004), 199–222.

36 Nels F. S. Ferré, *Swedish Contributions of Modern Theology* (New York: Harper and Brothers, 1939), 34–46; Murphy, *Theology in the Age of Scientific Reasoning*, 179.

37 Charles W. Kegley, ed., *The Philosophy and Theology of Anders Nygren* (Carbondale: Southern Illinois University Press, 1970), 314; Philip C. Almond, *Rudolf Otto: An Introduction to his Philosophical Theology* (Chapel Hill: University of North Carolina Press, 1984), 42.

38 Paul Tillich, *Systematic Theology* (London: Nisbet, 1953), 1:239.

39 Otto, *Idea of the Holy*, 19–21, 26–45.

40 Otto, *Idea of the Holy*, 194.

41   Otto, *Idea of the Holy*, 288, 296.

42   Almond, *Rudolf Otto*, 19, 31, 52, 57, 66; Rudolf Otto, "The Sensus Numinis as the Historical Basis of Religion," *The Hibbert Journal* 30 (1931–1932): 288.

43   Otto, "The Sensus Numinis," 415–18, 427; Almond, *Rudolf Otto*, 93; Otto, *Idea of the Holy*, 126, 157–59.

44   Berger, *A Far Glory*, 131.

45   Berger, *A Far Glory*, 133.

46   Paul Ricoeur, "Religion, Atheism, and Faith," in *The Conflict of Interpretations: Essays on Hermeneutics* (Evanston, Ill.: Northwestern University Press, 1974), 447–60.

47   Jacques Derrida, *The Gift of Death* (Chicago: University of Chicago Press, 1995), 3.

48   Caroline Franks Davis, *The Evidential Force of Religious Experience* (Oxford: Clarendon, 1989), 29–65.

49   Peter Berger, *A Rumor of Angels* (Garden City, N.Y.: Doubleday, 1970), 53–72.

50   Friedrich Schleiermacher, *On Religion: Speeches to its Cultured Despisers*, trans. Richard Crouter (Cambridge: Cambridge University Press, 1988), 90, 98, 114.

51   Tillich, *Systematic Theology*, 1:47, 18.

52   John B. Carman, "Religion as a Problem for Christian Theology," in *Christian Faith in a Religiously Plural World*, ed. Donald G. Dawe and John B. Carman (Maryknoll, N.Y.: Orbis, 1978), 87.

53   Herbert Richardson, ed., *Transcendence* (Boston: Beacon, 1969), 98–101.

54   Karl Barth, *Church Dogmatics* (New York: Charles Scribner's, 1956), 1:2:281–84, 298.

55   Berger, *Heretical Imperative*, 77; Ralf K. Wüstenberg, *A Theology of Life: Dietrich Bonhoeffer's Religionless Christianity* (Grand Rapids: Eerdmans, 1998), 51.

56   Barth, *Church Dogmatics*, 1:2:299, 308.

57   Berger, *Heretical Imperative*, 74.

58   Karen Carr, *The Banalization of Nihilism* (Albany: State University of New York Press, 1992), 2, 5, 39, 65–67, 72, 126.

59   Emil Brunner and Karl Barth, *Natural Theology*, trans. Peter Fraenkel (London: Geoffrey Bles, 1946), 71, 78, 97.

60   James Barr, *Biblical Faith*, 6–20, 148–50. Stanley Hauerwas argues that after writing *Nein*, Barth adjusted his thinking on natural

theology, under the influence of Thomas Aquinas' views on the role of analogy in religion. Stanley Hauerwas, *With the Grain of the Universe; The Church's Witness and Natural Theology* (Grand Rapids: Brazos Press, 2001), 167, 184–93.

61 Dietrich Bonhoeffer, *Letters and Papers from Prison* (London: Collins, 1959), 91.

62 Eberhard Bethge, *Dietrich Bonhoeffer* (New York: Harper & Row, 1970), 775; Wüstenberg, *Theology of Life*, 21–29; John W. deGruchy, ed., *The Cambridge Companion to Dietrich Bonhoeffer* (Cambridge: Cambridge University Press, 1999), 60–64, 229–31.

63 Carr, *Banalization of Nihilism*, 57, 70, 83.

64 Michael B. Foster, *Mystery and Philosophy* (London: SCM, 1957), 13–27.

65 Foster, *Mystery*, 67, 161 n. 40.

66 Foster, *Mystery*, 8–10, 122, 132, 140.

67 Quoted in Foster, *Mystery*, 101.

68 Milton K. Munitz, *Cosmic Understanding: Philosophy and Science of the Universe* (Princeton: Princeton University Press, 1986), 228–35.

69 Polanyi, *Personal Knowledge*, 193.

70 William Faulkner, *The Sound and the Fury* (New York: Modern Library, 1946), 310, 313.

71 See Steven J. Dick, *Life on Other Worlds: The 20th-Century Extraterrestrial Life Debate* (Cambridge: Cambridge University Press, 1998), 253.

Chapter 9

1 David Martin, "Towards Eliminating the Concept of Secularization," in *Penguin Survey of the Social Sciences, 1965* (Baltimore: Penguin, 1965), 169–82.

2 Larry Shiner, "The Concept of Secularization in Empirical Research," *Journal for the Scientific Study of Religion* 6 (1967): 207–20; Peter E. Glasner, *The Sociology of Secularisation: A Critique of a Concept* (London: Routledge & Kegan Paul, 1977); Olivier Tschannen, "The Secularization Paradigm: A Systematization," *Journal for the Scientific Study of Religion* 30 (1991): 394–415; Steve Bruce, *Religion and Modernization: Sociologists and Historians Debate the Secularization Thesis* (New York: Oxford University Press, 1992).

3 Richard K. Fenn, "The Process of Secularization: A Post-Parsonian View," *Journal for the Scientific Study of Religion* 9 (1970): 117–36; Karel

Dobbelaere, "Secularization Theories and Sociological Paradigms," *Sociological Analysis* 46 (1985): 377–87; Mark Chaves, "Secularization as Declining Religious Authority," *Social Forces* 72 (1994): 749–74.

4   C. John Sommerville, *The Secularization of Early Modern England: From Religious Culture to Religious Faith* (New York: Oxford University Press, 1992).

5   S. S. Acquaviva, "The Psychology of Dechristianization in the Dynamics of the Industrial Society," *Social Compass* 7 (1960): 209–25; Jean Delumeau, "Au Sujet de la Dechristianisation," *Revue d'Histoire Moderne et Contemporaine* 22 (1975): 52–60; Michel Vovelle, *The Revolution Against the Church* (Columbus: Ohio State University Press, 1990).

6   E.g., David Martin, *The Religious and the Secular* (London: Routledge & Kegan Paul, 1969), 49.

7   Thomas Luckmann, *The Invisible Religion: The Problem of Religion in Modern Society* (New York: Macmillan, 1967), 36.

8   *Pace* Peter Burke, "Religion and Secularisation," *New Cambridge Modern History* (Cambridge: Cambridge University Press, 1979), 13:293–317. See Sommerville, *Secularization of Early Modern England*, chap. 11.

9   E.g., Jeffrey K. Hadden, "Toward Desacralizing Secularization Theory," *Social Forces* 65 (1987): 587–611; but cf. David Yamane, "Secularization on Trial: In Defense of a Neosecularization Paradigm," *Journal for the Scientific Study of Religion* 36 (1997): 109–22.

10   David Martin, *A General Theory of Secularization* (Oxford: Basil Blackwell, 1978).

11   Nel Noddings, *Educating for Intelligent Belief or Unbelief*, 143.

12   Witte, *Religious Human Rights in Global Perspective: Religious Perspectives*, xxiv.

Index